WHAT WE GOT INTO

WHAT WE GOT INTO

THE POLITICS OF OUR WAR AND THE TRIALS THAT FOLLOWED

CASEY WESTENRIEDER

Copyright © 2013 by Casey Westenrieder.

Library of Congress Control Number:		2013915686
ISBN:	Hardcover	978-1-4836-9184-8
	Softcover	978-1-4836-9183-1
	Ebook	978-1-4836-9185-5

This book was printed in the United States of America.

Rev. date: 09/03/2013

To order additional copies of this book, contact:
Xlibris LLC
1-888-795-4274
www.Xlibris.com
Orders@Xlibris.com
126647

CONTENTS

ACKNOWLEDGMENTS...9
PREFACE...11
INTRODUCTION 13

ONE	Dead Men Walking..	17
TWO	Time to Fly	25
THREE	Early Patrols	31
FOUR	The Fighting Season Begins.....................................	39
FIVE	The Martin Tree Line	46
SIX	Just Another Day at the Office	54
SEVEN	Things Just Got Real	66
EIGHT	Martin Luck...	77
NINE	Frustration	84
TEN	A Painful Reminder: It's Still Real...........................	90
ELEVEN	The Beat Goes On	100
TWELVE	A Bend in the Road	108
THIRTEEN	Full Moon Reprieve...	116
FOURTEEN	Peshengan . . . Again	136
FIFTEEN	The Last Full Measure..	145
SIXTEEN	Final Missions	157
SEVENTEEN	Shenanigans..	168
EIGHTEEN	Mikey Zisha..	178
NINETEEN	When the Shit Hit the Fan	186
TWENTY	From Heroes to Zeroes	196
TWENTY-ONE	The Palace Eight . . . or Nine..................................	205
TWENTY-TWO	When Will This End?	214
TWENTY-THREE	By the Way . . . I Told You So!................................	223
TWENTY-FOUR	The Final Chapter..	233

EPILOGUE 243

DEDICATION

This book is dedicated to Doug Green, Brandon Mullins, and their families. Their ultimate sacrifice can never be forgotten.

Also to my family, including my children, William, DJ, Robert, Nick, and Abigail, for putting up with the time they have all spent away from me. Thanks to Kim for putting up with all the unnecessary nonsense from me; and to my mother and father for their continuing support, even when things were at their worst. I love you all.

ACKNOWLEDGMENTS

I don't even know where to begin when it comes to acknowledging everyone who made it possible to write this book. So many people were supportive of me through this process, and I don't want to drag this out.

I want to thank Lu Abbondanzio for her dedication in proofreading and editing the pages I sent to her. I couldn't have asked for a better editor. My proofreaders were great. Thanks to Sharibeth Niehaus for writing the summary on the cover and for making so many suggestions. She really understood what she read. Thanks, Shari! And I appreciate the time Gabi Vuichoud, DJ Hall, and Lyn Kelly put into making suggestions.

There were a lot of people who read this manuscript before it was published, including the families of some of the soldiers in this book: Laura Schwartz, Virginia Van Bockel, Merry Carden, and many others who gave me the confidence and reassurance that writing this book was a worthwhile project.

I especially want to thank Cathy and Tommy Mullins, Suni Chabrow, Krissy Green, and Dana Dumar. You have all opened up to me and allowed me to tell the story about your heroes. I hope I never have to understand the pain you've all endured.

Thanks to Robin Thompson of FlyHippie Photography for the great (and very flattering) author photo on the back cover of this book. Photoshop is a wonderful thing, but Robin has an amazing eye for great photography.

I also want to thank the soldiers of Third Platoon, who served with me in Afghanistan, particularly the men who served in Weapons Squad. I think of all of you like you're my brothers.

PREFACE

Before you read this book, I need to qualify the pages in this book as an experience of what I saw from *my* perspective. There are some stories told by other people, but I've made those stories obvious. In no way do I want to belittle anyone's deployment to Iraq, Afghanistan, Vietnam . . . or anywhere else, for that matter. I trash-talk POGs (Personnel Other than Grunts) a lot, but I honestly know that an infantryman wouldn't last a minute in combat without the work that other MOSs do. Don't take it personal, POG.

What I've written is my personal account of what happened to my platoon in Afghanistan and what followed. I actually started writing this at the suggestion of my shrink as therapy to get through the nightmares and my feelings of anxiety, paranoia, and the insomnia. There is some foul language because that's how infantrymen talk. There are some graphic descriptions because that's what happened. I have not embellished anything. I didn't have to. This story is crazy in and of itself. There was no need to make anything up.

In an effort to keep this story real, I've used the actual names of as many people as I possibly could. There are a handful of people who requested I not use their names for whatever reason. There are some that I couldn't contact for their permission. I've respected their privacy. For those of us that were there, we know who you are, and there's nothing wrong with not wanting to be associated with this.

A portion of the proceeds from this book will go to the Douglas J. Green Memorial Foundation and the Brandon Mullins Scholarship Foundation. I've listed the websites for more information on these organizations in case you would like to do more. Please support these worthwhile causes.

(*www.foundationfordcps.org* . . . click on "About" then "Mullins Scholarship")
(*www.douglasjgreenmemorialfoundation.org)*

INTRODUCTION

There is a love-hate relationship between an infantryman and a POG—Personnel Other than Grunt. First and foremost for me is the POG response to a combat soldier's complaints of how bad things are on the line, or in "the shit". The response I hear a lot is "You knew what you were getting into when you signed the dotted line." This statement is usually given by the guy that sits on the forward operating base (FOB) for a year, hiding in a bunker in full battle uniform (kit) when a firefight breaks out a click away.

The origin of the word *grunt* is disputed. Some say *grunt* was a term that was used in World War II that stood for "General Replacement Untrained." It is also said that the expression was coined during the Vietnam era describing an infantryman because he's always the guy who sleeps in the mud, does those thankless patrols, and puts up with all the Army's bullshit; and the most he can really do about it is grunt. At the same time, the POG is sitting behind a desk somewhere, pushing pencils, wishing he was in the infantry. The POG is usually the guy at the airport you hear telling all the war stories he's heard, or overheard, and inserting himself into the story. My friend, S.Sgt. Blaine Dugas, says they tell the stories of the things *he's* done.

It's true that most infantrymen despise POGs, but the truth is it's because we're just jealous. We all get paid the same whether we're putting paper clips on a stack of papers or eating shit in the woods. Almost all the noninfantry jobs exist to support the infantry, and despite the animosity, the infantry couldn't survive without the support positions. I have a level of respect for all POGs in different ways. Well, almost all POGs. I have no respect for the Criminal Investigation Division (CID), JAG prosecution lawyers, or parachute riggers. As you read this book, you'll see why I have no respect for CID and prosecutors. As for parachute riggers, that's a whole different book.

The guy that goes into combat and sees more than he could ever imagine didn't know what he was getting into when he signed that dotted line, whether he's an infantryman or a POG. (Sometimes POGs do see actual combat.) It does not matter how many books you read, pictures you see, or stories you hear, you can never imagine the horror of war until you see it for yourself. So how could anyone have known what they were getting into when they signed that dotted line?

I've argued that fact with several people, including fellow infantrymen, and the basic conclusion that I've always come to during these arguments is that when you sign the dotted line, there is an expectation that you're going to see horrible things. I agree with that because I've read books and heard the stories. My point is you don't know what you've gotten yourself into until you see the mutilated body lying in a ditch or the brains of a man sitting in the backseat of his car after he was shot in the head through a windshield. You can never imagine that a roadside bomb can actually take a man's face off and leave it sitting on the road like a Halloween mask. Is it conceivable that one could expect this going into the military? Yes. But what you can't conceive is the genuine revulsion of actually seeing such horror, nor can you predict how you will react when you see it. It's *not* something you know you're getting into when you sign the dotted line.

I first joined the United States Army in 1995 to pay back college loans. After Basic Training, Infantry School, and Airborne School, I joined the ranks of the soldiers of Third Brigade, 3-505 Parachute Infantry Regiment (PIR), Eighty-second Airborne Division at Fort Bragg, North Carolina. After three years and seventeen weeks, I decided the Army had nothing more to offer me. We were a peacetime Army, and it was my opinion that all the training we were doing was in vain. It was time for me to move on. I'd served my country, I'd paid off my college loans, and my Expiration Term of Service (ETS date) was poetic—July 4, 1998. Independence Day.

September 11, 2001, changed everything. We had a new president and a viable enemy. When the US invaded Iraq in 2003, I told my new wife I wanted to reenlist. She, in no uncertain terms, told me to go piss up a rope. So for five years I fought the urge to serve my country in a time of war. I always felt I hadn't done enough during my first enlistment. I'd read about all the glories of war. In my mind, it was something I had missed out on. I had some idealistic notion that fighting in a war was somehow . . . romantic. I wanted to be able to sit in the Veterans of Foreign Wars hall and tell my war stories. I wanted some kind of legacy to pass down to my children. It was late 2007 before I decided I had to convince my wife that it was something I couldn't live without, and after a long debate, she relented. In April 2008, I signed the proverbial dotted line . . . again.

After more than thirteen weeks of reintegration into Army life and retraining for something that hadn't changed in decades, I received orders for the Eighty-second Airborne Division. I felt like I'd gone full circle. I was headed back to Third Brigade, this time, in 2-505 PIR. I had lost one rank due to my ten-year absence from military service, so I reported to Fort Bragg as a specialist, hoping it wouldn't take long to get promoted back to the rank of sergeant.

My intentions and goals were simple. I planned to do a three-year stint in the Army, where I hoped to do three things: earn the Combat Infantryman Badge (CIB), attain the rank of staff sergeant, and become a jumpmaster. Two years into this enlistment, I achieved these goals. I spent a year in Iraq on a *fairly* uneventful deployment and graduated Jumpmaster School a few months after our return from Baghdad, which made me a shoo-in at the E-6 board in March 2010.

The first sergeant I had while deployed in Iraq was amazing; and as usual, when you lose something amazing, you rarely get it back. The first sergeant that replaced him after our return to Fort Bragg was no exception to that rule. We didn't get along from the day we met. I don't know what it was about me that rubbed that man wrong, and at first I thought it was just me. But sergeants from other platoons would come to me and ask, "What did you do to piss this guy off? Did you fuck his daughter?" I knew it wasn't all in my head. I tried my hardest to get a lateral transfer to a different company, but that didn't work out. I was walking by the company area one day when the first sergeant called me over.

First Sergeant: Sergeant Westernrider (He could never say my name correctly), I hear you're trying to go to Delta Company.

Me (standing at parade rest): Roger, First Sergeant.

First Sergeant: Well, I don't know where you got an idea like that, but I will say that will never happen. I'll make sure it never happens.

Me: But, First Sergeant, you hate my guts. Why not?

First Sergeant: Because I said (really mature). You need a haircut, and your uniform is dirty. (I had just gotten a haircut, and my uniform was brand new.)

Me: Roger, First Sergeant.

I still had almost a year until my ETS date. My marriage was faltering at the time, and the economy was in tatters. I needed a way to get out of where I was but saw no need to leave military service. After months of heavy drinking and feeling sorry for myself, I decided to exercise my reenlistment option. I made several trips to the retention office before I finally signed a new four-year contract that would take me from North Carolina to the interior of Alaska. I went from being in a prestigious airborne unit, less than a year back from Iraq, to a quiet Stryker unit with less than a year away from a deployment to Afghanistan.

I had no idea what I was about to get into.

ONE

DEAD MEN WALKING

*Few men are born brave. Many become so through training
and force of discipline.*

—Flavius Vegetius Renatus

10 November 2010-10 May 2011

After arriving at Fort Wainwright, Alaska, in November 2010, I reported to my new company—Charlie Company, 3-21 Infantry Battalion, First Brigade, Twenty-fifth Infantry Division. My new first sergeant held me back in his office after he grilled all the new privates, which was an experience of its own.

First Sergeant to a new private: Are you gay? (This was a legal question at the time because "Don't Ask, Don't Tell" had just been repealed, and the first sergeant was taking full advantage of it.)
Private: No, First Sergeant.
First Sergeant: How do you know? Have you ever had sex with a man?
Private: No, First Sergeant.
First Sergeant: How do you know if you're not gay if you've never had sex with a man?
Private: (No response.)
First Sergeant: Now I'm going to ask you again. Are you gay?
Private: I don't think so, First Sergeant.

When the private left to ponder his sexuality, I laughed along with the first sergeant, and I realized I finally had another good enlisted leader. He told me he was placing me in Third Platoon. The platoon sergeant, S.Sgt. Blaine Dugas, was at Ranger School, so I was going to fill the positions of Weapons Squad leader *and* platoon sergeant until he returned with a ranger tab. I'd spent some time in a weapons squad during my first enlistment, so I felt honored to be in charge of Weapons Squad. But I had absolutely no training in running a platoon, and my self-confidence took a nosedive.

The thing about being in the Army, particularly in the infantry, you don't (or can't) say, "No thanks. I'd rather not." Instead, I promised my new first sergeant I would do the best I could with what he'd given me.

My first charge as the new *acting* platoon sergeant involved pulling all the squad leaders into the platoon's office and telling them what I expected. After I briefed them on my standards, my platoon leader, Lieutenant Labowski, asked me if I wanted to meet the platoon. I hadn't expected this, but again, I couldn't say no.

It was the end of the duty day when I first met Third Platoon, Charlie Company. There I stood in front of an understrength platoon with some of the goofiest-looking rejects I could ever imagine. I introduced myself and gave my best Army "hooah" speech, hoping to scare the shit out of most of them so they knew I was in charge. I asked how many wore combat patches. Four hands went up. Two of those hands were from squad leaders. In the Army, once you've served in a combat zone with a unit, you are authorized to wear that unit's patch on your right sleeve. It's called a combat patch. (The Army is very big on patches and badges.) With six months left before the scheduled date of our deployment, I had a lot of work to do. Most of these kids were fresh out of basic training, and many of them couldn't pass a physical training (PT) test. Almost none of them had been deployed.

My motto around the platoon quickly became "We're dead men walking." Training these kids to do some of the simplest of tasks became maddening. Entering and clearing a room, for example, is a basic Infantry Battle Drill, and we would spend hours working on the basics of just entering a room. The young privates would make the same mistakes over and over. I wasn't much for yelling, but they would bring me to the point of rage.

"What. In. The. Fuck. Are. You. DOING?" I would yell, drawing a blank stare from the private who had just entered the room we were clearing. He stopped in the doorway. "If you stop in the door, how the fuck is the rest of your team going to make it into this room? Do you want to be in a room full of Taliban all by yourself? Are you that much of a fucking bad-ass that you can take them all out by yourself? If you do that in Afghanistan, you're a fucking dead man, and so is the rest of your team. Get back out that door, you fucktard, and do this again! This is not rocket surgery! Jesus H. Christ! You are all fucking retarded! We're fucking dead men walking! If you don't all pull your heads out of my ass, none of us will come back from this deployment alive! Do you fucking understand me?"

My intent was not to belittle the young privates but more to shock them into the reality they were about to face. I had one new goal, and it was simple: I wanted to absolutely scare these kids into the certainty that we were heading into a combat zone with almost no experience, and they had better start taking their training seriously. I wanted every one of these kids to come home after a year in Afghanistan and be able to say to me, "We are still dead men walking!" My goal was that simple: get everyone home alive.

I first met Staff Sergeant Dugas in December 2010. The battalion had taken Christmas leave, and since I had just arrived, I decided not to take leave. I was part of the rear detachment and was working in the platoon office one day when a stranger in civilian clothes walked in and started looking around the office. I would have been surprised, but he looked like he knew what he was doing. He didn't look out of place.

"You must be Sergeant Dugas," I said.

"Yes, I am," he replied.

And that was about the extent of the conversation.

Dugas had been given Christmas Exodus from Ranger School and had come home to be with his family for the holidays. Why he was tooling around at the office is beyond me. I know if I was on break from Ranger School, the last place I would want to be is at work. This made me worry that Dugas was going to be a gung ho noncommissioned officer (NCO) that would push the platoon to the limit, and at the same time, I hoped for that. I felt the platoon needed someone to kick it in the ass, and if Dugas could do that, I'd be OK with it. The problem was that he intimidated me. We were polar opposites. He was quiet. I was outgoing. He was built like a brick shithouse. I was just average in size. Dugas had a command presence about him. He was definitely intimidating.

After Christmas, Dugas went back to Ranger School, and Third Platoon prepared for our month-long training at the National Training Center (NTC) in Fort Irwin, California. I trained with the platoon the best I could. I focused mainly on my squad and let the other squad leaders run most of their own training. It was during this time I really started to get to know my squad and instill the Weapons Squad Attitude in them: "Weapons Squad doesn't take no shit from nobody!" And they caught on quickly.

Gun Team 1 consisted of Private First Class (PFC) Andrew Burke as the gunner and PFC Will Schwartz was his assistant gunner (AG). Burke and Schwartz were a great match. Both were athletic and muscular. Burke was a tall Black man from Corcoran, California. Schwartz wasn't much shorter and hailed from Monroe, Georgia. Both were competitive and worked hard.

After shuffling some people around and stealing a guy from another squad, Gun Team 2's gunner, PFC Theodore Thompson, and PFC Ronald Wyscaver was his AG. Thompson was the one we all were sure would become a serial killer one day. He came from a small town in Georgia, but I'm not exactly sure where because he was the most introverted soldier I've ever been in charge of. Wyscaver, on the other hand, was boisterous and fun loving. We'd later call him Lunchbox because he'd eat anything. He came from Lake Orion, Michigan.

Later, I would get PFC Tyler Alley as a driver, and PFC Brandon Hendrick was assigned as my vehicle commander (VC). Alley was really tall and just had a funny look about him. We called him Avatar, and his hometown was Pratt, Kansas. Hendrick was average, but he always had something funny to say. I wasn't sure if he was really as dopey as he came across, but he was fun to have in the squad. We never had a nickname for this kid because I had to give him up to the battalion mortar team not long after we arrived in Afghanistan. He still thinks it was a personal thing, but it was tough for me to give him up.

I had a strong group of guys, and it would turn out later to be the best squad in the platoon. Despite what other squad leaders thought of them, they remained the most loyal members of the platoon to me, and others around them, and I couldn't be more proud of this group of young men.

It was also during this time I acquired my new nickname. When I was at Fort Bragg, I was referred to as Greybush because I was the oldest guy in the company. When I got to Alaska, at forty-one, I was the second oldest man in the battalion and the oldest infantryman. I guess Greybush didn't catch on because one day, I walked into the platoon office and someone had written "Dusty Balls" on my keychain and on pieces of paper taped all over my desk. Nicknames come in strange wrappers.

A few weeks before we left for NTC, Dugas returned to Fort Wainwright with his Ranger Tab, and I knew things would get tough on Third Platoon. The PT regimen picked up and despite being out of shape, Dugas ran us into the ground with eight-mile runs and PT in full kit, which included weapon, body armor, and helmet. The weather in Alaska in January was brutally cold, but we still trained as hard as we could without putting anyone in danger of getting frostbite. Several times I warned Dugas that our platoon was inexperienced. I even told him once that we were all "dead men walking."

"Not me," he said. "Maybe all of you *turds* are gonna die over there, but I'm not! I'm coming home! You need to knock that shit off!"

Dugas, at the time, was a man of few words. He really liked the calling people turd. I had a great deal of respect for him, but I didn't know why. He wasn't a very large man, but he was serious and focused. I found out later he had reclassed to the infantry from Air Defense Artillery (ADA), and he knew his job well. Because of his knowledge, I felt comfortable with him as our platoon sergeant but, at the same time, was still worried he would be the one who would put the platoon out there to get the job done. I would find out later that Dugas was more concerned with the individual soldier than with the perception of the platoon. Dugas was the real deal. Once I figured that out, I realized he would be one of those Army buddies I'd always want in my corner. He would be a lifelong friend.

In February 2011, 1/25 infantry packed up and flew to Fort Irwin, California. After a week of training, getting issued Multiple Integrated Laser Engagement System, or MILES gear, and trying to adjust to the heat, we headed into the training area also known as the Box. We drove for several hours into the Mojave Desert to a simulated forward operating base (FOB) where we dropped off most of our gear. Our first mission was to go to a hilltop and set up a company defense. We loaded back up on the Strykers and headed to the hilltop, which was another two hours of driving. By the time we got there, it was dark, and we needed a ground guide to get up the hill with the Stryker. The ground guide walks in front of a vehicle to make sure it doesn't run over anything or anybody, and in this case, he made sure the truck didn't go off the side of the mountain. Typically, a lower-enlisted soldier would act as a ground guide. It wasn't a common job for a Weapons Squad leader.

"Sergeant Wes. Get out and ground guide, you turd!" Dugas yelled at me from the squad leader's hatch.

"Me? Are you serious?" I asked, wondering why he would put a staff sergeant out to do a private's task.

"Yes. You. Go!" he yelled back, and I knew it wouldn't do any good to argue with him.

The ramp dropped, and I climbed out of the Stryker in full kit into the dark. The headlights on the truck were on so I could see where to go. As the road started to get steeper, the altitude started to get to me. I was climbing up a steep road in front of the truck, and I was running out of air. I felt like I was going to die. I could feel my heart pounding inside my body armor, and I couldn't catch my breath. As I doubled over, putting my hands on my knees, trying to catch my breath, I heard Dugas laughing and decided the joke was on me. I walked around the back of the truck, banged on the ramp, and after it was down, I dragged myself back onto the truck. I'd either passed or failed Dugas's first test, and I didn't care. I wasn't sure if I was pissed or if I thought it was funny. At that point, I was just happy to still be breathing.

As we set in the company defense, I emplaced my two machine gun teams on the edge of the hill, and we waited. It was NTC, and we knew we were going to get attacked. We also knew that the opposing force (OPFOR) was much better trained for this environment than we were, so we had planned on getting hit and hit hard. And when we got hit, all hell broke loose.

Dugas ran to the position I was in with Gun Team 1. We started firing rounds into the OPFOR position and were doing a pretty good job when we started taking fire from behind us. The OPFOR had broken through the company perimeter and were *on* the hilltop. I started firing my M4 and took out two or three of the enemy before my MILES gear started screaming. I was "dead" and so was my gun team. Somehow Dugas was still alive. He grabbed the M240, turned to us, and screamed, "They're not taking me alive!" and ran off.

I looked at Burke and Schwartz in disbelief. Who did he think he was, Rambo?

"That motherfucker's crazy," I said. "But I'm dead. I'm just gonna sit here."

The desert nights were cold, so Burke and Schwartz followed suit, and we sat on the hilltop shivering until an index was called, signaling the end of the training exercise. We all piled into a Stryker, and I had the driver turn the heat up all the way. I was freezing. A few minutes later, Dugas climbed into the Stryker from the squad leader hatch.

"Turn that fucking heat off, turd," he told the driver. "It ain't cold in here."

And the heat went off. I looked back at all the sad faces in the Stryker, but I wasn't going to argue with the platoon sergeant.

"Great," I mumbled, just loud enough for Schwartz to hear. "We just have to have a fucking *Ranger* platoon sergeant, don't we?"

Schwartz laughed, and we all shivered ourselves to sleep for a few hours.

The rest of the NTC rotation was rather uneventful. My Weapons Squad really proved its worth during the live fire when both gunners and AGs dropped all the targets in our sector as soon as they popped up. We also spent four days defending a hilltop that was never attacked.

We were packing up to go home and were also packing a large shipping container with platoon equipment that would be shipped to Afghanistan. As we were doing the inventory of the container, we packed and unpacked it three or four times. I was completely disgusted. No one seemed to know what was going on, and I couldn't stand it anymore.

PFC Justin Christiansen was in First Squad, and during our four-day defense of the hilltop, he'd earned the nickname Dump after his team leader made him carry a large rock around as punishment for allegedly falling asleep on guard duty. The rock was named Dumpy, and we had planned on putting it in the container going to Afghanistan when Dugas put a stop to it and said we would bury Dumpy and give the rock full military honors. I told Christiansen to carry the heavy rock back to our tent. Specialist Matt Martin, a team leader in First Squad, started to carry the rock for Christiansen, and I made him stop. I wanted Christiansen to carry the rock. Martin tried to lobby for Christiansen, but I was undeterred. I wanted Christiansen to carry that rock back to the tent. Martin and Christiansen headed back to the tent with Dump carrying Dumpy.

After they had left, I decided I was fed up with packing the container and was going back to the tent. I was about halfway back when I looked up and saw Martin carrying Christiansen's rock. I was pissed, but I didn't feel like making an issue out of it. When I got back to the tent, I put my headphones on, and when Martin and Christiansen walked in, I took my headphones off and yelled at Martin.

"You're a piece of shit!" I screamed in front of everyone. "You're not doing a fucking thing to help that guy when you don't let him pull his own weight!" I was tired and frustrated, and honestly, I wasn't even sure why it was a big deal to me, but it pissed me off.

Martin held the rank of specialist (SPC) due to his education. Martin had graduated from the University of Missouri, and I wasn't happy about that since Mizzou had beaten my Texas Tech Red Raiders in a football bowl game a few years earlier. That aside, he didn't even have a year of service in the Army; but since he had earned a bachelor's degree before joining, he came in as an E-4. In the Army, we call them shake-and-bakes, which is a name I knew dearly as I was a shake-and-bake myself, but I'd never tell him that.

Martin wasn't a bad guy, but his education didn't provide him the practical military experience or qualifications needed to be a team leader. He was a team leader by virtue of his rank and the Army's lack of someone with enough experience to do the job.

As I put my headphones back on and was getting settled on my bunk, Martin came up to me and asked if he could speak to me outside. I knew what was coming, and quite frankly, I didn't want to hear it, but I got up and went outside so he could talk to me. It didn't go well for him.

"I want you to know I respect your rank and all the things that you've done," he started. "But also, I don't really appreciate . . ." and that was as far as he got.

"You don't appreciate?" I screamed in his face. "Honestly, I don't give a fuck *what* you appreciate, Martin! You suck as a team leader, and it's not your fault. It's because you're a fucking college E-4, who got stuck in the position of team leader, and you don't fucking deserve it. You don't know how to lead soldiers because you don't have enough time in service, and you haven't done shit. Whether you appreciate it or not, I don't give a fuck. You'd better learn to lead your men before we get over to Afghanistan and you get them all fucked up!"

I did apologize to him for yelling at him in front of his peers. I shouldn't have done it, but I wanted to make a point. I couldn't believe he didn't *appreciate* that. Despite what I thought of Martin at the time, he would later prove, in my opinion, to be one of the bravest soldiers in the platoon . . . twice.

Upon our return from NTC, we received several new NCOs to augment our platoon, including two from the Eighty-second Airborne Division, Sgt. Davin Dumar and Sgt. Adam Holcomb. Sgt. Andrew Van Bockel came to us from Tenth Mountain Division.

Dumar and I had been in the same platoon at Bragg, and I knew him well. He was a loyal friend and a good soldier. He was always the one who would show up at my house for a cookout, and I could always depend on him for anything. I was excited to have someone I knew in the platoon. As far as Van Bockel and Holcomb, I didn't know much about them. Holcomb was in the same battalion as I was at Bragg, but our paths rarely crossed there. Sergeant Van Bockel took over as trusted squad leader for Second Squad.

In the six months prior to the deployment, Third Platoon worked hard. Cohesion grew inside squads; PT scores improved, marksmanship and battle drills were honed. The bad seeds were weeded out. The focus of the platoon aimed at deploying to, fighting in, and returning from Afghanistan. I felt, under the circumstances, we couldn't be more ready. I'd really become confident in my squad, and I started to look at them as my children. Only Wyscaver and Hendrick were older than my oldest son, so it was only natural that I wanted to look out for them like I would my own children. I adopted an approach in the platoon that required other squad leaders to let me know if someone from my Weapons Squad made a mistake. The other squad leaders weren't allowed to discipline or "smoke" my squad. It caused a lot of bad feelings among some of the leaderships, but Weapons Squad was *my* squad, and I had become rather territorial when it came to *my* squad. "You leave my guys alone, and

I'll leave your guys alone" was my mantra. Weapons Squad knew this, and it helped them polish the attitude I wanted to see them portray. Eventually, the Weapons Squad motto became "If you're not Weapons Squad, fuck you!" and I liked it.

In the two months left before deployment, tensions mounted, and the guys were chomping at the bit. We found out where we were going and who we'd be replacing. We were ready to go and get our war started. We were ready to fight. We were ready to get into the fight. We were ready to make a difference. Whenever guys from my squad started talking about how they would do this or that, I'd tell them they wouldn't do anything. I'd tell them that none would earn their Combat Infantryman Badge, the CIB. In the infantry, the CIB is a badge of honor. To earn the badge, you must have received fire from the enemy and returned fire. An infantryman who returns from a combat rotation without a CIB is often mocked. Weapons Squad was eager to earn theirs.

"None of you guys will get your CIB over there," I would say, kidding with them and dashing their infantryman dreams.

"Are you serious? You really don't think we'll get our CIB?" they would desperately ask.

"No, you won't because I'm gonna be doing all the killing over there, and you'll all be behind me hiding because you're gonna be scared shitless," I told them, laughing inside, knowing how eager they were to get a CIB.

"I ain't scared," Burke would say. "I'll be killing them right alongside you, Sergeant Wes."

"We'll see about that, Burke," I would tell him with a smile on my face.

I knew most of them would return with the badge, and I'm pretty sure they knew they would too. They were ready to go to war, and I told them on many occasions to be careful what they wished for. They just didn't know what they were getting into. Neither did I.

TWO

TIME TO FLY

*Leadership is the art of getting someone else to do something
you want done because he wants to do it.*
—General Dwight D. Eisenhower

11 May 2011-24 May 2011

I woke up a little after seven o'clock the morning of 11 May 2011 and still had
stuff to do before I had to report to work. I slept on a mattress in the living room
because I'd taken the bed apart and thrown it away. The mattress was all that was left.
I figured I would deserve a new bed in a year.

I got up, took a shower, brushed my teeth, and shaved. I gathered up what was
left of my belongings and loaded them into the rental car. I tied the mattress to the
top of the car and would take it to the transfer station, or the dump, on my way into
town. After everything was out of the cabin, I did a last-minute cleanup of the place.
It was important to leave it in good condition for a couple reasons: I may need to rent
from this landlord when I got back, and I wanted my deposit back.

After all was done, I drove to the landlord's home, dropped the key off with a
goodbye note, and drove to the transfer station where I tossed the mattress and any
trash I had gathered from the cabin. I headed into town and went by my storage
unit and put the last of my stuff in the tightly packed closet. It's sobering when you
realize everything you own in life, minus what you drive, can fit into a five-by-ten
space. What's really sad about it is that I didn't even efficiently pack it or I'd have
more space. My dad, a master packer, would have a heart attack if he ever saw how I
carelessly stacked stuff into this small unit. God forbid something should happen to
me on this deployment and he had to empty my storage unit. I made a mental note to
make sure he didn't get the spare key.

Having some time before I had to report in, I went to a local diner in Fairbanks and ate breakfast. I noticed a few military families gathering at the diner to eat their last meal together before departing for a year. Maybe even their last meal together. I felt lonely and anxious. I'd dreaded this day as much as I looked forward to getting it started. I wanted to deploy, but I wanted to get it over with and come home. I was ready, but I wasn't. When my meal came, I ate what I could and left the rest sitting on the table with the tip. I walked out of the restaurant and drove to work.

I'd made arrangements for the car to be taken back to the rental agency, so I walked away from the car and went upstairs to the off-post locker room. I cleaned out my locker, taking all my bags out and getting rid of all the trash I'd accumulated over the past six months. The locker room looked empty with all the cleaned-out lockers. It was really here. It was really time to go. I carried my bags downstairs and placed them in the formation area and waited for the boys to show up. I was early.

After drawing weapons and making copies of hand receipts, which would show accountability for the equipment we drew out, we waited longer. It gave those with family there a chance to prolong their inevitable goodbyes. Wives and girlfriends clung to their soldiers for a last chance to embrace before they left for a year-long deployment to Afghanistan.

At 1500, our bags having already been loaded onto trucks and shipped off, we loaded the busses. I grabbed my carry-on bag and counted out my guys as they walked from the back door of our company building toward the waiting busses. I climbed onto the bus and looked back at the company building and saw all the family members waving at the busses, not sure where their soldier sat on any of the several busses it took to transport Charlie Company.

The busses took us south to Eielson Air Force Base. When we got off, I was hungry. Burke, unloading right behind me, said, "I smell sandwiches." I laughed, but surprisingly enough, there were peanut butter and jelly sandwiches in the holding area. I learned then I would probably take Burke's nose more seriously. So we ate sandwiches and chips and watched a TV show projected on the wall while waiting for the time we would fly away from Alaska. Some for the last time.

After we loaded the commercial airline, everyone got situated for the long flight. Our first leg would take us to Bangor, Maine. We'd stop there to refuel, reload, and then continue on to Leipzig, Germany for another layover. From there we'd stop at Manas Air Base in Kyrgyzstan, a former Soviet province. I learned from my last deployment that the worst part of going to war is actually getting there and then getting back. On the way there, you just want to get there and get started. On the way back, the plane can't fly to freedom fast enough.

I don't remember much from the flights or the layovers, but I couldn't help but notice that when we arrived in Maine, all the cell phones were coming out, and soldiers were getting their last chance to text or talk to their loved ones. I would have called my wife, but it was late, and I didn't want to bother her. In Germany, our battalion sergeant major practically stood guard over the alcohol shelves, making sure no one got brave enough to buy European liquor. I remember landing in Kyrgyzstan and noticing the Russian words on the terminal entrance. I wasn't even sure where in the world we were.

We arrived at Manas Air Base on 12 May, where we stayed for three days. The first full day there, we had to get the plates from our body armor inspected. After that, it was a waiting game. I slept as much as possible. No one was sure how long we would be there. I thought if I slept, the time would go by fast. It worked.

On 15 May, the call came, and we gathered all of our gear and marched to the holding area where we would get locked down until it was time to take the final leg of our journey to Afghanistan. We carried everything to the holding area and waited in the hot sun. When we left Alaska, the warmest weather we had been in for months, NTC excluded, was fifty-eight degrees. At Manas Air Base, it was in the upper nineties, and we were feeling every bit of it. We huddled in the shade to keep from becoming heat casualties. Staff Sergeant Dugas was yelling at everyone. We were all on edge. We knew our next stop would be Kandahar Airfield. I was not excited. I was suddenly dreading every day of the upcoming year. I'm not sure if I was the only one who abruptly had a change of heart because at that point, I wouldn't dare admit something that could be construed as a sign of weakness or of being afraid.

We waited for what seemed like an eternity in the holding area at Manas. I sat alone and didn't really want to talk to anyone. I couldn't sleep and envied all the guys that were able to lean against the wall and catch a few winks. I was a jumble of nerves. I wasn't sure what I was nervous about, but I knew once we got on the air force C-17 to Kandahar, things would be different. When we finally boarded the cargo plane and took off for Afghanistan, I was exhausted. I don't remember much from the flight or even how long it was, but I'm pretty sure I didn't sleep. If I did, it wasn't much.

We landed at Kandahar Airfield (KAF) on 15 May, and all our palletized baggage was unloaded from the bird. We were piled into a small briefing room where some POG gave us the guidelines we were supposed to follow while staying at KAF. One of the things she talked about was rocket attacks and how, in the event of such an attack, we should "lie on the ground facing north for two minutes." I laughed when I heard her say that, like any infantryman worth his salt is going to lie on the ground and look at his watch for two minutes. I'm sure at the moment no one even knew which direction was north.

After the briefing, we went outside and waited on busses to take us to the transient tents. It was dark, but it was still hot. I was waiting next to Burke and Schwartz. The flight line was to our right, and seemingly, from nowhere, a loud screeching sound bellowed from the sky. I have to be honest; my first thought went straight to the briefing we'd just received about rocket attacks. Burke almost hit the ground before we all realized it was the sound of a jet making a pass over KAF. I made fun of Burke, but I almost hit the ground right beside him facing north, whichever direction north was, anyway.

Charlie Company was assigned a transient tent with a faulty air conditioner. I shouldn't have been surprised, but I wasn't happy. But misery loves company, and as it was, we shared that tent with Bravo Company. With about two hundred and fifty soldiers crammed into a tent with almost no air, it got a little cramped. The chow hall was really close to the tent, but the food wasn't even good enough for Burke to sniff it out. To make things worse, the smell from the sewage tanks wafted over to our side of the compound, and the heat was unbearable. Dust was everywhere, and it was impossible to stay clean because of the sweat and dirt that constantly clung to our bodies. The Boardwalk at KAF is a large area with a lot of stores and restaurants, but it was about a mile away, and I wasn't a fan of walking in the heat. I figured I'd get enough of that later on. Little did I know.

We stayed at KAF longer than I thought we would and a lot longer than I hoped we would. Inside the tent during the day, it felt like a sauna. I would lie on my Army cot and just sweat. I was miserable. One day, I decided to do something I thought would make my life better, so I went to the boardwalk and found a store that sold fans. For thirty-five dollars, I bought an oscillating fan, and I walked back to the tent. True story. I had this fantasy that I would put this fan together and everyone would cheer. I would be a hero. Things didn't exactly work out that way. I put the fan together and plugged it in using the adapter I also bought to convert it from the European plug to the American-style outlet. I turned the fan on, and it didn't work. Everyone sat looking at me, then looking at the fan, then looking back at me. I picked up the instructions and finally found the section where it said it was made for 220 volts; not the American-style 110. Instead of cheers, I got jeers. Later, I still had to go back to the boardwalk to get a converter, and when the fan finally worked, I still didn't get any pats on the back. I think the heat was getting to me.

Eight days had gone by and we were still waiting at KAF. Tempers were flaring, but I hadn't seen any fights. I wished a fight would break out just to break up the boredom and even tried to instigate a few, but to no avail. I was going out of my mind. Rumors and speculations were running amuck. I can't count how many times Schwartz or Burke or Wyscaver would come to my cot and say something like "I heard we're going to be here for two more weeks."

"Where did you hear that from?" I'd ask every time.

"Some kid in Bravo Company said," was usually the reply.

Tired of hearing the rumors, I put out to my squad, "If you don't hear it from me, it's not true, so quit asking me stupid questions."

Early that evening, Schwartz came to my cot and said he'd heard another rumor and asked if I'd check it out.

"What did you hear this time?" I groaned.

"I heard we're going to be stationed at the battalion FOB, and we're gonna be pulling force protection. I heard we won't even be doing patrols." He looked nervous, and I could tell he wasn't happy about this rumor.

Force pro was not much more than bitch work on a FOB. We'd take shifts pulling tower guard, sergeant of the guard (SOG), and possibly a roving guard. We'd be in charge of the Entry Control Points (ECPs), where we'd control who entered the FOB on foot or in a vehicle. Not to mention the details that would come down as a result of being the FOB bitches. I could understand where he was coming from with his disappointment, but at the same time, I wasn't too worried about it.

I got up and found Dugas to ask if there was any merit to this rumor. It turned out this one was true. First Platoon was slotted for a remote Combat Outpost, Second Platoon would be stationed at the Sperwan Ghar, the company FOB, and we would be going to the battalion's FOB Zangabad, where we were scheduled to do tower guard and SOG duty. It looked like it was going to be a boring deployment for us. This news was both good and bad. Good because if we were stuck on the battalion FOB, we'd have good food and a good chance of having Internet and phone service. We would have a link to the outside world. The bad part was that we probably wouldn't see much action. But how bad could that really be?

I went back to my bunk, where Schwartz was waiting, and told him he was hearing it from me, so it's true. We were going to be Fobbits at Zangabad.

"Man, that's bullshit," Schwartz said, legitimately pissed off. "I didn't join the fucking Army to sit in a guard tower. I don't want to spend a year pulling guard duty."

"Look on the bright side," I said. "We'll have Internet and phones. We'll have a good chow hall. The best part is we'll all come back alive."

"Fuck that shit," he argued. "I want my CIB. I didn't want to come to Afghanistan to be a bitch for battalion. I was hoping this deployment would be more like some of that *Restrepo* shit!"

Schwartz, as well as most of the men in the platoon, had seen the movie *Restrepo* and decided that living in the "suck" was some kind of romantic way of spending a combat tour. It seems I wasn't the only one who thought fighting for my country would be some kind of glorious adventure.

"Did you see the look on those guys' faces when they interviewed them?" I asked Schwartz. "Do you want to come home with that look on your face? Do you want to see your buddies cut down in a fucking firefight? Schwartz. Be careful what you ask for. You think it would be cool to be stuck on a small COP (Combat Outpost) fighting the enemy every day, but let me tell you something, that kind of shit will steal your soul, man. You don't want that. Just be happy you're going to go home in one piece."

As it turned out, Schwartz had a buddy in First Platoon who had ribbed him about this assignment, laughing that he would never get his CIB. Schwartz and his friend were very competitive, and Schwartz said he just wanted his CIB before his buddy. I couldn't blame him, but it was becoming more and more comfortable to know we'd be sitting on an FOB for a year, not pulling patrols. Little did I know how fast that would change.

That night, we finally got live rounds to load into our magazines. When the ammo truck pulled up, each platoon grabbed what they could and passed the rounds out to each squad. We spent less than an hour loading our magazines. This was a sign that we would be leaving soon. After we all had a combat load or as close as we could get to it, the word came down to pack our stuff. We'd be leaving the next day. I was elated. I couldn't wait to get out of that hot tent and away from the smells of KAF. That night was an uneasy sleep. I knew the next day we'd be headed into the heart of Kandahar Province. We were going to the Panjwei'i District at a FOB that was less than one hundred miles from the Pakistani border. We'd be deep inside the Kandahar Province, which was also the birthplace of the Taliban. Even though we were supposed to be pulling force pro for the FOB, something didn't sit right with me. I couldn't believe that it would be that easy.

On 24 May, we loaded vehicles and convoyed to FOB Zangabad. It was a three-hour trip that took five and a half hours because of all the delays. It was early afternoon when I finally stepped off the back of the Canadian troop transport and saw my new home, and I wasn't impressed. The entire FOB was small. It was less than three-quarters of a mile in circumference. It was still full of Canadian soldiers, and we barely had room to turn around. Our platoon of forty soldiers was given two tents. Talk about sardines. The only good news at that point was that the air conditioners in these tents blew arctic air, so I wouldn't need my fan.

The rumor of us pulling force pro turned out to be just that—a rumor. The Canadians would be there for three more weeks, and two days after our arrival at Zangabad, we were scheduled to send eight men out on joint patrol with our new temporary counterparts. So much for sitting on an FOB for a year.

The amenities at Zangabad weren't much to write home about. The Canadian cooks did a good job, but the porta-johns smelled. There wasn't much water for the shower trailers, and there was no Internet or phone service. Actually, that's not true. The Canadians had an Internet tent, but we weren't allowed to use it. Additionally, of the three clothes washers in our vicinity, we were told we could only do laundry on even-numbered days. It seemed at first that we were going to have a great deal of tension with the Canadians. That turned out to be untrue. Other than the language barrier that sometimes caused some confusion, the Canadians couldn't have been more helpful in getting us accustomed to what we would be up against while fighting in Panjwei'i. They offered more than enough advice, and later we would learn that when we steered away from their guidance, we would pay a hefty price.

The Canadians offered us food, ammunition, and supplies. For everything they gave us, it was less that they had to pack up and send home. It made sense, and we were thankful. The transition was going well, and in a few days, we'd be going on patrols and learning how to live in our new home.

THREE

EARLY PATROLS

> *Let every nation know, whether it wishes us well or ill, that*
> *we shall pay any price, bear any burden, meet any hardship,*
> *support any friend, oppose any foe, to assure the survival and*
> *success of liberty.*
>
> —John F. Kennedy

24 May 2011-19 June 2011

The first few days at Zangabad were spent with us just getting adjusted to being on a FOB. For most of the platoon, it was a new experience, and a lot of them were enjoying themselves thinking this was what it was like to be in a combat zone. It reminded me too much of being in Iraq with the cramped living quarters, the work details being called for, and all the other mindless military nonsense that goes with being deployed. Going a little overboard myself, I decided I would be a cigarette butt and toilet seat Nazi.

Every morning, I would walk around the two tents that our platoon was housed in, looking for cigarette butts thrown on the ground. It was inevitable that I'd find at least one, so I'd pull the whole platoon outside to do trash pickup. It really wasn't fair to the guys who didn't smoke, but I figured that when they saw smokers throw their butts on the ground, they'd say something. In actuality, it wasn't fair to any of them, because the unit that was housed in the tents behind us would smoke by our tents and throw their butts on the ground. But it was something for me to do, and I was intent on keeping our area clean.

The porta-johns we used were also shared by other units, but if there was anything I've learned from being in the military, you have to keep the lid down, and at night you need to use a light to see where you are pissing. I let my platoon know that if I walked into a shitter that had the lid up or had piss all over the floor, I would make a guard roster for members of the platoon to pull guard duty on the toilets in full kit.

"But, Sergeant Wes, that's not fair," many of the guys said to me. "We're not the only ones using them. What if someone else leaves the lid up?"

"Then you'd better make sure it gets down before I see it," I told them.

It worked. It got to the point where I wasn't finding cigarette butts on the ground, and the porta-johns didn't smell like sewage depots. Things were looking good, and the guys were starting to understand that we needed to take care of the areas we inhabited. These lessons would come in handy later when we moved to COP Palace.

The patrols with the Canadians started slowly, mainly with the platoon leadership going out with the Canadians to get a feel for the Area of Operations (AO). Dugas and Lieutenant Labowski went on the first patrol with the Canadians, and they brought Burke and Schwartz along to act as air guards for the Stryker. The air guard hatches in the Stryker are two openings in the back that provide rear security for the vehicle. Though Burke and Schwartz never left the truck on that patrol, I still worried about them going out and me not being able to be there in case something happened. Nothing happened, and they were disappointed. I was relieved.

The first patrol I went on with the Canadians was to Lakani on 29 May. Before we left, the Canadian leadership told us to expect enemy contact since they had a lot of difficulty getting into this village. On this patrol, we would roll in from the south, through the Red Desert, in Strykers and the Canadian version of the Stryker— the LAV. Also involved were several tanks from the Canadian side and some MGSs from our Fourth Platoon. The MGS is a Stryker with a 105 mm cannon on it and is manned by tankers, not infantrymen. Needless to say, we were rolling in with some serious armament.

When I got off the Stryker outside Lakani, an air force A-10 Warthog fired into a wood line not far from where we were. It scared the crap out of me, and if you've ever heard the noise an A-10 makes when it shoots its 30 mm cannon, you'd understand why. Later, we heard they killed five Taliban in the tree line, and apparently, that set the stage for our patrol. We didn't make any contact that day. Instead, I sat at a road intersection in the village with Sergeant Van Bockel and a Canadian soldier and played with some kids while the rest of our unit talked to some of the villagers. What I learned from the patrol is that the kids in Afghanistan are thankless and bold. I'd give them bottled water, and they'd pour it out on the ground. They would get right in my face and try to take equipment off of my ballistic vest.

I also learned that the heat in our AO was not something to take for granted. I was sweating so much that it poured into my eyes, and I couldn't see. I didn't do any more patrols after that without wearing a headband or a bandana on my head to soak up the sweat.

The next day, 30 May, Dugas, the LT, and all the squad leaders went on an afternoon mission with the Canadians. It was another sweltering day in Panjwei'i, but at least the movement was short. We walked about five hundred meters to a local village where a Canadian patrol had earlier found a Taliban trench. From the trench, there was a clear view to the FOB, and it was multileveled so after firing shots at Zangabad, the fighters could jump into the lower level and take cover from any incoming rounds fired in return. It was dug tightly into the tree line, shielding it from aerial view. A group of Canadian engineers wired some serious explosives to the trench, and when we were all clear, all the work the Taliban had put into this fighting position was covered up by rubble and a tree.

We walked through the village and were talking to some villagers, using interpreters, or terps, and I was attempting to "make nice" with some children in the area. I was learning that the kids in Afghanistan were not like the children of Iraq. In Iraq, if you gave a child something as simple as a pen or a piece of paper, they would grin from ear to ear and thank you profusely. Some of the Iraqi children spoke broken English and attempted to make us laugh. It was different in Panjwei'i. The children would give us dirty looks and appreciate nothing. I gave one child a bottle of water, and he poured it out on the ground in front of me and flipped me the bird. All I could do was roll my eyes.

Despite the poor manners of the Afghan people, particularly in this district, the coalition forces were in constant competition with the Taliban to gain local sentiment. The Canadian troops told us that when children were around, they had yet to be engaged because the Taliban were afraid of shooting kids and losing local favor. So even though they were rude, I was happy the children were present.

I was attempting to play with a child while standing on a road in front of a mud wall that was about five feet tall. Shots rang out, and I could hear the rounds from the automatic weapon breaking over my head. I ducked and took cover behind the wall while the kid ran away in fear. Over the radio, someone was saying that we had taken fire from a compound north of our position. So much for the Taliban not firing at us with kids around. I ran to an area where I could see where the shots had come from, but no more shots were fired.

I was on a road that ran north and south and was waiting behind a wall. My heart was still pounding from being shot at which, at that point was something that didn't happen every day. The wall I was against had a large break in it about ten meters in front of me to the north. As soldiers were moving further north, they'd bound past the break to avoid getting shot. I was one of the last men to go past the break and felt like it was all over, so rather than hurry past it like everyone else, I took my time. When I was halfway past the break, I heard a round crack that came really close. I think that one had my name on it, and it didn't take me long to hurry past that break in the wall. My heart had been pumping before, and now I could feel it beat against the Kevlar plates in my body armor. I knew I was in combat zone, and as crazy as it sounds, I started wondering why someone would want to shoot at me. What did I do to them?

We made it to an intersection just north of the village. Sergeant Holcomb, a team leader from Third Squad, was on a wall with an M14 rifle looking for the sniper that had been taking shots at us. I moved into the intersection with Lieutenant Labowski and Sergeant Moreton. The road heading west was lined on both sides by mud walls, so we took cover along the north side of the road, which was only about fifteen feet wide. It was quiet. Moreton and I started moving east on the road, which made a left-hand turn about one hundred meters in front of us. Not having a mine detector, we decided it wasn't a good idea to go further, so we turned around and headed back.

As we got back to the rest of the element, a small firefight broke out; and since I didn't see where the enemy fire was coming from, I didn't return fire. The incident was enough to get my heart pumping, but that was about it. The decision came down to return to Zangabad, so we started heading west on the road that would take us to Route Q, the main paved road that ran north/south by FOB Zangabad. When I was about fifty meters west of the intersection, what seemed like a huge firefight kicked off. It wasn't really that huge, but at the time, it was the most fire I'd heard since we arrived. I ran back to the intersection just as it was dying down. Dugas and the LT had been right in the thick of it and were coming from around the corner of the intersection when it was done. It was Lieutenant Labowski's first time engaging the enemy, so it meant he would be the first member of the platoon to earn his CIB on this deployment.

On 05 June, Dugas came into the tent. I could tell he was bothered by something, but I didn't know what. I figured if he wanted to say, he would. Eventually, he did.

"I don't know what to do about Christiansen," he said. Christiansen, also known as Dump, was the soldier from NTC that had to carry the rock. His team leader told him to do something, and Christiansen mouthed off, making some kind of threat. His shoelaces were taken away from him, and the bolt from his M4 was removed. He was considered a suicide risk.

"I'll take him," I said to Dugas.

"What are you gonna do with him?" Dugas asked.

"I don't know, but I'll find something for him to do," I said. So Christiansen became the newest member of Weapons Squad, and when I got him, I pulled him off to the side and let him know where I stood.

"I don't know what was said," I began my speech to Christiansen. "But I will tell you this: If you threaten to kill yourself, you might as well just do it. I've taken you into my squad because I believe that you can become a good soldier. I'm the only one in this platoon that thinks that, so at this point, you have nowhere left to go. Threatening to kill yourself will not get you moved to another squad. If you have a problem with anyone, you come to me. You need to start going to the gym and working out because if I take you on a patrol and you fall out, it will be your last patrol. Do you understand me?"

"Yes, Sergeant," he said timidly. But I could see he was happy he had been transferred to my squad.

Christiansen, a young guy from the Dales, Oregon, was very understanding, and he knew he had reached the end of his line. I changed his nickname from

Dump to Sticks and defended him when people picked on him. He soon became a very loyal member of my squad. He later became known as the Enforcer. According to Christiansen, he had been a cage fighter before he joined the Army, and he was known as the Enforcer. No one believed him, but it was funny.

On 08 June, we went on another patrol with the Canadians. Weapons Squad's task was to provide a blocking position north of a village the rest of the platoon was going to clear. The Canadians played adviser roles for this mission, making this the first US-led patrol. Our takeover was nearly complete. I took Christiansen on this patrol and gave him a very light load, reminding him that if he fell out, it would be his last mission I also told him to let me know if the load, as light as it was, got to be too much, and I would carry what I could. He promised he would be fine. I believed him.

My squad, with the help of our Canadian counterparts, managed to get to the blocking position. The landmarks we found were nothing like the map or the outdated aerial photographs showed when we planned the mission. I realized then that in the future I would have to be ready for anything. I emplaced both guns on the road to stop any traffic, including pedestrian traffic. We sat in the position for several hours while the rest of the platoon did their jobs in the village south of us.

Before we left, a Canadian Special Forces unit came to our position and warned us that they had a tip that an Improvised Explosive Device (IED) had been placed in a grape hut to our northwest. We got a visual location of the grape hut, called in the tip, and the decision was made to do nothing because it could have been something to lure us into an ambush. I was frustrated with the decision, but it turned out later to be a good call.

When it came time to leave the area, the Canadians took the lead with their minesweeper, and right behind the Vallon was Gun Team 2, Thompson on the M240 and his assistant gunner, Wyscaver. I looked up and saw the Canadian throw the minesweeper in the air and run for cover. In trail were Thompson and Wyscaver. Christiansen was with me, and Burke and Schwartz were behind him.

What the fuck? I thought as I ran up to see what was going on. I thought the Canadian had found an IED. He was standing near one of his buddies, and his lip was quivering. He was obviously frightened.

"There are two men with RPGs around that corner," the Canadian said in broken English and a French accent as he pointed to a corner where he'd seen the men with the rocket-propelled grenades. I looked down at Thompson and Wyscaver in disgust.

"Why did you run? Why didn't you blow those fuckers away?" I asked.

"We didn't see that," Thompson said. "We thought he found an IED, and when he hauled ass, we just followed him."

I went to the edge of the corner and peered around. There was a large open doorway on the left-hand side leading into a compound where the Canadian said he'd seen the armed men. But I didn't see anything. My Canadian counterpart told me that the best thing to do was to change course and leave as quickly as possible. After radioing the situation up my chain of command, our elements changed course and started a hasty movement away from the danger area. The first part of this movement involved climbing a twenty-foot berm into a grape field. I wasn't sure Christiansen would make it, but he surprised me as he scampered up the side of the hill and got into the grape field.

We moved west to get back to Route H, walking through dense grape fields and climbing over walls to get from one field to the next. At one point, Christiansen was getting tired and turned to me.

"Sergeant Wes, I don't think I can carry this anymore," he said.

"Look, Christiansen. I told you I'd carry that stuff if it got too much, but you picked a really bad time to try to dump it off on me," I told him. "We just ran into two guys with RPGs that could be tracking us right now. We need to get the fuck out of here before they decide to open up on us, and I don't have time to take on your gear. You're going to have to dig down deep and find a way to carry that back."

Never again did Christiansen complain about a load he had on his back. He made it all the way back to the waiting vehicles without a word of complaint. Luckily, we were not targeted by the men with RPGs, and we made it back safely.

Our next patrol was on 12 June, and I wasn't involved, but Schwartz, Burke, and Alley were. The following is what Schwartz told me about that patrol.

I was attached to Third Squad with Burke and Alley. We crossed an open field and got into a wadi. Burke and I were watching the road while Alley pulled rear security. We were only there for about fifteen minutes when a fighting-aged male (FAM) dressed in all white started walking down the road from north to south. Burke had eyes on him first, and he told me he was walking toward us.

The FAM put a hood over his head and jumped into a break in the wall that ran along the road. The wall was only about forty meters away from us, and as soon as he got behind the wall, the Taliban opened up with small arms fire from two different positions. One was straight in front of us at our twelve o'clock. The other position was about at our two o'clock by the corner of a building. All enemy fires were focused on our gun team. Dirt was kicking up in our faces. You could hear the cracks, zips, and whizzes from the rounds going right by us.

It took a few seconds to register mentally for everyone that we were actually getting shot at. But as soon as it did, Burke opened up with the gun on the position by the building, and I was firing my M4 at the position straight in front of us.

The enemy contact stopped, and Alley said he thought he saw a spotter to our rear. We switched positions because I have an ACOG (a sight optic for an M4 rifle) and could see further away. As soon as we switched, the enemy contact started up again. Burke opened up with the M240 again, and Alley returned fire with his M4.

The contact stopped again, and we didn't hear any more enemy fire until we started our exfil (exfiltration), and by that time, it was so far away we didn't even bother. We just continued our exfil.

Burke, Schwartz, and Alley each earned their CIB on that patrol, just days after getting there. I thought of how I kidded them about going home without earning the badge and how quickly they actually earned it. Though I wasn't there, I heard a lot of praise from the leadership that was present about their professionalism and courage under fire. I was proud of my boys. I was upset that I had missed this patrol and wasn't there when they had earned their CIBs, but I should have been happy for the break. It would be one of the last patrols I would miss until September.

Our final patrol while based at FOB Zangabad was a fiasco. On 13 June, we left on our own with no Canadian support elements. It was an afternoon presence patrol in the area northwest of the FOB. Being new to the area, we didn't know much. Dugas put me on one of the Strykers and told me I was going to be the vehicle commander, so I would have little part in this mission, other than watching over their movement and relaying radio commands.

The patrol started around 1500, and the heat was unbearable. I sat on the truck, sweat pouring from my body as the rest of the platoon ventured into a grape field. The first sign that things were going wrong came when one of the team leaders from First Squad climbed over a wall and twisted his knee coming down the other side. Doc Smith, our medic, said it was bad enough that he wouldn't be able to walk out. Dugas called in a nine-line medevac message, a communication with nine lines of information for helicopters to pick up wounded, and when he did, members of the platoon started falling left and right from heat casualties.

When the Blackhawk came in to pick up the wounded team leader, it also picked up five members of the platoon who had gone down as heat casualties. Two of those were from my squad: Specialist Bedient, the platoon radio operator (RTO), and Wyscaver.

The mission was a failure. The rest of the platoon made it back to the trucks, and we went back to Zangabad with our tails between our legs. Dugas was livid. So was Lieutenant Labowski. The six men were evacuated to KAF. We wouldn't get the team leader back because he had torn his ACL. We wouldn't see the other five for almost a week, and Dugas told me that none of these soldiers would be allowed to patrol again until the weather got cooler. That would be a long time because it was just June, and it wasn't going to cool off until October or November, from what we'd been told. I knew that would change, but it was heartbreaking for Wyscaver, who still hadn't earned his CIB, and when the weather cooled off, the fighting season would be over in Panjwei'i.

Additionally, Dugas rounded up all the workout supplements that the soldiers had been taking, banning any kind of substance that might cause anyone to be dehydrated. As it turned out, the five that were taken on the medevac to KAF had low nitrate levels, and it was basically because they had skipped meals. When I heard this, I was fairly certain I'd be able to get Wyscaver back out when Dugas cooled off.

Our time at Zangabad was nearly up. A platoon of Canadians had occupied a small combat outpost approximately a mile north of Zangabad on Route Q. Lieutenant Labowski had somehow talked someone into letting Third Platoon take this COP over, which would put our element away from the headquarters, also known as the proverbial flagpole, and give us some room to relax. At the time, I thought it was a fantastic idea. In hindsight, it may not have been. Regardless, on 19 June, Third Platoon packed its bags, and we moved from FOB Zangabad to COP Palace.

Things would never be the same.

FOUR

THE FIGHTING SEASON BEGINS

I learned that good judgment comes from experience and that experience grows out of mistakes.
—General Omar N. Bradley

19 June 2011-20 June 2011

The move to Palace was pretty simple compared to most Army endeavors. We loaded up our gear onto Strykers and dropped it off when we got there. We couldn't move in yet because the Canadian platoon that occupied this site was still there, and surprisingly, they weren't in a big hurry to move out. I expected them to be lined up at the gate, but they casually started moving their gear out, and as they did, we started moving in.

There wasn't much to Palace. There was more parking area for vehicles than anything else. If you walked the perimeter, it was right at five hundred meters, so this place wasn't very big. The living area consisted of eight Container Housing Units. A CHU is a metal shipping container that is roughly eight feet wide and about twenty feet long and is adapted for living instead of shipping vehicles, which is generally how I've seen them used. Most had been reinforced to withstand gunfire and blasts. They had bunks built into the sides of them, some of them on both sides. They were air conditioned, and each one had power running to it. The one I chose was on the very south end of the COP. It had three double bunks on one side and shelves on the other side. Since I was a squad leader, I only had one roommate while team leaders and squad members crammed into the CHUs with twelve bunks. As the highest-ranking leaders in the platoon, Lieutenant Labowski and Dugas had their own CHU, and the remaining containers were divided into Squad CHUs. That sucked for Weapons Squad since we had ten people in the squad at the time, and that was the most people crammed into a single CHU at Palace.

Sergeant Moreton was my roommate, and I was happy living with him. He was a very tidy person, almost to the point of being OCD. He was pretty quiet, and we were both considerate of each other's privacy while we were there together. Though this arrangement would only last a month, that time with Moreton helped build a strong friendship with him that will likely last a lifetime.

There were four guard towers at Palace. The main tower, Tower 1, was at the front gate on the east side of the COP, and when we started manning towers, we had two men in that tower. Tower 2 was directly over my CHU, which was good, and bad. It was good because my "can" had an extra layer of sandbags over it. It was bad because when it was shift-change time, I could hear the relief climbing the stairs outside, sometimes hitting their weapon on the side of my home, and plodding across the top of the can to the tower. But after the changeover was complete, it was quiet. Tower Three faced west and overlooked an Afghan National Army (ANA) compound, and because of the trees, the fields of fire were obstructed, making it a rather useless tower. Tower Four was on the north end of the COP, and we didn't start using that until later.

We had a small aid station where our medic slept, a small tent we used for snacks, a small kitchen tent, a small structure that acted as our platoon command post (CP), and a small area with some gym equipment, which we referred to as our prison gym. And that was our new home. That was our Palace. All the CHUs had tarps over the entry ways, and most of them had picnic tables or some kind of seating under the tarps. There wasn't much to this place, but it was home. It was away from the flagpole, which gave us a little breathing room on daily shaving, uniform wear, and the other details we would have to worry about if we were closer to the "brass." Things could have been worse.

The biggest thing we had to worry about when we first started to settle in were the contracts for the porta-johns, garbage, and the generator, which provided us our electricity. When the Canadians' time expired at Palace, their contracts ran out as well. We had to dig a slit trench to shit in, and we had to steal fuel from FOB Zangabad to keep the generator running. The garbage started to pile up quickly, so Dugas had me supervise the digging of a burn pit. Things eventually ironed out when the new contracts kicked in, but there were chronic issues, and we never stopped burning trash at Palace.

One other issue was water. We had a little structure with laundry machines and a small shower building with three small shower stalls. Right next to the shower structure was a large bladder which supplied the laundry and shower with water. The water supply for this bladder was a large tank that was gravity fed, but had to be refilled with water from a larger tank which was about thirty meters away. Originally, we had a pump and hoses to pump water from the big tank to the little tank, but the motor on the pump burned out, and we would run out of water in the bladder. When the water in the large tank ran out, we found ourselves with no water, putting an end to all showers for more than a week because the contract with the local Afghan vendors for water had not yet been secured by our command.

More importantly, we faced significant inadequacies with the essentials—food and ammunition. Third Platoon was starting to feel like the battalion's red-headed stepchild. We were at Palace for more than a month before we were resupplied with food and ammo. Luckily, the Canadians left enough behind that we had our beans and bullets and everything else we were able to steal from FOB Zangabad, including drinking water and fuel. Typically, I'd be against stealing, but it was literally a matter of life and death. If we didn't take it from Zangabad, we were going to starve or run out of ammo.

Despite the lack of resupply, we made our compound as comfortable as we could. We hung a dart board, played cards, and did what we could to entertain ourselves between patrols. But the patrols we launched from Palace would often push us to our limits.

In Afghanistan, there is something referred to as the fighting season. Apparently, the season begins when the crops start getting harvested. The three main cash crops in our area were poppies, grapes, and marijuana. The poppy crop is the first one to go, and the Afghan farmers are rather protective of this illicit plant. That harvest takes place starting around April. We showed up right at the end of the poppy harvest. The grapes and marijuana harvests last until late September or early November, and that is when the fighting in this region slows down.

I developed a theory as time went on as to why there is a fighting season in Afghanistan. How valid this theory was, I'll never know, but it made sense to me. It seemed most of the fighters we were hit by, or that we hit, were Pakistani. If they weren't Pakistani, they had Pakistani money, and some had identification paperwork indicating they had come from Pakistan. These Taliban fighters would be in our area long enough to protect the harvest of the crops, the poppy, and marijuana in particular, because they were able to get a portion of these drugs and sell them, which in turn would bank roll their Taliban operations. When the crops were harvested, it was starting to get cold, and it was the Pakistani Taliban's cue to go home. The season was over.

I don't, in any way, intend to say that Pakistan is fronting the Taliban cause in Panjwei'i, or anywhere else in Afghanistan for that matter. I don't have that kind of evidence, nor do I have the knowledge it would take to make such a claim. And in truth, it would be like saying Mexico backs all the illegal immigration into the United States. That is just absurd.

Our small sector in Panjwei'i turned out to be the most active AO in the entire brigade and, as we learned later, was the most active area in all of Afghanistan that summer. Though we were lucky enough to suffer fewer casualties than other units, we definitely saw more action than any other member of our task force that summer. At first, it was just us doing our jobs. But soon it got to the point where the stress was too much for some of us, and it showed in some of the actions that would take place at Palace as the fighting season wore on.

20 June 2011-First, and Last, Air Assault

We barely had enough time to divvy our bags before we started our first patrol out of Palace. This mission was a joint mission with the Canadian Special Forces that were still operating in the area and a small contingent of ANA. Using two CH-47 Chinook helicopters, we would be transported or conduct an air assault mission into an area in the farthest area west in our sector. It was a place very few coalition forces had been, so we were told. Apparently, the Taliban pretty much had freedom of movement in this area, and we were supposed to go in and put a stop to it.

Just after midnight, we started getting ready, loading our Strykers to go to Zangabad. By 0200, we were waiting at the Helicopter Landing Zone (HLZ) on the south end of the FOB, waiting for the Chinook CH-47 helicopters that would ferry us to our mission. We had rehearsed getting on and off the birds and had separated each squad into "chalks" (or team) depending on which helicopter they would load. There were two drop-off LZs, so it was important that everyone was in the right chalk.

I had a Meal Ready to Eat (MRE), several bottles of water, and since we were low on squad radios, I took the larger manpack radio with several batteries because we had planned to be there all day. The platoon had also prepared two body bags per chalk, one filled with MREs and the other with bottled drinking water. The plan was to stash the body bags at the insertion point and still be able to go back for the resupply when we needed food and water. It sounded like a good plan when we made it, but the bags turned out to be too heavy to carry through the grape fields, and a lot of those supplies, including the bags, were left behind with the hopes that our supplies would still be there if we needed to get back to them.

When the birds came in, we climbed on and put the resupply bags near the ramp so we could get them off quickly. As the huge cargo helicopter took off, I felt the nerves building inside of me. A Chinook is not a quiet helicopter, so when we landed, it was going to be no surprise where we were. I couldn't help thinking about how the soldiers in Vietnam felt when they had to go into a Hot LZ when being inserted into the jungles. I was really hoping our LZ would be cold.

After a short flight, my bird started making its descent to drop us off. I'm sure my heart was pounding in hopes of dismounting the bird to no gunfire, but I couldn't tell from the noise and the rattle of the large helicopter. When it touched down, the men nearest the ramp pushed off the body-bag resupply, and we all made our hasty retreat from the Chinook. As I was going off the ramp, something from my equipment snagged on the side of the bird, but I was so amped up, I just pushed through. I got off the bird, made it about fifteen meters away from it, and got into the prone, just like we'd rehearsed. The bird took off, and it was quiet. It was a cold insertion, and I started to stop shaking.

Dugas was in my element with a few attachments and a small group of ANA soldiers. Our mission was to take over a compound about eight hundred meters from the HLZ and set up a blocking position to our south in case any Taliban decided to move to that position. Thompson manned our Vallon, and I was directly behind him navigating. Burke and Schwartz were behind me, and Alley was behind them. The ANA and one Canadian Special Forces soldier followed while Dugas took up the rear. The movement was quiet, and we made good time. At one point, Dugas came up behind me, and he was a little agitated.

"Hey, turd . . . can you fucking hear me?" he asked in a whisper.

"What are you talking about?" I asked back.

"I've been trying to get you on the radio, and you're not responding," he said.

"I haven't heard anything," I told him. "Try doing a radio check."

Dugas did a radio check, and I heard him loud and clear.

"There must be something wrong with your radio," I told him.

In the Army it's never *your* fault when equipment malfunctions; it's easy to point fingers. So Dugas went back to his position, and we kept moving. When we made it to our compound, it was still dark, but the sun would be coming up soon. I called Dugas on the radio to tell him we'd made it to our objective, but he didn't respond.

Our intent was to kick in the door of this compound and take it by force. A lot of us still had the Iraq mind-set of smashing down a front door and taking the compound by force, so it still made sense to us. When I brought up my team that was set to kick down the front door of the compound, I realized we weren't going to kick this door in. It was a large steel door, and it looked pretty solid. Dugas came up to me, still bitching about the radio problems we were having, and I simply pointed to the door and said, "We ain't kicking that thing in."

"Well, we didn't bring any explosives, so we can't blow it," Dugas said. "Take a team around the perimeter of this compound and see if there's a place we can climb over the wall. One way or another, we're gonna get in there."

I rogered him and took about three guys, including Thompson on the minesweeper and a terp, in case we ran into someone who spoke no English. As we encircled the compound, I was looking for a low spot in the wall or something we could climb to get up and over the wall, but there was nothing. I was getting a little frustrated at our lack of planning.

"Why don't we knock on the door and ask if we can go in," the terp asked in broken accented English. I didn't want to hear that.

"Why don't you shut the fuck up and let us do our jobs," I barked back at him as quietly as I could. "You just interpret for me when I need you. That's your job, so do *your* job."

As we got back around to the front of the compound, it was apparent that the interpreter's suggestion was the only one that made sense at the time. So, much to my chagrin, we knocked on the door, and an old lady answered. The terp talked to her and told her we needed in and that we would be on her rooftop. She was not happy about us being there and started to argue, but when twenty armed men show up at your door and say, "Let us in," what can you really say?

We went into the compound, cleared the bottom level for any kind of booby traps, and then set up on the rooftop. When I got on the roof, Dugas looked at me and told me to turn around. I thought I'd ripped my pants or something.

"Where's your antenna?" he asked.

I dropped my assault pack on the roof and looked. Sure enough, there was no antenna, and I realized it must have been what snagged when I was exiting the bird and probably tore off.

"Yeah," Dugas chided me. "There must be something wrong with *my* radio. Enjoy carrying that useless piece of shit around for the rest of the day, turd."

He laughed and I tried to act like I thought it was funny, but I wasn't going to enjoy lugging around a useless piece of equipment, not to mention all the batteries I had brought with me.

When the sun came up, we started to bake on the roof. As it got hotter, we quickly started going through the water we had packed for ourselves. Dugas called me over and told me to take a gun team back to the HLZ and pick up the resupply. He also told us we needed to resupply Second Squad, who was in a compound about five hundred meters north of us. He gave me his radio, and I took Burke, Schwartz, and Alley, and we set out for the body bags with empty backpacks we could load up with water and food.

The site where we'd dropped off the bags was plotted on my handheld GPS, so it didn't take long to get there. We were nervous because it was the first time we'd been out as just a fire team alone. When we got to the resupply, we took turns pulling security while we filled the bags with as many bottles of water and as many MREs as we could carry. There was no way four people were going to carry those heavy bags back through the grape fields, so we got what we could and left the remainder in the field along with the two canvas body bags. On the way back, we stopped at Second Squad's position and lightened our load before heading back to our compound.

At the compound, Dugas had started rotating guys from the roof into the shade in thirty-minute shifts. It was way too hot to sit on the rooftop, and we were going through too much water. I alternated one-hour shifts with Dugas on the roof so there would be an NCO up there at all times. We also attempted to take refuge in the shade of a poleless litter, which is made of a strong nylon mesh but offered little shade from the pounding sun. Our time there was miserable.

Around noon, we got a call to move to the position of the mission's main effort, which consisted of First and Third Squads and Lieutenant Labowski. I couldn't believe someone had the bright idea of moving in this intense heat, and we were already starting to run low on water again. This was starting to look like it was a bad idea. But we followed orders, and along with Second Squad, we linked up with the rest of the platoon.

As a platoon, we moved from the link-up position to the southern end of our objective where we sat in the sun and set up security. I put Burke and Schwartz on a rooftop with the M240, and I know they hated life in the sun. We all grumbled to ourselves, and as much as I hated it, when someone would tell me how "stupid this shit is," all I could do was tell them to "shut the fuck up." We were all miserable, and I didn't want to hear about it from anyone else. My only thought was getting through this day and waiting for the birds to come back in and pick us up so we could go back to Palace. We were all low on water, and the day was dragging out. None of our searches had been productive, and I was beginning to think this mission was a waste of time.

At about 1600, the change of mission (also called a FRAGO) came down to let us know that the birds weren't picking us up, and we had to walk back to Zangabad. I thought it was joke, but no one was laughing. We were already dehydrated from the heat, almost out of water, and it was probably three clicks (three thousand meters) back to Zangabad. It just sounded like a bad idea. The plan called for us stopping at Belambay, a village about a mile and a half from Zangabad that had a Special Forces outpost. There we could resupply on water and make it the rest of the way. The question was how many people would go down from dehydration in the movement there, which was more than a mile in the heat through the grape fields.

We started the movement back and split the platoon, the ANA elements and the Canadians into two long files to get across an open field. When we got to the grape fields, we collapsed the two columns into one and kept moving. I don't remember seeing this tactic in any handbook, but someone made the decision, and all I could do was plod along and hope I didn't pass out on the way to Belambay. When we were about halfway across the open field, I heard a loud pop. It took a second for my mind to register that the pop was actually a gunshot. As I looked up at a grape hut nearly two hundred meters to our north, gunfire exploded, and there were rounds falling all around us. I immediately hit the ground, as did everyone else in the movement. We were pinned down.

It was a strange feeling lying in the prone in an open field with spouts of dust popping up where bullets were landing just a few feet away. I looked to my right and saw Schwartz and Thompson and yelled for them to return fire. Both of them opened up on the large grape hut, as did the rest of the platoon. The mud hut immediately looked like it was on fire with all the dust floating around it due to all the rounds smashing against the side of it.

This was the first time the platoon had taken fire as a full platoon. When we ceased fire, the grape hut looked untouched, other than all the dust floating off of it. The enemy had ceased fire as well, and the Canadian Special Forces were bounding across the field in an amazing display of combat teamwork. I was impressed. I don't know what they were going after, but they were moving with a purpose. After waiting there for what seemed like an eternity, pulling security all around, we determined that we'd done what we could there and started moving out again.

We didn't get hit again that day, but it proved to be the first in a long line of patrols that Third Platoon would go on resulting in contact with the enemy. For us, this was the first day of the fighting season, and it didn't seem to have an end in sight.

FIVE

THE MARTIN TREE LINE

If you are going to win any battle, you have to do one thing.
You have to make the mind run the body. Never let the body
tell the mind what to do . . . the body is never tired if the mind
is not tired.

—General George S. Patton

23 June 2011

We were all still feeling a little bulletproof. We'd been through a decent firefight, and no one even got a scratch. On the morning of 23 June, we set out to do a patrol in one of the larger villages in our sector. One we'd been to before with the Canadians and one we would get to know fairly intimately over the next couple months. We were going into the village of Lakani.

Planning patrol routes became the duty of the squad leaders, and First Squad's squad leader, Sgt. Austin Moreton, planned the route to Lakani. The route took us into the village in a much different way than the route we used when we went in with the Canadians. We left Palace on the Strykers and drove a short distance south on Route Q, where we dismounted and planned to walk the distance to Lakani. First Squad was in the lead, followed by Second and Third Squads. I had Gun Team 1 with me, Burke and Schwartz, and Dugas was pulling rear security. He said he preferred to be in the rear so he could keep an eye on things, but I think the truth is it's safer in the rear. I didn't blame him, and I didn't mind because I was second to the last in the order of movement.

We traveled along the route Sergeant Moreton had planned with his squad. When we were just north of Lakani, we crossed a bridge and took a turn headed west. The turn took us through a dense tree line on a small trail that put us near Lakani. We'd planned on jumping a wall in a low spot to get into the village which was less than two hundred meters south of us. Walking along the trail, I noticed a small pile of rocks. It looked as if it could have been a trail marker for an Improvised Explosive Device (IED). I brushed it off, thinking, *I'm second to the last man. Surely someone else had seen that.* It was a mistake I would never make again.

The path was narrow and had mud walls and vegetation on each side. The tree line was pretty thick, and if we had been ambushed on this path, we would have had nowhere to go and had no cover to hide behind. It made me nervous. As I was thinking, *This is very canalizing*, I heard Dugas say behind me, "We need to get off this fucking path." I was in complete agreement with him, and less than two minutes later, there was an earth-shattering boom.

"What the fuck?" I said, looking back at Dugas. "Was that an IED?"

"I don't know," he said and got on his radio. I didn't have a radio that day because at the time, we didn't have enough for everyone, and since I was so close to Dugas, I figured I wouldn't need one. I couldn't hear what was being said, and finally, Dugas reported what he heard.

"It was an IED," he said. "No one was hurt, so it's all OK."

"Thank God," I said and walked up to Schwartz and Burke, who were both taking a knee on the path.

I told them it was an IED and everyone was OK when I heard Dugas yell, "Shit! I'm moving up time now!"

"What's going on?" I asked, but he didn't answer. He moved to the front of the formation, around a curve and out of sight. I took up rear security while talking to Schwartz and Burke.

About twenty minutes passed and information started spilling from the front to the rear. First Squad had been hit by the IED. Martin was minesweeping, and Specialist Curtis was right behind him navigating. Specialist Hurley was behind him pulling security, and Moreton was right behind him. No one could say the extent of the injuries, and since I didn't have a radio, I was still clueless.

I looked up the path and saw Doc Smith escorting Martin who was followed by Curtis, Hurley, and Moreton. Martin was disoriented. He had blood on his face and neck, and his shirt had been shredded. His eye protection had been blown off, and one of his eyes was swollen and red. Honestly, though, I thought he looked pretty good for having just been blown up. At least he was still alive and had all his pieces. As he walked by, I ragged him a little since I was really thankful he was alive.

"Would you look at that?" I said. "That's a Purple Heart. You son of a bitch, you stole my Purple Heart. If you're gonna get one, that's the best way to get one if you can walk away from it."

I know Martin heard me, and I wasn't offended that he didn't answer. He was still in a shocked daze from the blast. Doc pulled him back to the rear of the formation and continued performing first-aid measures on him. He had suffered a contusion on his right leg from about midshin to midthigh. He had several wounds from shrapnel, but there was a spot on his right arm that was completely unharmed.

It turned out it was an area protected by a Bible he was carrying in his sleeve pocket.

"I guess I'm not very good at minesweeping," Martin said.

Lieutenant Labowski laughed and said, "Don't worry, man. We're going to get you a medevac out of here. Just relax."

"Fuck that," Martin said. "I don't want a medevac. I want to walk back. I don't want those fuckers to see they got the best of me."

That took everyone by surprise. I have to say if I had just been blown up, I'd welcome a helicopter ride back to the rear. But Martin didn't want anything to do with that, and he did what I thought was the bravest thing I'd seen on the deployment thus far—he walked back to FOB Zangabad bandaged up, including his eye, with no weapon so he could prove a point. They hadn't gotten the best of him.

When we set out for the FOB, we left the LT, Second, and Third Squads back to pull security on the site. My gun team, the tattered First Squad, and Dugas made the trek back. It took a long time to get back, but we finally made it through the north gate at Zangabad. When we got there, the Explosive Ordinance Disposal team (EOD) was already waiting at the gate. I was exhausted. I dropped my bag off on one of the Strykers and started guzzling water. I was eating some bits and pieces of a MRE, hoping it would take some of the cramps away. The EOD team asked how far the IED site was, and I told them it was about two to three hundred meters away. Then, after looking at my GPS, I realized I was wrong. We had just walked more than a thousand meters.

"Sorry," I told them. "It's more than a *click* away, and that's straight-line distance."

I hadn't realized how far we'd gone. I think I was a little dehydrated and surprised at the events of the day. But it wasn't over yet. Dugas had taken First Squad to the aid station so they could get evaluated. They had all been very close to the IED when it had gone off, and Martin had to have some injuries evaluated.

When Dugas came back, he wasn't alone. He brought an element of the battalion Recon Platoon with him, and he told me we were going back.

"You need to get your gun team together, and you'll be leading this thing back," he said. He must have read the look on my face. "Do you have a problem with that?"

I wanted to say, "Fuck, yes, I have a problem with that," but I couldn't bring myself to do it. I wasn't feeling confident about navigating an area where I had never led a patrol and hadn't had time to plan a route. Nevertheless, *no* was not an option under these circumstances, and I was about to start a pattern of not being able to tell Dugas no to anything. I pulled out the map, plotted where we were and where we needed to go, and started to plan a hasty route. I spun up my gun team and grabbed Alley to be the minesweeper on the way back out to the site. Before we left, I sat down with Dugas and showed him the route I had planned, which would take us out the south gate.

"I don't think we should go back the way we came," I told Dugas. "If they watched us leave, they'll be waiting for us to come back, knowing we still have guys out there. If we leave out the south gate, we can cut through grape fields and end up on the northwest side of the objective."

Dugas nodded, I got a radio from Moreton, and we got everyone together. Alley was in the lead, and I was right behind him. Burke followed me with the M240, and Schwartz was right behind him. Dugas was next followed by the three-member EOD team, including a female operator. The Recon Element took up the rear. It turned out this was their first mission since arriving in sector, and they were sorely unprepared.

After we left the south gate, we crossed a small stream called a wadi and moved into the grape fields. I was feeling some pressure and wanted to move as quickly and safely as possible. I didn't want to mess up, and we needed to get back to the soldiers we had left behind to guard the path and the detonation site. According to the route I had planned, we would cross two tree lines heading south and then turn east for about one hundred fifty meters before heading northeast, which would bring us back to the vicinity of the blast area. It was a hasty route, and I just wanted to get us close enough where we would be back with the rest of the platoon.

We had moved about three hundred meters when I began to doubt our location. I knew something wasn't right, so when we climbed over a fairly high wall, I moved up about fifty meters and had Alley stop. The wall was a significant obstacle that would take time for everyone to cross, and it gave me an opportunity to do a map check. I pulled out my GPS and compared our location to the map. We were off course. The tree line we had just passed was not the first tree line on the map, but the second. In my haste, I'd missed seeing the first tree line which actually started further east than I thought. I had to tell Dugas and anticipated a good ass chewing for screwing up the route.

As people were climbing over the wall, I walked back to his position with the map.

"Here's where we are," I said, pointing to the map. "Here's where I thought we were. We're about 150 meters off course."

I expected him to at least call me an idiot, but instead he just said, "So what are we going to do about it?"

By not yelling at me, he gave me some confidence, and I was able to quickly point out a new route that would pull us further north. The terrain was rough. In addition to the grape rows we had to navigate through, we had to climb numerous mud walls, walk through dense marijuana fields, and ford some deep, wide wadis. It was taking some time.

The Canadian Special Forces (CanSOF) unit was still stationed at a small base outside Zangabad, and they were able to intercept transmissions from Taliban radio sources. As we were moving, they started calling up some of the chatter they heard. The first thing they called up to us was that the Taliban was using children in the grape fields as spotters, reporting back our position. This was not uncommon as the Taliban knew we wouldn't likely shoot an unarmed child, so we kept moving.

As we were crossing a road, Alley stopped and turned to me.

"Sergeant Wes, there are some kids on this road," he said.

I got on the road, and west of us, less than fifty meters away, were two small children with an adult woman. I didn't see any weapons, nor did I see any radio. I yelled at them to move out using the only Pashto word I knew.

"Za!" I yelled. "Za! Get the fuck out of here."

Of course, they just looked at me. I guess my accent was off. I didn't know what to do, but as luck would have it, right at that moment, an F18 fighter jet came screaming overhead. By the time I heard it, it was already gone, and the noise was deafening. It was enough to scare the shit out of the woman and two children, and they ran off. It was also enough to give me a chance to breathe and laugh.

We crossed the road and continued moving northeast through a field of marijuana. The plants were so dense, and I'd never seen so much marijuana in my life. Then CanSOF came back online. They had radios that that would intercept Taliban communications (ICOM), and they had some news for us.

"Three-seven, this is CanSOF," the voice over the radio said, calling Dugas. "We have ICOM chatter that states the Taliban have a four- to five-man element with eyes on your position. They are setting up an ambush to hit you."

I stopped the movement in the middle of the pot field and walked back to Dugas. I didn't say why we had stopped because I didn't want the rest of the guys to get nervous.

"Did you hear that shit?" I asked Dugas.

"Fuck yeah, I heard that," he said. "What do you think we should do?" This was the first time since I'd known him that he didn't have an answer.

I could tell he wasn't scared, but I wanted to fuck with him.

"You ready to go out in a blaze of fucking glory?" I asked with a smile on my face.

"Fuck you, turd!" he quickly responded, and I could tell he wasn't in the mood to joke.

I figured with the amount of personnel we had, we could handle the small ambush, but I thought it would be better to change course.

"We can keep going this direction," I said, motioning to the northeast. "Or we can turn north here, jump that wall, and get back into the grape fields. This marijuana provides good concealment, but I think it's shit for cover."

Dugas didn't hesitate.

"Let's get out of this shit," he said, looking at the map. "Turn north and get into that grape field. I want you to zigzag through those fields up there and get us to the objective."

"Roger that," I said and walked back to the front, telling Alley what the plan was.

We turned north and got into the grape fields, going up one row, crossing over to another row, and going back down. The logic behind this made sense. The grape rows provided undeniable coverage, and if we made unpredictable turns, there would be no way for the enemy to know where we'd be, providing a sense of security for us from IEDs.

When we were nearly one hundred meters from where I had plotted the end point, I got on the radio and called Lieutenant Labowski.

"Three-six, this is Three-four," I said. "Do you have eyes on our position?"

After a brief pause, he came back. "Negative."

"Can you give me a grid to your current location?" I asked.

The LT came back with an eight-digit grid coordinate, and after consulting with my GPS, I realized we were still two hundred fifty meters away. That's not a far distance unless you're moving through grape fields and climbing mud walls. I was frustrated, but we kept moving. When we finally got near the position we had been given, we were about fifty meters north of a mud compound. I called back again asking for "eyes on," and still they didn't have eyes on us. I was really starting to get frustrated. I had brought us within fifty meters of where the LT had reported his location. I was tired, thirsty, hungry, and wanting to quit, but we had to drive on. There wasn't a choice. I halted the movement to check the map one more time.

"Three-four, this is Three-six," called the LT. "We're going to fire a pen flare from our position. Stand by."

When you carry a radio, you sometimes take it for granted that everyone hears what you hear, so I didn't bother to relay that information back. When the flare went off just behind the compound wall, I realized I should have let everyone know what it was. I turned around and Schwartz was already in the prone. I think that was the fastest I'd ever seen him move. I laughed out loud, relieved that we had found our platoon, and told everyone it was a pen flare. Schwartz looked pretty embarrassed, and the first thing he did was look behind him to make sure the EOD female hadn't seen him dive to the ground.

We linked up with Lieutenant Labowski and the rest of the platoon. They led us back to the path, and I took Burke and Schwartz to the farthest east end of our position and put them in place.

"If anything comes up that path, I want you to blast the fuck out it," I instructed them, then walked back to where EOD was setting up to do site exploitation of the IED site. As they were setting up, a loud pop came from the east end of the trail. Everyone froze.

"Medic!" someone yelled from that direction, and the first thing I thought was that Burke and Schwartz were blown up. I ran down the path. When I got to their position, I saw they were safe, and the relief felt like a weight lifted off my back.

"What the fuck was that?" I asked.

"I don't know," Burke said. "Recon's LT went down that path, and we heard the pop and someone called for a medic."

"What the fuck was he doing going down there?" I asked, almost pissed. "You two are the far left limit. No one should have gone past you."

"I know, Sarge," Burke said. "But we can't tell a lieutenant not to do nothin'. We just privates."

I couldn't argue with the logic, but in combat, these privates had a job to do, and they should have stopped that lieutenant. I went down the trail where the medic was already working on Recon's LT. He had stepped on a pressure plate, and the IED had been a partial detonation. With all the moaning and crying he was doing, I expected him to be legless. Instead, since it was a partial detonation, it had broken his ankle. Brave or not, he wasn't walking back to Zangabad. We were going to have to medevac him out of there.

As I surveyed the position, I realized something that made me question my own existence. The spot where he had stepped on the pressure plate was right next to where Schwartz had taken a knee when Martin had been hit. In fact, in the trail, you could see the knee prints from Schwartz's and my knee pads—both less than a foot from where the pressure plate had been located. How had neither of us stepped on it? Not just us, but the rest of the platoon had walked by this area too.

The EOD team made its way back to the new site and dug up what was left of the jug of homemade explosives. I was tasked with pulling security with one of the EOD operators while he mineswept an open field we would use for the medevac site. After it was cleared, I pulled security on the northwest side of the helicopter landing zone and waited for the helicopter to arrive. When the bird made its first pass, we marked the HLZ with a smoke grenade, signaling where the Blackhawk could land. It came in, landed, and the crew chief dismounted the bird to help load the wounded LT. After a few minutes, the medevac took off, and we continued to pull security until it was out of sight.

I made my way back to the rest of the platoon, and the decision was made that we would return to Palace. There were too many IED threats in this tree line. We had already set off two explosions, and the risk was too great.

We started moving back to Palace. I was near the center of the movement with Schwartz, Alley, and Burke right behind me. CanSOF started reporting more ICOM chatter.

"They watched the medevac bird come in," they reported. "They even said it was a Blackhawk and that one man got off the bird and helped load another man on. They definitely have eyes on your movement."

The idea of the Taliban watching us so closely gave me the creeps, and the accuracy of the CanSOF report just made me angry. I wanted to make contact with the enemy at that point and blow them away, but there was nothing we could do but move out. As we kept moving, the CanSOF operator continued to relay intercepted Taliban messages, each time relaying exactly what we were doing and where we were. It was unnerving. I felt a little reassured knowing that we had close air support including two Kiowa Warriors and one Apache helicopter. I wished the Taliban would try something and give the pilots some target practice.

When we were two hundred meters from Route Q, the CanSOF message came across that the Taliban "has you surrounded and is about to initiate an ambush." The thought of that made me laugh. At this point, we were approximately forty soldiers moving in a file on a road through a small village. How could they have us surrounded? And would they really be foolish enough to try to ambush us with three lethal helicopters flying overhead? Suddenly, I wasn't worried.

We made it to Route Q, where three Strykers were waiting. We loaded as many people onto the trucks as we could fit, and the rest of us walked between the trucks the rest of the way back to Palace.

We learned a lot from this patrol. First and foremost, we learned we weren't bulletproof. We had been really lucky. Secondly, we learned to never ignore anything that looked like an IED marker.

Later, I learned that Martin, while minesweeping with the Vallon, got a large metal detection. When he did, he turned around to backtrack and stepped onto an area that hadn't been swept. As luck would have it, he stepped on a pressure plate. Luckily, the explosives wired to the pressure plate were further up the trail, and when the explosion went off, no one was directly in the kill radius, but Martin had been injured. And luckily, none of his injuries caused him loss of life or limb.

I never had much regard for Martin, the college E-4 who had carried Christiansen's rock for him earlier that year at NTC. I remembered that I had called him a piece of shit. After he walked back to Zangabad in the state that he was in, I had a newfound respect for him.

As far as the Recon LT, I didn't feel so bad for him. Apparently, before we left Zangabad with Recon and EOD, a soldier asked him who had been blown up. This LT allegedly said, "Don't worry about it. It was just a fucking private." If that was an accurate account, Karma just reared her ugly face for the first time since we got in sector. I decided to consciously swallow comments like that from then on, and if he had really said that, he got what he deserved.

Karma, at least in Afghanistan, is a bitch.

From that day forward, we referred to the tree line north of Lakani as the Martin Tree Line, and as much as an honor as that may have been, it became our intent that the Martin Tree Line be burned to the ground. Unfortunately, we never saw that happen. No matter how hard we tried.

SIX

JUST ANOTHER DAY AT THE OFFICE

All right, they're on our left, they're on our right, they're in
front of us, they're behind us . . . they can't get away this time.
— Lewis B. "Chesty" Puller, USMC

30 June 2011—Lakani Firefight

Our first attempt to bring down the Martin Tree Line came days later as we set out for another patrol in the Lakani area. Again, the intent was to get to the center of town and hold a *shura* or a town meeting with the villagers. I wondered if we would ever realize these shuras were, in reality, a waste of time. The Taliban influence was so deeply engrained with the locals, and the fear of reprisal for perceived cooperation with us was so real that it rendered most shuras futile.

But we were still new in Panjwei'i, and we had a lot to learn. Gun Team 1, Burke and Schwartz, carried extra ammo on this patrol. I talked Dugas into letting Wyscaver come out to redeem himself from the fall-out patrol. He carried an M249 Squad Automatic Weapon (SAW) to add a little kick to our firepower. His gunners, Thompson and Christiansen, had gone on leave, or I may have brought them along as well. I wanted to hit the Martin Tree Line with everything we had. I thought if we took fire from that area again, we'd be able to call in enough fire to burn it down, taking away the enemy's use of the tree line as a fighting position.

The role of Weapons Squad in this patrol was to take over a compound west of Lakani, where we would have fields of fire to a southern tree line and to the north, the Martin Tree Line. The plan was for Dugas to stay at the compound with us while the LT and the rest of the platoon advanced toward the center of town to conduct a shura, assuming they made it that far.

They wouldn't make it that far.

As we approached the compound we planned to overtake, Third Squad loaned us their minesweeper to scan the area for IEDs. Private First Class Padilla, a member of First Squad from New Mexico, had started to take his job of manning the Vallon seriously, and as time went on, he became the best minesweeper in the platoon. Padilla was really good about exaggerating things and often referred to himself as the product of Zeus, or something crazy like that, so sometimes it was hard to tell when he was serious. When he was clearing a path on the western side of the compound along the wall from south to north, he searched the path and along the walls. I was right behind him, pulling security and set Wyscaver in a small clearing to have more cover to the northern tree line. As Padilla turned right to continue clearing the northern side of the building, he froze.

"Uh . . . Sergeant," he said. "I think you might want to look at this."

"What is it?" I asked.

"I think it's a pressure plate," he said.

The Taliban had gotten pretty adept at making pressure plates from various objects, including old tires, pieces of wood, and even scraps of military garbage left behind. When Padilla said that, I thought he'd found something with the Vallon. As I came around the corner, I realized it wasn't a completed pressure plate, and it wasn't buried. It was sitting on the path north of the compound and it looked like someone had been constructing it, and as we walked up, they ran off, leaving their work behind.

After inspecting the partial pressure plate, we took pictures of it and bagged what we could for evidence. I was now pretty wary of what kind of compound we had encountered. It could easily be some kind of holdup for the Taliban, and considering the area we were in and what we'd just found, I wasn't sure it was a good idea to get on top of this compound. Padilla continued searching the outskirts of the building, and when we made it to the east side and cleared to the door, I was more watchful of our surroundings. I saw a lot of potential bomb-making material in the area, including wire and discarded batteries.

Dugas walked up with an interpreter, and after a short discussion about whether this was a safe compound to overtake, Dugas made the decision to knock on the door. An older Afghan lady opened, and through the terp, we gained access to the compound. Weapons Squad, minus Wyscaver, who was still pulling security in the clearing, headed to the west wall using the wall to gain access to the roof. Schwartz went first then helped Burke get up with the gun. I followed Burke, and we set up in a position on the northeast end of the wall.

This rooftop was perfect. There were large humps built into the roof, and although they were a little tough to maneuver over, they provided great cover. Additionally, the rooftops had a raised section of wall about three feet tall on the northern side, adding even more cover should we take fire. Our sectors of fire on the Martin Tree Line were perfect, and we could see into the grape fields between us and the tree line to the north. We also had a good view of the southern tree line, but we still had friendly troops in the area, so we concentrated on the north. I was hoping we would take fire from that direction because all we needed was an excuse.

By 0700, we were in place, and the humps on the roof doubled as cover and something we could lean against. I always enjoyed getting into these blocking positions with Burke and Schwartz because they were really good about carrying on conversation. Thompson was so quiet that it was hard to talk to him. So the three of us talked for about twenty minutes, making jokes and hoping we'd see something from the northern tree line. We even contemplated a fake firefight so we could call in an airstrike and burn the fucker down. It turned out that wouldn't be necessary.

At 0730, I was standing up to walk to the western side of the rooftop so I could look down on Wyscaver and make sure he was doing OK. As I took a step toward the top of the hump, shots rang out, and some bullets whizzed past my head while some hit the short wall in front of us. I fell in between two humps and called out to Gun Team 1, "Where the fuck did that come from?"

"I think it was from that wall out there in front of the tree line!" Burke yelled back.

"Light that fucker up!" I screamed. "He almost fucking shot me!"

Burke opened up with the M240 and put almost one hundred rounds into that wall. I was feeling pretty ballsy, as you usually do standing behind a machine gun, and as Burke finished his round of firing, I stood up and yelled, "How do you like that, motherfucker?"

I guess he didn't like it too much because another volley of AK-47 fire hit the side of the building and put me back on my ass.

"Burke, you'd better fuck that dude up!" I said. "He wants to kill me. Do you want him to kill me?"

"No, Sarge," Burke said, laughing. "I don't want that. If you get killed, who would be Weapons Squad leader?"

"Probably Dugas," I called back. "Do you want Sergeant Dugas to be your squad leader?"

"Hell no, Sarge," Burke said back. "I think it'd be good to keep you as squad leader."

"Then what the fuck are you waiting for? Shoot that motherfucker!" I yelled.

Burke let out another burst of machine gun fire, and it got quiet for a few minutes. I hoped that if Burke hadn't shot the guy, at least he'd run him off. That wasn't the case because less than ten minutes later, we got hit again. This time I heard Wyscaver open up with the SAW from the clearing while Burke sent another shower of lead onto the wall and the tree line. Hearing Wyscaver open fire made me feel good because now, Christiansen was the only member of the squad who hadn't earned his CIB since Thompson got his the day we were hit in the open field on the air assault mission.

As Burke was firing toward the north, our forward operator, Sergeant Keelslice, came up on the roof to get a better vantage point to call in fire. Keelslice, later to be nicknamed Kill Slice, had radio communications with the mortar systems at Zangabad and also with any aerial assets we had. I was happy to see him, hoping he would be able to call in fire on the tree line. He stayed low on the roof as he plotted the area from where the enemy fire was coming. As he was working, we started taking fire from the southern tree line. I trained my M4 toward where I thought the rounds were coming from and opened fire. This was the first firefight we'd been in where we took fire from more than one front. It wasn't surprising because the Canadians told us that it was common, but living it for the first time was a little unsettling.

When the fire calmed down, I called Wyscaver up from the clearing and told him to get on the roof. When he made it to the top, I put him on the southwest corner of the building with instructions to "smoke anything in that tree line that moved." No sooner did I say that, we began to take fire. On the southern end Wyscaver and the northern end Burke sprayed their respective tree lines, giving us a lull in the fire. By now we'd been in contact for almost an hour.

My adrenaline was still pumping pretty hard. I started making jokes to Schwartz about getting my Purple Heart on the rooftop. He didn't think my jokes were very funny at first, but eventually, he'd get in on it too. I wanted to get Dugas's opinion, so I called him on the radio.

"Three-seven, this is Three-four," I radioed. "Can I stand up on the rooftop and taunt them into firing at us again?"

"No, Three-four," Dugas called back. "I don't want to carry your fat-ass body back to the FOB. Just give me another distance and direction, and we'll call in some mortar fire."

"Buzz kill," I said and then gave him the distance and direction.

Keelslice radioed back to the FOB to get a fire mission started with the 81 mm mortar team. It took forever, but finally they started to drop rounds. This is what I'd been waiting for. When the mortars got a bead on the tree line, we would call "fire for effect," and they could turn it to glass. When the first round hit, it was too far north, so Keelslice called in the adjustment and called in "Fire for effect . . . three rounds."

All three rounds hit the tree line. One hit at tree so hard, it looked like it was going to collapse but somehow remained standing. I was excited because I knew we were about to burn it down when the FOB mortar team called Keelslice and said they were told to cease fire because, according to the proverbial "them," we had been targeting compounds.

"Are you kidding me?" I asked Keelslice. "Those rounds were right on target! We could knock that fucking tree line down with those mortars. Who said we're hitting compounds? All I see are trees!"

Keelslice couldn't answer who "they" were that said that, but his job was done. I was pissed. I guess we wouldn't burn down that tree line today. I'm not sure if I was the only person in the platoon that felt a personal obligation to take down that tree line. Of course, with it gone, it would deny cover in that area for Taliban fighters, but we had also sustained our first serious injury from that tree line. Maybe it was personal.

Lieutenant Labowski made his way to the roof carrying a light antitank weapon. The US Army no longer carried these small shoulder-fired rockets in its inventory, but the Canadians had left us with a small supply. The LT asked me where the fire was coming from and extended the LAW, placed it in action, and fired it, landing a direct hit on the tree line. We whooped and hollered, "How do you like me now, motherfucker?" I think we may have been having too much fun at this point, and it was turning into a carnival.

There was a lull in the fire, and Schwartz was leaning against one of the humps close to the northern edge of the roof. We had been talking for a few minutes, and it seemed like the shooting had ceased. A loud crack broke up our conversation, and a piece of the small wall on the rooftop burst into dust about two feet directly in front of Schwartz's face. Had it not been for the wall, that bullet would have been the end of him. His eyes got wide, and he slinked down between two humps, and Burke defended his AG with a fifty-round burst.

"Did you see that shit?" Schwartz yelled at me. "Did you see where that fucking round hit? That would have hit me straight in the grill! Holy shit!"

"I'm telling your mom," I said to him. I had promised his mother I'd watch out for him on this deployment, and I teased him about that often. "I'm telling her you were sitting up on this roof and you weren't paying attention, and *that's* why you almost got shot. You'd better pay attention from now on or she's gonna spank you when you get home."

He was still bedazzled by his near-death experience. "Did you see that?" he asked again. "If that wall wasn't there, I'd be fucking dead right now."

"No, you wouldn't be dead," I said. "I'm here and I'm a combat lifesaver. I would save you. And what would really piss me off is that you'd get a Purple Heart, and I wouldn't get one. I wouldn't get shit."

"Well, if you couldn't save me, I'd still get a Purple Heart, but I'd be dead and wouldn't get any of the benefits from it," he responded, still breathing a little hard.

"Well, if you died," I said, still joking with him, "could I get your Purple Heart benefits? I think that would be even better than getting the Purple Heart if I didn't get hurt but still got all the benefits from it. Would that be OK with you? Do you think your mommy would mind if I got the benefits?"

We laughed just as another round of incoming fire hit the side of the building from the south side. We took cover while Wyscaver returned fire. From the ground, someone handed us another LAW. Schwartz felt like getting a little payback and asked if he could shoot it, and I said, "Fuck yeah."

Since the LAW isn't something we trained on in garrison and it's no longer taught at Basic Training or Infantry School, I helped Schwartz get the weapon into firing configuration. He got where he could see the southern tree line, and after clearing his back blast area, he fired the LAW into the southern tree line with a direct hit. It was beautiful.

It was nearly 1100 hours, and after three and a half hours, we were getting tired being targets. I wanted to come down off the roof, but if they were still watching us, we'd be easy targets as we handed down all of our equipment. We got hit again from the northern side, and Dugas called up to tell me to spot rounds for our 60 mm Mortar Team. I didn't trust our mortar men. The gunner, Private First Class Manley, was unpredictable and tended to do what he wanted rather than do what he was told. His assistant gunner (AG) was just as worthless. But since we had that asset and Dugas was controlling it, I told him I'd spot rounds.

As Burke fired another volley at the wall in front of the tree line, the first 60 mm mortar round hit. Burke yelled out, "Holy fuck! Manley just killed that motherfucker!" He said with excitement in his voice, "I just saw a fucking body flying through the air. Manley killed him! It was just like in the fucking movies, man! Boom! And a body flying through the air!"

We all laughed our asses off, and though it was a lucky shot, our mortar team had actually taken out the northern sniper. I thought maybe I'd misjudged the two guys, but I later realized my gut instincts were right on target.

We were still taking fire from the southern tree line, so Keelslice called up an airstrike from an A-10. Since the tree line was only about two hundred meters from our position, anything fired from an aircraft would be considered danger close, and I was surprised that Keelslice, and whoever authorized it, would have the balls to make that call. We had plenty of cover on the rooftop, so I wasn't worried, and I told my crew to get down. We watched as the plane circled around and came in for the shot. The pilot launched two Hellfire missiles on the tree line, both of them landing about thirty meters short, and it looked like he was going to come around for another chance, but someone called him off.

It didn't matter because if nothing else, it was an effective show of force, and at 1130, all fire ceased. We'd been on the rooftop for five hours, and four and half hours of that time had been under intermittent fire. I was worn out. Lieutenant Labowski went into the grape field to the north of our position to do Battle Damage Assessment (BDA) on the mortar strike. He returned when he didn't find anything, denying our mortar team of a confirmed kill despite Burke witnessing the body flying through the air.

We dismounted the roof, and all the squads linked up for the movement back to Zangabad. I was tired, hungry, and thirsty. It was a good day because no one had been hurt, Schwartz still had all of his teeth, and we had just been in the longest firefight of the deployment. Even though BDA on the northern and southern tree lines had come up empty, I trusted what Burke said and felt like we'd taken at least one Taliban fighter out of the game. We still hadn't burned down the Martin Tree Line, but I hoped we'd be back for that another day.

01 July 2011—An HME Factory?

We had received a tip that a compound just northwest of Palace was a site where the Taliban was producing Homemade Explosives (HME), so Lieutenant Labowski had us organize a patrol to the area and somehow managed to get an element of ANA to go with us. We hadn't had much luck partnering up with our ANA counterparts, and there was a lot of mistrust between us and them. A Special Forces unit had been to Palace about a week earlier and set up some surveillance equipment to monitor incoming and outgoing cell phone calls. It turned out that every time we left Palace, someone from the ANA compound would make a call to a suspected Taliban number and report where we were going and how many soldiers we were taking with us on patrol. This information made Dugas nervous, and when he got nervous, I got scared.

The LTs response to this was to get them more involved in our patrols. His thought process was that if they were with us, we were less likely to get hit since some of them were obviously corrupt. Despite the reasoning behind it, we were all pretty wary of having the ANA on patrol with us, but we didn't have a say in the matter.

We made our way on foot to the alleged HME factory and Weapons Squad consisting of me and Gun Team 1, took over a small uninhabited compound, and got on the roof to cover the search. Getting on the roof wasn't an easy task since we had to climb on a wall to get on the roof that had a large tree overhang. It was difficult maneuvering the M240 through the branches, but we got in there and pulled security. The ANA took the lead in searching for HME, and no one was surprised when the search came up empty.

When it was time to get off the roof, I looked over the roof, and it looked like a long drop down. I decided we'd have to go back the way we came, and it was a slow process getting down. Instead of going back into the compound, Burke and Schwartz weaved through the tree branches of the overhanging tree and dropped down outside the compound. I followed their lead, and after handing my weapon down to Schwartz, I grabbed a tree branch and held on, releasing my feet from the wall and dangling from the branch.

"Just drop, Sarge," Burke said. "You can make it."

I don't think he realized that despite the fact I was an airborne jumpmaster with the Eighty-second Airborne Division, I am deathly afraid of heights.

"How far down is it?" I asked.

A burst of laughter broke out with all the soldiers on the ground. I had no idea what was so funny.

"How fucking far is it?" I asked a little irritated, realizing I was becoming the butt of some joke.

"It's about two inches," Burke said, laughing his ass off.

Sure enough, when I let go of the branch, I dropped about two inches to the ground. If I had reached with my toes, I would have touched the ground. I felt like an idiot, but I realized how funny it must have looked, so I laughed at myself. As we walked around to the front of the compound we had been overwatching from I realized that the wall was only about eight feet high, and we probably wouldn't have had any problems getting down from there. I started to wonder if I wasn't just getting scared, not just of heights but of making a bad decision.

We made it back to Palace without a skirmish. Those days were becoming increasingly few and far between. It felt good to have not seen any action, but at the same time, it felt like the patrol was a waste of time. I started to wonder if there was some correlation to having the ANA with us and our not getting hit. I'm not saying all of our counterparts were crooked, but there was something to be said about having them with us and not getting sprayed with Taliban bullets.

When we got back from this patrol, we had a sweet surprise. I was walking by the kitchen tent, and there was a huge BBQ grill with wheels put in front of it.

"What the fuck is this?" I asked.

"The cook brought it with him," one of the privates said.

"We got a cook?" I asked. "Bullshit! There's no way they sent a cook to Palace. That's way too good to be true."

But sure enough, we were assigned Sgt. Terrell Miller to prepare our meals. We'd spent so long scavenging food the Canadians left behind, including rotten Canadian MREs, and trying to figure out how to keep from starving that having a cook was too good to be true.

Miller was the cook of all cooks. We'd give him a hard time if he didn't have a meal ready from time to time, but I don't know how that deployment would have gone without him. He had connections wherever we went, and when he went to a FOB, he'd come back to Palace with a Stryker full of food. And don't get me started on Rib Night on Friday nights.

In addition to cooking, Miller would fill in for us on patrols. We never asked him. He wanted to go out with us, and as we started to thin out on personnel, we didn't argue. When I was in Iraq, we took our supply sergeant on a few missions, but our area wasn't very dangerous. Panjwei'i was not safe, and Miller was the only cook I'd ever seen willing to go on an infantry patrol. Dugas used to kid him because of all the noise he'd make walking through the grape fields. He used to ask Miller, "Do you have all your pots and pans in your assault pack?"

I had, and today still have, a lot of respect for Sergeant Miller.

02 July 2011-04 July 2011—A Night in Lakani

Third Platoon was planning a cookout at Palace in observance of the Fourth of July, and we had invited the Canadian Special Forces unit to join us since they were leaving soon. They had done a great deal to support us. In a war zone, there are no four-day weekends for holidays, and two days before our shindig, we had to do a snap patrol with the ANA into Lakani.

The squad leaders were told to get our people together and prepare for a two-day patrol into Lakani on 02 July. A battalion push into Lakani complete with engineers, found seventeen IEDs from the village, two of which they couldn't remove because of the Taliban threat in the area. With about an hour's notice, we were going into the area with the ANA to search more compounds.

We got everything together, and I took Alley, Burke, and Schwartz for the mission. Since this was billed as an ANA-led patrol, we piled into the backs of their Ford Rangers and let them ferry us out to Lakani. I didn't mind getting a ride, and since the roads to Lakani were too narrow for a Stryker to get there without causing damage, it was much faster to go out in the back of a pickup truck. But I wasn't comfortable riding in the truck for a couple reasons. The first was because growing up, my dad had always warned me of the dangers of riding in the back of a pickup truck, and it was a warning I'd always heeded. Secondly, I had to wonder how much protection a Ford Ranger would provide if we hit an IED. Surely it couldn't be much. So the ride to Lakani was quicker than walking, but I can't say I was any more comfortable riding in the back of a pickup truck.

When we got to the area, we pulled security while the trucks went to get the rest of our men from Palace. It took a long time, but when everyone was ready, we set out to search the compounds. Weapons Squad's job was to pull security along the roads while the other squads accompanied ANA troops on the search. Things went south rather quickly.

Two groups were searching different areas simultaneously, and I was nearer the group with more ANA than US soldiers. A fuss started coming over the radio that our interpreter had gotten into an argument with the ANA commander about what US troops were *allowed* to do. The ANA commander threatened to call the whole patrol off, and inside, I was hoping he would because I'd rather just go back to Palace. I didn't feel comfortable being in Lakani, and I sure wasn't thrilled about the ANA trying to push us around. I really just wanted to make it back for the Fourth of July cookout.

One thing led to another, and soon enough, none of the US soldiers were searching any of the compounds. Instead, we all pulled security for the ANA while they hastily searched the buildings in the area. It was no surprise to us when their searches turned up nothing.

It was on this patrol that Burke and Schwartz received their nicknames from me. Burke always wanted to be called Black Mamba, but I thought that was too overplayed. Schwartz was still searching for a moniker. While pulling security at an intersection, I heard Schwartz call me.

"Hey, Sergeant Wes," he said. "Come look at this. There's a mongoose running on this wall over here."

As I started to walk toward them to see this mongoose, Burke made a correction.

"That ain't no mongoose, nigga, that's a weasel!"

I burst out laughing and almost pissed my pants. It was the funniest thing I'd ever heard Burke say, and he always had something funny to say. Burke always has a smile on his face, and he's very quick witted, so the comment alone was funny. But how did someone from Corcoran, California know the difference between a mongoose and weasel? I couldn't contain myself, and I repeated that quote for the rest of the deployment. Burke was now Weasel, and Schwartz's new name was Mongoose. Like I said, nicknames come in strange wrappers.

As the search continued, it was obvious we weren't having any success. We were in a road entertaining some small children, and we were just relaxed. It worried me a little because I figured when we least expected it, we should expect it. Schwartz handed a little girl a bottle of water, and before I could tell him not to, she opened the water and poured it out right in front of his face.

"You stupid cunt!" he yelled at her. "You're wasting our fucking water."

She laughed and ran off. That story would be told over and over as the deployment went on.

We ended up in the center of Lakani, one of the few times we'd ever make it there. I wasn't surprised we got there since we were with our ANA buddies. While we were waiting for further instructions, the ANA commander told Lieutenant Labowski that they were going to go back to Palace for the night. I heard Lieutenant Labowski tell him that if he was going back, we would have to go back with them. I was relieved because my back was giving me problems, and I would rather sleep in my CHU than in some mud compound on the floor. When the LT called in that we were going to return to Palace, the word came back that we had to stay out there, even if the ANA went back. I was pissed.

The ANA commander surprisingly volunteered his element to stay with us, and that relieved me a little. I was already pretty sure we hadn't seen any action because we were with the ANA. If we had to spend the night out here, at least we had them with us.

We moved further west on the road until we came to an abandoned compound. As members of First Squad cleared the compound, another spat arose among the ANA, and it turned out they refused to enter the compound. I never learned the reason why, but that meant they would sleep on the road. Lieutenant Labowski told me if they were sleeping on the road, we would have to leave some men outside to support them. The ANA didn't have night-vision equipment, and we would have to help defend them in the event of a firefight. That meant Weapons Squad would be sleeping on the road with them.

I was done complaining. I partnered up with Schwartz while Alley and Burke teamed up, and we took turns pulling guard shifts while our buddy slept. We were on the road near the firefight that had just taken place a few days earlier. I didn't like the idea of the whole thing, but I was tired and took advantage of my time to sleep and pulled guard when it was my turn.

The next morning, we got ready to go back to Palace. Mongoose made fun of me for farting in my sleep and did a pretty good impression of what it must have sounded like. It was Independence Day, and I was looking forward to the cookout that night, so all I wanted to do was get back to Palace without incident.

The ANA shuttled us back to Palace in the Ford Rangers, and we made no contact. We had our cookout and it was good. The camaraderie in the platoon was building, and for a while, it felt like we were starting to become a family. Thanks to Sergeant Miller, we ate shrimp, lobster tails, and steak, and our spirits were high.

05 July 2011—Gharandai

If we had been at home, we might still be on a holiday break for Independence Day, but in the war zone, there's no rest for the weary. It was just another day at the office. We were going into a village southwest of Zangabad. Gharandai was within eyesight of the Operation Delta Attachment (ODA), and the Special Forces team there would cover our movement, so there was some level of comfort.

The movement to the compound Weapons Squad and Second Squad would occupy was uneventful. I was starting to think we'd run the Taliban off because we'd been on two patrols with no action. When the rest of the platoon split off to go to their objective, we boosted Wyscaver and Keelslice onto a roof. Mongoose and Weasel were getting in position to cover the west side of our strong point when Sergeant Hurst called me.

"Dusty Balls!" Hurst yelled. "We need you over here for some of your Vietnam expertise."

I was constantly getting ribbed about my age, and I've always been a pretty good sport about it. I thought it was funny when my peers would ask me what it was like to be in Vietnam or World War II.

I walked over to where Hurst and Van Bockel were standing, looking up at a pipe sticking out of a wall.

"Does that look like some Vietnam shit to you?" Van Bockel asked, pointing at the pipe.

I looked up at the pipe that was probably eight inches in diameter; and sticking out of the pipe was, what appeared to be, the tail end of some kind of rocket. My first thought was that we had found an IED. My second thought was that it would go off any second. I did an about-face forward march, yelling, "Fuck, fuck, fuck, fuck!" and called Dugas over to check it out. The consensus among us all was that it was indeed an IED, and we needed to call EOD. The good part about that was that we would get to see our favorite female EOD operator, and the thought of that raised everyone's spirits a little.

As Dugas called up the IED, we were standing between two buildings. One was a grape hut, and the other was the small building Wyscaver and Keelslice were on top of. A burst of AK-47 fire opened up, and the echo from between the two buildings made it impossible to tell where it was coming from.

Wyscaver opened up with the SAW, and Burke and Schwartz put their gun into action, returning fire on a grape hut that was to our northwest. The ODA opened up from their position with a Mark 19, and the enemy fire stopped momentarily. I was still worried about the possible IED in the building right next to us, so I stayed as far from it as I could.

When the Taliban opened up again, we realized it was coming from a grape hut about two hundred meters north of our position. Hurst came around the corner of the building he was behind, carrying a LAW. Our small arms weren't going to penetrate the enemy grape hut, and I didn't think the LAW would either, but hopefully it would be enough to scare the Taliban away. Hurst fired the LAW, hit the grape hut, and it didn't seem to make a dent. The firefight continued. Dugas got into it and started firing his M4 while Burke was blasting the grape hut with his M240. There were helicopters flying overhead, but Keelslice wasn't having any luck communicating with them. We continued to fire at the grape hut along with the ODA Mark 19, and as I was standing back, I heard Dugas yell, "Here comes a missile!"

When he said that, I thought he meant from the grape hut, and I dove for cover. When I looked up, I could hear the explosion and realized the missile came from the Apache helicopter flying overhead. I looked toward the grape hut; it was engulfed in a cloud of dust and smoke. We all cheered and watched as the dust settled, revealing a huge section of wall missing. I was pretty confident that if the Hellfire missile hadn't killed them, the remainder of the Taliban that had been shooting at us had run off. All firing ceased.

We waited for EOD to show up, and when they did, we all crowded around as they inspected the IED and said they would blow it. They had to confirm that the compound was uninhabited before they set their charge.

When they started the countdown, we all took cover in a small ditch about fifty meters from where the IED was emplaced. When the C-4 explosives went off, it shook the earth; and when the dust settled, we carefully walked over to inspect the damage.

The IED turned out to be a large piece of steel pipe. I couldn't determine what it actually was, but the blast from the C-4 didn't even scratch it, but it did blow it out of the pipe and onto the ground. It was pretty heavy, and no one volunteered to carry it back. We felt a little silly about calling EOD out to blow this steel pipe, but Dugas reassured us that it was better to be safe than sorry. Not to mention, we got to see Ms. EOD.

At approximately 1145 hours, we linked up with the rest of the platoon and started our walk back to Palace. Spirits were pretty high. We'd just endured another firefight, and we walked away unscathed. We were starting to feel bulletproof again.

That wouldn't last long.

SEVEN

THINGS JUST GOT REAL

The foot soldier has a special feeling for the ground. He walks on it, fights on it, sleeps and eats on it; the ground shelters him from fire; he digs his home in it. But mines and booby traps transform that friendly, familiar earth into a thing of menace, a thing to be feared as much as machine guns or mortar shells. The infantryman knows that any moment the ground he is walking on can erupt and kill him; kill him if he's lucky. If he's unlucky, he will be turned into a blind, deaf, emasculated, legless shell. It was not warfare. It was murder . . . we had begun to feel more like victims than soldiers.

—From *A Rumor of War* by Philip Caputo

07 July 2011

We woke up and got ready for the patrol which was intended to simply be a disruption patrol where we planned on going into a few villages to make our presence known and hopefully push the Taliban away from any actions they had planned.

As I was getting ready, I did a radio check and couldn't reach anyone. I had to get my radio reprogrammed or filled. I took it to our command post (CP) and had the radio operator fill my radio. When I got back, I found Dugas standing outside my CHU. He started handing me papers.

"What is this shit?" I asked.

"It's the nine-line information," he said, referring to the information that was required to call in a medevac in the case of serious injury or death. "I'm not going out. I need a break, so you're going to be the acting platoon sergeant today."

I was OK with that. Dugas was getting pretty worn out, and I figured he could use a break from a patrol or two. He hadn't missed one yet, and with all we'd seen, it was about time we all started getting a day off from patrolling here and there.

After he handed me the list with the platoon's names and battle roster numbers, he hung out while I was getting my gear on. He was acting like a father who was worried about his son taking the car out for the first time. I kept laughing at him and finally said, "Don't worry, Dad. We're gonna be OK." He quickly responded with a "fuck you" and walked off.

We weren't going far that day, so we didn't need the Strykers. When we crowded together at the front gate of Palace, it was First Squad, Third Squad, and a gun team consisting of Burke, Schwartz, and Alley from Weapons Squad. We also had our Forward Observer, Sergeant Keelslice, and the platoon medic, Private First Class Smith. Including Lieutenant Labowski, there were twenty-five of us going out. It was a typical size for one of our patrols. So far, nothing was out of the ordinary.

We left COP Palace and walked south on Route Q for just more than five hundred meters. First squad was in the lead, Third Squad was behind them, and Weapons Squad picked up the rear. The interpreter, the LT, the FO, and the medic were near the center of the movement.

When we took the turn west toward the first village of Shapozai, I was surprised at the tall sunflower plants that were growing alongside the road. Usually, when we traveled on Route Q, we were in vehicles and rarely walked along this route during daylight hours, so it was the first time I'd noticed these plants. It struck me as ironic that there can be spots of true beauty in a country so full of hate and pain.

We entered Shapozai and set up blocking positions on each end of the small dirt road in front and to the rear of our formation. I put Burke and Schwartz on the gun facing our six o'clock to pull security while the LT talked with some locals. I moved toward the center where the meeting was taking place and took some pictures while the LT was talking to them through an interpreter.

The meeting was pretty funny. Lieutenant Labowski was trying to get information about where the Taliban was and who was providing them with a place to sleep and food to eat. The locals were cooperating, but it was obvious they didn't want to give out too much information. Finally, in frustration, Lieutenant Labowski told the interpreter, "The next time they see the Taliban, tell them that I said they are cowards, and they are gay."

The interpreter laughed. Lieutenant Labowski reiterated and continued saying, "If they aren't cowards, tell them they need to stand out and fight us in the open with weapons."

The interpreter stumbled, trying to find a word in Pashto that corresponds with *homosexual*, and when he got it out, the locals laughed. I'm not sure if Lieutenant Labowski was trying to be funny, but it loosened the villagers up. One of them started saying something to the interpreter who relayed the conversation to the LT.

"He said there are Taliban that operate out of Peshengan," the interpreter said in broken English.

"Where is Peshengan?" Lieutenant Labowski asked.

"It's about two hundred meters that way," he replied, pointing to the west.

Lieutenant Labowski looked at me and told me to radio to our CP and find out exactly how far Peshengan Village was and what the terrain looked like between where we were and the village. I called up the radio operator at the platoon CP. After looking at the map, they relayed that the village of Peshengan was actually about five hundred meters away, and to get to it, we just needed to follow the same road we were on. We verified the route using the outdated maps we had available.

Lieutenant Labowski told me to get everyone ready; we were going to go see if we could find some Taliban. I was a little upset because I had been hoping this would be a really short patrol. With the LT adding this FRAGO, a change of mission, it was going to be longer than I had hoped, but I didn't complain. Instead, I called the squad leaders and my gun team together to let them know what we were doing.

We picked up, and Padilla led out with the minesweeper, searching for IEDs. We passed the area where we had our first contact of the deployment, and I felt like I was starting to see the same places over and over. We kept moving past the intersection, and at about three hundred meters into the movement, the platoon stopped. I was at the rear and called First Squad's squad leader, Sergeant Moreton, on the radio to see what caused us to halt.

First Squad had come upon a compound that looked abandoned, but there were footprints and motorcycle tracks leading up to the door. The door was locked, and Sergeant Moreton, after searching with the metal detector and looking for wires, started to breach the door. As he was doing this, I moved Private First Class Budd in front of the platoon with his M249 SAW to pull security and kept the M240 gun team at the rear. About thirty meters in front of Budd, the road made a left turn. I brought Padilla up to sweep for mines to the corner of the road so Budd could get in position and pull security around the corner. It was clear, and Budd got set.

A few minutes later, Budd called back, "Sergeant Wes, you should come see this."

I walked up to his position. The road turned right about fifty meters in front of his position, and there was a door to a house in the corner of the turn. Two small children and an old lady were packing up as much as they could carry, hastily moving out of the house and headed west down the road in the opposite direction of our patrol.

I called back to Lieutenant Labowski and told him what I saw. He told me to keep up security while they were inspecting the compound where they were located. When they finished, they pushed Padilla up to the front, and he cleared the road to the right turn and about twenty meters farther west on the road. Budd followed on and continued to pull security toward the front of the element. A group went inside the home, which was left unlocked, and searched it. They came up with nothing. I was standing outside when Lieutenant Labowski came out of the house.

"I want you to take some guys and clear up this road while we finish looking around this house," he said. "There's probably something since that family took off so fast."

I called up my gun team from the rear and had Alley pull out his metal detector. After he got it ready, he took point, and I pulled security for him while he cleared the road, looking for IEDs.

The next intersection was about one hundred meters west of the house being searched. We crossed over a small culvert and into an area shaded by trees. The road came to a small T intersection. The left side ran south. Going north, there was only about five meters before the road made another left turn going back west. There was a trail leading to the north on the other side of a small creek.

Alley cleared the intersection with the metal detector, and I had him pull security with his M4 up the trail to the north. I set in Budd with the SAW to pull security along the south-running road, and I pulled up Burke with the M240. I was standing in the middle of the intersection facing west.

"Set in right here," I told Burke, pointing west in the direction I wanted him to pull security.

As Burke set in the gun, I looked up, and a burst of machine gun fire opened up less than fifty meters up the road. I could see the gray smoke from the weapon billowing behind a tree branch, and leaves were falling from the tree from where the fire was coming.

"What the fuck?" I screamed as I spun to my right and got behind a wall for cover. From behind the protection of the wall, I peeked around the corner and could see leaves still falling from the trees. As close as the shooter was, I'll never know how I didn't get shot. Maybe I was lucky.

I looked down and saw in the middle of the intersection, Burke's M240 sitting there all alone. He had obviously dropped it when the firing started and darted behind cover. I can't say I blamed him, but now we had to get that gun back.

"What the fuck, Burke?" I yelled. "You need to get out there and get that gun! I'll cover you!"

From cover, I aimed my M4 at the spot where the firing had come from and shot about fifteen rounds into it. When I looked down, the gun was still sitting on the ground in the middle of the intersection.

"Goddammit, Burke! Why the fuck is that gun still out there?" I screamed.

"Dang, Sarge," he said. "I don't wanna go out there and get it."

"Well, it ain't gonna get itself, Burke," I said. "Now get your ass out there and get it!"

Burke moved as fast as I'd seen him move, and before I could even provide any cover fire, he'd darted out, grabbed the gun, and made it back behind the wall.

By this time, Lieutenant Labowski had made it to the intersection to see what had taken place. It all happened so fast, and I was so worried about losing our machine gun I'd forgotten to call it up on the radio. I told him we had been engaged by what appeared to be a lone gunman, pointing out the tree where I had received fire. He called up First Squad to push further west down the road.

Weapons Squad continued pulling security to the north and east, and Budd continued pulling security to the south. About one hundred meters further up the road, a massive firefight broke out with First Squad trading a substantial amount of bullets into a fighting position just south of the road. The squad was using a mud wall for cover while they rained 5.56 and M320 rounds into the fighting position. The firefight lasted almost ten minutes, and I can't imagine the amount of ammunition they put into the fighting position.

When things calmed down, I told my guys to hold their positions. I moved up to where First Squad was still poised for another volley. By this time, our air support had come in so I pulled out my VS17 panel and placed it over the wall, orange side up, so the helicopters could differentiate between us and the bad guys. Lieutenant Labowski walked over to me.

"The birds said they saw guys leaving that wood line and stashing weapons in a grape hut," he said, pointing to the tree line where the firefight had just taken place. "I'm going to take some guys to the grid coordinates they sent and see if we can find those weapons. I want you and Dumar to plan an exfil route to get us out of here. When I get back, we'll beat feet."

Dugas was monitoring the action from the platoon CP back at Palace. He came over the radio and made a suggestion.

"If you guys want to head north, I'll spin up some trucks and pick you up on Route H," he said. "It's only about a five-hundred-meter movement, and you'll have cover in the grape fields."

"Roger, Three-seven," I called back. "I'll look at the map and advise you of our exfil route when we have it determined."

He rogered me back, and I sat down against a mud wall with Dumar, and we looked at the map together. From where we were to Route H was indeed only about five hundred meters, but we would have to cross at least five tree lines during the movement. It was an area we were still unfamiliar with, so I didn't feel comfortable taking that direction. Dumar agreed.

"We should just go back the way we came," Dumar said. "I don't like the idea of crossing all those tree lines, and I think it'll just be safer to go back the same way. Not to mention it'll be faster."

At this point, we'd already been in contact twice, and I was ready to just leave. This area was obviously a hotbed for Taliban, and we weren't expecting it that day. I just wanted to go back to Palace, where we could plan a patrol against this village for a later date.

I called back to Dugas that we were going to exfil on the same route we had come in on, giving the reason that the tree lines made it much too dangerous to head north. He concurred, and I sat against the wall next to Dumar, waiting for the LT to get back from his mini patrol.

"Whatcha gonna do when we get back?" I asked Dumar.

"I'm gonna kick your ass at darts, for starters," he said.

Dumar and I had some history together. We'd been in the same platoon at Fort Bragg. He came to Fort Bragg and the Eighty-second Airborne Division from Fort Wainwright. When I reenlisted, he was sad to see me leave Fort Bragg but gave me a warm coat to use when I got to Alaska. Three months later, he received orders to return to Alaska, and I'd pulled some strings to get him into my company, and luckily, he'd landed a team leader spot in Third Platoon. When he got there, I told him he wasn't getting his coat back.

Someone back home had sent me an electronic dartboard, and it was hanging outside my CHU. It was a source of stress relief to play darts with Dumar, but every time he played, he'd hit the side of the dartboard with a dart, and somehow the electronic counter would reset.

"I'll play darts with you when we get back, but if you reset that dartboard one more time, I'm never gonna play with you again," I told him.

We sat against the wall talking for about thirty more minutes before the LT showed up. His recon mission came up empty, and I had Dumar pull out the map. I explained that I didn't think it was a good idea to head north, and we should go back the same direction that we had come in. Lieutenant Labowski agreed, and we formed up the platoon for the march back to Palace.

At about 0800, First Squad took the lead, followed by Third Squad, and Weapons Squad was in the rear. We traveled east along the road toward Route Q. When we'd gone about three hundred meters, we came across a compound that was just south of the road, and a family of locals was outside. Lieutenant Labowski stopped the movement, and a handful of us went into the compound to talk to the people.

Through an interpreter, Lieutenant Labowski talked to the inhabitants for about thirty minutes, and all we got from them was that they were upset that US troops were walking through their grape gardens and tearing their crops up. Lieutenant Labowski argued that if they wouldn't allow the Taliban to mine the roads, we wouldn't have a reason to walk through their gardens, but all that did was start another line of complaining from the locals, and finally the LT promised we'd tread more lightly through their gardens from now on. We picked up our gear and headed out of the compound.

As soon as I stepped out the door of the compound, we took fire for the third time that day. Rounds from Taliban fire ripped over my head, causing me to duck behind the mud wall that ran along the north side of the road. The platoon lined up on the wall and returned fire toward a mud structure that was about three hundred meters to the north. From our vantage point, we couldn't identify the source of the enemy gunfire. This lasted about fifteen minutes.

Dumar asked the LT if he could shoot the SMAW-D, which is a shoulder-fired weapon and, when extended, looks a lot like an AT-4. Lieutenant Labowski gave him the go-ahead, and I pulled out my video camera. When Dumar fired the weapon, the concussion from the back blast was so immense that it kicked up dirt and dust all around us. I couldn't see a thing. I looked over to the compound, and Dumar had landed a direct hit on his target. There was a burst of cheers.

"I'm taking First Squad, and I'm moving around to get a different look at that compound," Lieutenant Labowski said to me as I was stowing my video camera. "I want you to stay here with Third and Weapons and provide cover for us."

"Roger that, sir," I said, and he gathered up First Squad.

His intent was to move about one hundred meters into the grape field to a mud wall that ran north and south. From there, First Squad would have a better vantage point to return fire on the compound. Private First Class Blake took point with the metal detector, followed by Dumar, Moreton, Budd, Lieutenant Labowski, and the remainder of First Squad. The rest of us sat against the wall with weapons pointed toward the compound where we had received enemy fire.

First Squad went into the grape field and was headed north when I lost sight of them. The lush foliage on the grape walls provided a lot of concealment for our guys as they walked between the grape rows. The fact that I could no longer see First Squad because of this concealment actually brought some relief because it meant they were well hidden from the enemy as well. About fifteen minutes later, Lieutenant Labowski called me on the radio.

"Three-four, this is Three-six . . . Do you have eyes on us?" he asked.

I looked up and saw Blake climbing a grape wall next to a small group of trees. I responded back to the LT that I did have eyes on the element moving. I continued to watch as the next man cleared the top of the wall, and as soon as he was on top of the wall, it happened.

BOOM!

A huge explosion engulfed First Squad, shooting a cone-shaped cloud of debris at least a hundred feet into the air. I remember seeing pieces of clothing, probably parts of someone's body armor, flying through the air, and my first thought was that Lieutenant Labowski was dead.

"Goddammit!" I yelled and reached for my hand mic. "Three-seven, this is Three-four . . . we just hit an IED! I think we just lost Six! I think we just lost First Squad!"

"What the fuck?" came Dugas's response over the radio. "I need a situation report! Stay calm!"

Stay calm? I was freaking the fuck out! It was like one of those surreal feelings of watching yourself calmly go through the motions, appearing composed on the outside but having the eerie feeling of internally feeling out of control as you watch yourself from a distance. It was almost an out-of-body experience. This was something you see in the movies. This is not something that happens to other people. Not to me.

I pulled the nine-line paperwork out of the pouch on my body armor and pulled out a map to find a suitable helicopter landing zone (HLZ). My hands were shaking. I was scared to death!

The only HLZ was right where that IED had just gone off. I was afraid to make that an LZ since it was so close to the blast. Unfortunately, we had no choice, and time was ticking.

A voice came over the radio.

"Three-four, this is Three-six. We need a medic up here now, and I need you to start prepping the nine-line!"

Lieutenant Labowski had survived. I felt a surge of relief pulse through my body, but I was still very flustered.

"Six, this is Four," I responded. "I'm sending doc to your position time now. The closest HLZ is the field just to your north. I'm getting a grid for it now."

I sent the medic with Sergeants Holcomb and Keelslice to the blast site and continued prepping the nine-line medevac report. After I'd gotten the first five lines, which was enough to get the birds off the ground, I gathered the remaining members of the platoon, and we began to advance toward the blast site to help our wounded soldiers. Alley led us with the mine detector, and I was right behind him. Burke and Schwartz were behind me, followed by the rest of Third Squad.

When we got to the wall south of the proposed HLZ, I saw Padilla sweeping the field for mines—a standard operating procedure when calling for a medevac. I sent Alley into the field to sweep, so this task could be done faster. I looked over to a soldier pulling security and asked, "Who go hit?"

"It was Sergeant Dumar," he said.

"What the fuck!" I said as I felt my heart sink. Dumar was my best friend in the platoon. Now he was lying in a grape field about thirty meters away from me. I had no idea how badly he was injured.

I ran toward him and found three guys hovering around him. Budd was at his feet, Keelslice was cradling his head, and Doc Smith was frantically working at his side. As I came up, Smith came up to me and, in a hushed voice, said, "See if you can find his foot."

"Are you fucking kidding me?" I said, almost in shock. Dumar had lost his foot! "Did you see the size of that explosion? His fucking foot could be anywhere."

Doc turned away from me and quickly went back to Dumar. I looked around at the site. Suspended in one of the trees was a tube. It was likely the IED that had just exploded, and the remnants of the tube had been blown into the tree branches. It looked like a spent Light Anti-tank Weapon, which was probably fired by the Canadians then discarded, only to be found by the Taliban who stuffed it full of homemade explosives and used it for an IED. I could see wires running through the trees toward the compound from which we'd been taking fire. They'd lured us in, and we fell for it.

I got next to Dumar and put my hand on his chest. He had tourniquets on both of his legs. His left foot was gone, severed from about midshin down. His pants were shredded. Doc was working on his right arm, which looked like hamburger meat all the way down. Dumar was obviously in shock, and Doc had just administered ten milligrams of morphine.

"Hey, man," Dumar said almost too calmly. "I think things just got real."

"The birds are on the way, Davin," I told him, calling him by his first name to try to keep him relaxed. "Just stay cool. You're gonna be OK."

His head tilted back onto Keelslice's lap, and he gritted his teeth in pain. Tears rolled down the side of his face as he groaned in agony. I held his left arm with my hand and kept my right hand on his chest as I noticed he was also missing his middle finger on his left hand. His pain subsided momentarily as Doc Smith wrapped his right arm.

"I don't think I'll be playing darts with you today," he said to me. My heart wrenched as I looked over his ravaged body. "If I do, I'll have to throw left-handed."

I held his arm and told him not to worry about playing darts right now.

"Just keep calm, Dav," I said. "We're gonna get you out of here, and you and me will be playing darts soon enough."

"I got to shoot the SMAW-D," he rambled. "You didn't. You guys suck."

"You sure did," I told him. "I think you got one of them faggots. Now just relax."

We sat in the field waiting for the UH-60 Blackhawk to pick him up. While we waited, we slid a poleless litter underneath him to transport him when the bird arrived while Dumar went through fits of pain and moments of what seemed like relief. I can only guess that the morphine, coupled with the shock, helped him from feeling the wounds he received. He would mumble something, and then he'd writhe in pain again, constantly asking for the "fucking birds."

"They're on their way, Davin," I kept telling him. "Just relax. You're going to be OK."

"Tell Dana I love her," he told me, referring to his fiancé back home.

"Tell her yourself, motherfucker," I shot back. "You're going to be OK."

A few minutes passed, and Dumar said, "My dick is burning."

His pants had been shredded and his testicles were exposed to the hot sun burning down upon us. I grabbed a flap from his pants to cover his balls, and as I did, the flap on the other side of his pants fell off, exposing his penis. It wasn't his balls that were burning. His dick was burning because the head of his penis had been sliced down the middle. It was my worst nightmare revealed. I was speechless, and I almost started to cry for Dumar.

About this time, we could hear the thumping of the rotary-winged aircraft coming to pick up Dumar. Lieutenant Labowski made contact with the Blackhawk on the radio, and we threw a green smoke grenade into the field to mark the HLZ. As the bird was coming in, a barrage of Taliban gunfire spit from behind the compound, aimed at the helicopter. Lieutenant Labowski had to wave off the medevac.

Sergeant A, one of the team leaders, rallied the troops. I saw him stand up and walk across the open field with his M4 raised at the Taliban compound, shooting, and he was yelling, "Get the fuck against this wall and shoot these motherfuckers!"

The rest of the platoon lined up on the wall following A's lead, and it sounded like a company-sized element opening up on the incoming fire, which quickly receded, at least long enough for Lieutenant Labowski to call the bird back to land.

When the UH-60 landed, we covered Dumar with our own bodies to protect his wounds from the dust and debris kicked up by the helicopter. Once it subsided, five of us grabbed the litter and headed for the bird. I was on the front right side, doing the best I could to keep from making brash moves that might cause Dumar even more pain. When we were about fifteen feet from the bird, the crew chief dismounted and ran to me, grabbing my side of the litter and carrying it the rest of the way. I didn't see his name, but I saw his Screaming Eagle patch, noting that he was either in the 101st Airborne Division or had at least done time there. I've always had respect for the 101st, so I felt more at ease after seeing his unit affiliation.

When the bird lifted off, the five litter bearers ran back to our concealed position in the grape field and gathered our gear. I was completely out of breath. I sat with my head in my hands trying to regain my composure as the firing line, led by Sergeant A, started filtering back toward the grape field. I looked down at where Dumar had been lying, and amid the bandages and medical wrappers littering the ground was a pool of blood. I looked at my boots sitting in my friend's blood. I tried not to cry. My hands were shaking. I wasn't sure how this had all happened so fast.

"We have to get out of here," Lieutenant Labowski said, snapping me out of my trance. "I want you to pull up the rear and cover our exfil with two mortar rounds."

The rest of the platoon started pulling back. When I was left with Manley, I had him drop two mortar rounds, and we hauled ass to catch up with the rest of the guys. Back on the road, my head was on a swivel. We had close-air support covering our movement, but I was sure we'd get hit again on the way out. Luckily, we didn't.

We finally made it to Route Q. Dugas had spun up our trucks, and they were waiting when we arrived. First Squad mounted a Stryker and headed to FOB Zangabad for blast assessment since they were all so close to the explosion. The rest of us loaded the other trucks and went back to COP Palace. As I sat in the back of the Stryker, I could feel the sweat pouring off my head and into my eyes. I figured it would be a good time to cry because I could blame any tears and red eyes on the sweat. I was about to cry when I looked up at Keelslice who suddenly burst into tears. I reached up and grasped his shoulder and held on to him. When we got back to Palace, I went to my CHU to unload my gear. Lieutenant Labowski walked in, and after we made eye contact, we embraced.

"Shit, sir. I thought you were dead!" I told him. He just looked at me, took a step back, and started to cry. It was our first serious casualty of this deployment, and it hit him hard. I told him he could stay there as long as he needed to. He quickly composed himself, thanked me, and left.

I had to collect myself and pull my squad together for a meeting. When everyone was there, I asked if anyone wanted to say anything. No one said a word. I had to give the bullshit speech you always see in the movies.

"I know this sucks, and I know it probably scares the shit out of you guys. I totally understand, and I am with you all 100 percent. But we have to go back out there. It would be easy to sit here at Palace and let the rest of this deployment go by, but we can't do that. For every day we sit on this COP, it gives the Taliban a chance to get closer to us and emplace more IEDs. We can't let them do that. We have to get out there. We have to do patrols. We have to stick it to them before they can stick it to us.

"I know everyone liked Dumar. I've known him for a long time, and he's always been a good friend to me. So when we go back out, we need to keep in mind what happened today. We need to watch what we're doing and not make mistakes. Today wasn't anyone's fault. I don't blame anyone. It's a fact of war, and Dumar was a victim. But don't let this bring you down. Don't let this scare you. You need to grab your balls and be men. And the first chance we get to give some payback, we need to grab it. Does everyone understand?"

Everyone nodded, and I told them I would leave them alone. I also gave them the opportunity to come talk to me anytime in case they were too afraid to show their feelings in front of their peers. Then I walked back to my CHU, sat on my bunk, and closed my eyes. All I could see was the explosion in slow motion. My thoughts kept going back to Dumar lying on the ground in a pool of his own blood. I didn't sleep that night or for several nights following that. And when I did sleep again, I woke up in a pool of sweat, having had nightmares of what happened.

We had been lucky until this point, and with everything considered, you could say we were still lucky. Dumar survived. He would never be whole again, but he lived. It could have been any one of us lying in that grape field that day.

Back at Zangabad, Moreton was diagnosed with Traumatic Brain Injury (TBI) from being so close to the blast, and he had a dislocated shoulder. Blake, who was minesweeping, had abrasions on the back of his neck from the blast. One other soldier had a laceration on his arm. Moreton wouldn't come back to us.

I found out later that in addition to all his other injuries, Dumar's colon had been dislodged and he would have to shit through a colostomy bag for an undetermined amount of time. His left leg was amputated from the knee down, his right leg was saved but in bad shape. His right elbow was so damaged that it was eventually fused together, preventing him from bending it.

It was weeks later when I was finally able to talk to him on the telephone. He was still in a drug-induced state. He told me they sewed the head of his penis back together and "it looks like a viper." That was just like Dumar to make a bad situation funny. He was alive, and he was away from Panjwei'i.

In a sick way, I was jealous.

EIGHT

MARTIN LUCK

> *Do not interfere with an army that is returning home. When*
> *you surround an army, leave an outlet free. Do not press a*
> *desperate foe too hard.*
> —Sun Tzu, *The Art of War*

11 July 2011

We were supposed to do a patrol in the Peshengan area on 10 July, but we had communication problems with our company HQ, and when Dugas cancelled the patrol, no one complained. On 11 July, we set out on our first patrol since the day Dumar was blown up. Only four days had passed since our first serious casualty.

We were headed to Lakani so the LT could make it to the center of town to hold a shura. I was starting to think Lieutenant Labowski was just trying to prove we could get into Lakani, and all the missions there were just a point he was trying to prove. I couldn't blame him if that was the case, because why shouldn't we be able to get into a small village? I understood his frustration for our inability to reach the center of this village.

The night before the patrol, the Third Squad leader drew up the route to get into Lakani. When I saw it, it made me sick to my stomach. There were several portions of the route that led us through large open fields, and part of the route called for us to travel parallel to the Martin Tree Line. One thing I thought we'd learned at this point is not to parallel the tree lines, but move perpendicular to them if we had to get near them. Third Squad's leader disagreed, and when I pointed this out, he said, "They don't hit you from the tree line if you're that close." I was in shock. Since when did these guys cower from us because we're close to them? Just four days earlier a guy shot at me from less than fifty meters. I didn't argue the point because I wasn't leading the patrol. I later wished I had held my ground.

We got up at 0245 and loaded trucks an hour later. We drove to Zangabad, and by 0430, we were exiting the south gate headed for Lakani. Weapons Squad's part in this patrol was to get on a rooftop that would overlook both the Martin Tree Line and the center of Lakani. I'd chosen the rooftop according to the aerial map I used to plot my routes. The movement went smoothly on the way out there. We didn't receive any fire from the tree lines, and we successfully crossed the open fields without being hit. We made it to the release point where Weapons Squad would split from the rest of the platoon to complete our part of the mission.

After crossing a small open field to get to the compound we were overtaking, we boosted each other up the ten-foot wall that we needed to get on. Burke went first, followed by Blake, who was acting as AG for Burke because Schwartz was sick, and then Alley. The two snipers we had from Fourth Platoon with us mounted next, followed by our forward observer. I was the last one to get on the roof, and had I been the first, I might have changed the plan.

The rooftop was completely flat. We had an excellent view of the Martin Tree Line, but we couldn't see the center of town because the trees were blocking our view. Since the rooftop was flat, we would have almost no cover from incoming rounds if we took fire from the tree line. It wasn't a good position, but we were all up there, and the rest of the platoon was already moving out to the center of Lakani. I called up that I didn't have eyes on the center of town, but it made no difference at that point.

As the rest of the platoon made its way into the village, shots were fired from the cemetery that was located in the middle of Lakani. No one was hurt, and after calling in air support, we learned that whoever had fired at us was long gone. The birds covered the entire town and found no signs of anyone bearing arms.

Weapons Squad and our attachments spent only about an hour on the roof before the LT concluded the mission. He'd made it to the center of town, but I don't think there were enough people around to hold a shura, so he decided we'd done as much as we could. The platoon started filing out of Lakani while Weapons Squad covered their movement from the rooftop. When everyone had made it to the grape field adjacent to our position, we dismounted the rooftop while being covered by the troops in the field. It was all going as planned.

On the way back to Zangabad, we were walking parallel to the south side of the Martin Tree Line when the front of our element took fire from a compound about three hundred meters to our south. We were walking through a marijuana field, so the concealment was fantastic, but I can't say the same for cover. The element taking contact fired back with some serious violence of action. I was proud of our platoon when I heard the amount of fire we returned. When it got quiet, we started moving again. I thought we'd run the Taliban off, but it surprised me that they would hit us on our way out. I looked at Burke, who was moving about ten meters in front of me.

"Why do they hit us when we leave?" I asked rhetorically. "We're fucking leaving. Leave us alone, and we'll leave. It just doesn't make sense."

Burke chuckled as he plodded along through the pot field. I heard Specialist Curtis from the lead element say, "You'd better run your ass across that field," and I assumed we had made it to the last open area of the movement. I looked back at Alley, who was right behind me, and said, "Here's a news flash for you guys: I'm not running my old fat-ass across any field. Whoever just yelled that can suck my dick," and we all had a short laugh.

Blake was the first man in the Weapons Squad movement, and as he was crossing from the marijuana field into the open field behind Second Squad, all hell broke loose. There were still four men in the open field when enemy fire opened up from the south again. Burke was on the edge of the field and positioned the M240 facing south and opened fire. His rounds were dead-on, and he pelted the wall from where the fire was coming with about two hundred rounds of 7.62 mm. While he was doing that, I was yelling to everyone behind us to "get the fuck down and keep your heads down" because we were still in the marijuana field, and the incoming rounds were close. You can always tell the rounds that are really close because they have a distinctive cracking sound when they whiz by your head. It's not a comfortable feeling when you hear that sound, and I wanted to make sure everyone was as low as they could get.

As Burke dominated the southern sector, the Martin Tree Line opened up with more enemy fire. We were caught in a crossfire, getting hit from the north and the south. We still had four men stuck in the open field and no way to get them out.

"Burke! Turn that gun on the tree line to the north!" I yelled. "We have men covering the south already, but if we don't dominate that tree line, those guys in the field are dead."

Burke picked up the gun and turned it around, staying as low as he could. The pot plants were probably five feet high, and the tops of the stalks were dropping on top of us. These rounds were close. As Burke looked up and started to open fire, he paused and looked at me.

"Sergeant Wes," he said, "I think they're shooting at us from that grape hut too."

I looked up, and to the northwest, there was a grape hut, and I couldn't disagree with Burke. It seemed like the fire from the tree line had died down, but we were still taking a lot of fire, and it seemed to be coming from that grape hut, so I told Burke to light it up. At this point, the most he could have done is provide covering fire because there is no way an M240 round is going to penetrate a grape hut wall which is made of dried mud and roughly four feet thick. So Burke provided covering fire while the men in the open field were able to get up and move.

Martin was one of the men lying in the field. This was his first patrol since coming back to the platoon from getting hit by the IED. While Burke was suppressing the northern enemy fire, it allowed a small break for Martin and the others to get up and move. As Martin got up, a round entered through his left butt cheek, exited his left cheek, and was lodged in his right butt cheek. We would later say that Martin was a real pain in the ass, but right then we weren't making jokes.

Sergeant Hurst, a team leader in second squad, saw Martin go down and ran into the field to retrieve him. Hurst dragged Martin into the cover of the grape field where Doc Smith started first-aid procedures.

Meanwhile, Burke was continuing to suppress the enemy fire. It seemed to be coming from all around, and it was more accurate than any other fire we'd experienced prior to this firefight. The rounds were cracking overhead, and the tops of the marijuana plants kept getting shorter and shorter. I was lying so close to the ground, trying to get as small as I could that I thought I was going to actually become part of the ground. How were the Taliban able to shoot at us so accurately with Burke and all the SAW gunners in the grape field laying down so much suppressive fire?

"Hey, Burke," I said. "How the fuck are we gonna get out of this one?"

"Dang, Sarge," Burke said, looking a little desperate. "Don't say stuff like that."

"Well, if you wanna get out of this, you'd better turn that gun on that enemy fire, or we're not making it out of here!"

I was trying to sound funny when I asked it, but I seriously doubted our chances of getting out of this one unscathed. The incoming fire was so close, and we still hadn't received any close air support. I was starting to get worried.

On the other side of the open field, Doc was working on Martin, and the SAW gunners were firing from the edge of the grape field in the direction of the incoming fire. Sergeant Hurst had an M320 mounted on his M4 and started lobbing 40 mm rounds toward the incoming fire. After he ran out of high explosive rounds, an air force A-10 was on station, and Hurst fired three red smoke rounds at the incoming fire to mark the target for the birds. For some reason, the A-10 ignored these rounds and dropped a Hellfire missile on the southern side of our position where we had originally taken fire.

Something that needs to be said for all of our air assets is that they are very picky about the targets they hit. Typically, they won't open fire unless they have a visual confirmation of enemy action. It's pilots covering their own asses, and it's something I appreciated most of the time. So when the A-10 hit the southern sector, I took it for granted that he saw enemy action to our south despite most of the fire coming from the north. The good news was that the missile explosion was enough of a show of force that all fire ceased.

I still wasn't aware that Martin had been shot. I was still in the marijuana field, and when a status report had been called for, I gave Weapons Squad status as "up" as did the other squad leaders. Martin was moving under Second Squad, and his squad leader, Van Bockel, was one of the soldiers pinned down in the field, and I don't even remember if he called up his status. I don't blame him if he didn't. As the remainder of the platoon started hustling across the open field, the message came over the radio that someone had been shot.

Burke and I stayed in the marijuana field to cover the rest of the platoon's movement across the open terrain. When Dugas, the last man in the movement, started running across the field, I told Burke to pick up and go. When he was about halfway across the field, I stood up, and yes, I ran as fast as my forty-one-year-old legs could carry me; and carrying about eighty pounds of equipment, I have to say it wasn't very fast. It was more of a quick shuffle than a run. But I made it. I was completely out of breath when I got to the grape field. When I made it across the field, I was yelling for all the guys bunched up in the grape row to get out of my way, and I rolled into the grape row. It was a good feeling to finally get behind some cover.

Over the radio, I could hear the nine-line being called up. There was a pause when it came to the line that gave the location pick-up site. As it turned out, the only suitable HLZ anywhere near us was the open field we'd just crossed. It was the same field where our wounded man had just been shot. It doesn't take a rocket surgeon to realize it was not a good idea. Our only choice was to carry Martin out of the grape field back to Zangabad. We weren't very far, so it was doable.

The movement began, and I was near the end of the element with Weapons Squad and Dugas pulling up the rear. We made it to Route Q, where some vehicles had been waiting to transport Martin the remainder of the distance into the FOB. When I finally made it onto Route Q, I learned that no one had actually carried Martin out of the grape field. He walked!

Less than three weeks prior to this, Martin was blown up by an IED and walked more than a thousand meters, partially blind and limping, back to FOB Zangabad. Now the man had been shot in the leg and the ass and was able to do a repeat. I thought about the time I'd yelled at him back in NTC, and now I felt like an idiot.

I walked back to the FOB, entered the south gate, and grounded all my sweaty gear. I told Burke to watch my stuff, and I made a beeline to the aid station. When I got there, Lieutenant Labowski, Dugas, and Hurst were all standing around outside, talking to the battalion sergeant major, who did not look happy. I bypassed all of them and went straight into the aid station where Martin was lying on an elevated table.

Martin noticed me, sat up, and said, "Sergeant Wes, do you want this one?" referring to his second Purple Heart in less than a month. I laughed.

"You crazy son of a bitch," I said. "You keep this one too. You fucking earned it. I can't believe you walked back. You're one hard motherfucker."

Martin smiled, obviously feeling the effects of the morphine and probably still in a state of shock. As he lay back down, I walked out of the aid station feeling like Martin was going to be OK. I felt like this would finish his part of the war. I thought he'd get sent home, but I was wrong. He would come back to us about four weeks later, but Dugas wouldn't let him patrol anymore.

"He's used up all of his luck," Dugas said. I agreed.

Eventually, Martin moved up to the company headquarters where he was assigned administrative duties. I think he had proven himself, and he could use the work in the rear. He was definitely qualified for it and did a great job for the remainder of the deployment.

When I left the aid station, there seemed to be an additional concern on the faces of the leadership outside. Hurst walked up to me and pulled me off to the side.

"You know those 320 rounds I fired?" he asked. I nodded.

"Two of the HE rounds landed in the wire outside the FOB, and the three red smoke rounds landed *inside* the FOB," he said.

"What the fuck?" I asked. I was in shock, and it hadn't yet registered, so Hurst continued.

"It turns out when we took fire from that northern tree line, the ANA in the guard tower opened up on us with their 240, thinking we were Taliban," he said. "And wait. It gets better. Someone ran a Stryker up one of the run-up ramps and started firing at us with a fifty cal. The red smoke rounds hit right by the Stryker, so I'm hoping that's what made them realize they weren't shooting at the fucking Taliban. That Stryker was hit with more than twelve hundred rounds of SAW and 7.62 mm, so you can tell Burke he's a badass shot!"

It still hadn't registered with me. I heard Curtis say, "We must be a bad fucking platoon to push back a fucking Stryker!" And that was true. But why should we, an American platoon, have to fend off an American fighting vehicle stationed at an American FOB? And was that 7.62 mm round that was lodged in Martin's ass from an American weapon? I was beside myself.

The sergeant major seemed pretty pissed that we had lobbed 320 rounds into the FOB, and at one point, I heard him get very possessive.

"This is *my* FOB, and you fired on it," he said. "There's going to be a full investigation, and some heads are gonna roll!"

That's when the talk started surfacing about Lieutenant Labowski and Dugas being relieved for cause. I didn't want to even think about that because I was next in line behind Dugas, and I wanted nothing to do with being the platoon sergeant out here. I couldn't help thinking that all we were doing was defending ourselves. The sergeant major's logic was that we didn't have positive identification (PID) of our targets. My logic was "neither did the men on *your* FOB, and if they had not fired at us, we wouldn't have had to defend ourselves against them." Really, what did they expect? We had four men pinned down in an open field while we were taking fire from three directions. The most effective fire was probably coming from the FOB, from American soldiers and ANA, and we had to do something to get our men out of that field, one of them having already been shot.

What a load of shit.

When the investigation kicked off, there were rumors floating around about how Third Platoon was going to get pulled out of Palace and replaced by another platoon. I didn't like being at Palace anymore, but I didn't want to get pulled. I told Captain Allred, our company commander who said it was his decision, that if he pulled us from Palace, we would all be happy to leave; but in the long run, we'd look back at our mission there as a failure.

I don't know the specifics of the results of the investigation, but what I heard through the Private News Network (PNN), the major source of all military rumors, is that when our battalion commander read all the sworn statements, he threw the investigation out. It got swept under the rug.

If that was true, in my mind, that was nothing more than the higher-ups covering their own asses. If Lieutenant Labowski and Dugas were going to get relieved because they were responsible for the actions of the platoon that fired on the FOB, who would have been relieved for the actions of the soldiers on the FOB? The words of the battalion sergeant major came back to me.

"This is *my* FOB," he had said.

The FOB also *belonged* to the battalion commander. True or not, the cover-up rumor made sense.

NINE

FRUSTRATION

> *Holding on to anger is like grasping a hot coal with the intent of throwing it at someone else; you are the one who gets burned.*
>
> —Buddha

13 July 2011

We were supposed to start patrol (SP) out of the front gate of Palace at 0445. I rolled over in my bed and looked at my watch at 0443. I sprang out of my bed and threw my uniform on, wondering why no one had gotten me up. My first thought was that the patrol had been scrubbed. I was still trying to put my boots on as I went out the front door. Schwartz came around the corner of my CHU in full kit.

"Is this thing a scratch?" I asked.

"No, Sergeant. I came over here to get you," he said, sensing I was pissed.

"Why didn't anyone wake me up?" I asked, obviously agitated.

"We never have to get you up," Schwartz said. "You always get us up."

I was pissed. I threw on my kit, grabbed my rifle, and headed for the front gate. On the way out there, Dugas gave me a shit-eating grin, and I'm pretty sure he said something snide. He was probably calling me a turd. I didn't pay attention to him. Luckily, our interpreter was running late so they couldn't blame the late departure on me. I gave my squad a hard time for not waking me up. I knew it wasn't their fault, but it was fun making them feel like shit.

We finally got everyone together and started out. Our plan was to circumnavigate the problem areas west of Palace, including Peshengan and a few other villages in the area. It was going to be a long movement, and my day hadn't exactly started out on a good note. I was worried about making contact because we would be in the area where Dumar had been blown up. The IED threat was intense.

Sergeant A took point on this mission, and he would do so for most of the upcoming patrols. I trusted Sergeant A, especially after he had proven his courage in rallying the platoon to protect the helicopter for Dumar's medevac.

At about 0515, as the sun was starting to push its way over the horizon, we pushed into the grape fields and reached a release point where Lieutenant Labowski and a small element had planned on going to recon a small area for fighting positions before linking back up with the platoon. After a short security halt, the recon element decided not to go out, and we kept moving. I was near the back of the movement, and when we passed the release point, we took fire from a machine gun to our west. The shots were coming from a grape hut, and we all got down. I couldn't see where the shots were coming from, so I just lay low while the elements at the front of the patrol returned fire. A few minutes later, I heard Lieutenant Labowski calling in air assets. I looked up and saw two A-10s air force jets circling our position.

Within a few minutes, the A-10 opened up, shooting its 30 mm cannon into the grape hut and putting an end to that firefight. We weren't asked to do Battle Damage Assessment (BDA) on this site, so we moved on. As I passed the grape hut, I could see the thatched roof burning, and I knew whatever was inside there was dead.

I wondered if the owner of the grape hut would be angry or if he would just think of it as collateral damage. I almost felt bad for the farmers in the area for having to put up with the Taliban and us destroying their crops and structures. I wished they would just stand up to the Taliban and keep them out of their fields. But then who was to say that the farmers weren't Taliban themselves? There was no way to know. As I passed the burning building, I inhaled deeply through my nose, hoping to smell a burning carcass. All I could smell was smoke.

"Who's smoking?" I asked rhetorically. When no one answered, I said, "The Taliban!"

That got a few laughs, mostly from me.

We pushed onward maneuvering through the grape fields until we were far enough west of the villages then turned south. We were climbing grape walls, taking halts, and trudging through mud; it was a slow process. While we were moving, I looked up and saw a large wall in front of me that ran along a tree line. The tree lines made me nervous. I knew they were used by the Taliban for cover, but after what happened with Dumar, I also realized they used the trees as markers for IEDs. Schwartz was directly in front of me, and Burke was in front of him with the M240. Alley was right behind me. I felt comfortable knowing my squad was close to me, and we were toward the end of the file. When I got to the wall, I smelled smoke. This time, for real.

"Schwartz," I called forward. "Are you smoking?"

"Hell, no," he called back. I knew Burke and Alley didn't smoke, but I turned to look at Alley and told him I smelled cigarette smoke. He stopped to sniff as I started climbing the wall. Before I could get to the other side of the wall, the tree line to our east opened up with automatic weapons fire, and I rolled back down the near side of the wall. Alley came running up to me.

"Sergeant Wes! Are you OK?" he urgently asked me.

A piece of my equipment had snagged on the root of a grape plant, and I was hanging off the wall. To be honest, it felt nice to just hang there for a few minutes, and I didn't try to struggle.

"I'm fine, Alley," I said. "Help me get my fat-ass down off this wall before I get shot."

"Damn, Sergeant Wes," he said. "I thought you were dead! You were just hanging there!"

"Alley, I'm getting too old to do this shit," I said as he helped me off the wall. "When that shit kicked up, I just rolled over. I thought I was going to break my hip!"

"Well, don't scare me like that again," Alley said with that goofy smile of his.

"Did you smell that cigarette smoke?" I asked.

"I did after you said something," Alley told me.

"Yeah, well, none of us are smoking," I said. "Those fuckers are close by. Make sure you're careful where you step. There could be IEDs or pressure plates out here."

"Roger that, Sergeant," Alley said as his eyes started scanning the ground.

Alley and I set up on the north side of the wall. We didn't have eyes on where the gunshots were coming from, and we were separated from Burke and Schwartz. A few moments later, I heard Burke open up with the M240, and I wondered if he had taken the initiative to do it on his own. I found out later that he and Schwartz realized I wasn't able to give them direction, so they took it upon themselves to set up and return fire. My boys were turning into men.

When we reached a lull in fire, I crossed the wall with Alley in tow. We linked up with the rest of the platoon and were moving south again. It wasn't long before we were attacked from a small tree line to our southwest. This time I didn't say anything but watched as Burke and Schwartz found a position to set up the gun and opened fire on the tree line. We only had one gun team on this patrol, but a SAW gunner from another squad set up closer to me and started "talking" his SAW with Burke's gun. The sound of one gun firing a burst, stopping while the other fires a burst, and so on, is music to an infantryman's ears. Inside I was cheering, but I knew we still had to get past that tree line. Luckily, we still had A-10s in the area.

The air force rained down on the tree line with Hellfire missiles, and Dugas made the decision that the area was too hot. We had already taken fire from two tree lines and a grape hut. We weren't sure how long the A-10s would be able to remain on station, so Dugas spun up the trucks from Palace and told them to meet us on Route H. The movement to Route H from where we were was just a little more than five hundred meters away. Inside I was cheering again. I was starting to recognize that Dugas was more concerned about the welfare of the soldiers in the platoon. My first thought was that he was scared, but the more we walked through the grape fields toward Route H that day, the more I realized that if he was scared, it was fear of someone else getting hurt.

As we made our way west to Route H, we took fire again. No one returned fire because it was a short blast of gunfire, and we weren't sure exactly where it had come from. About five minutes after that, we heard a large explosion from the same direction of the gunfire. Everyone froze. Dugas wasn't far behind me, and I turned to him and asked what he thought that was.

"I don't know," he said. "Wouldn't that be funny if the Taliban was trying to emplace an IED and blew themselves up?"

I laughed and agreed that it would be funny. We later found out that is just what happened. Apparently, the Taliban had set in an IED and tried to bait us into a firefight with that short burst of small arms fire. When we didn't fall for their trap, they were recovering the IED, and it exploded. Dugas was looking smarter and smarter to me.

We made it to Route H, and the trucks were waiting for us. We loaded the trucks and returned to Palace. As I was cleaning my weapon, another A-10 gun run near Palace shook me. The sound of that awesome aircraft opening up is startling. It makes two sounds: One sound is the loud buzz of the 30 mm cannon firing; the other is the "back burp," and I'm not sure what makes that sound. I jumped for cover when I heard it. When I realized what it was, I cursed. The loud sudden noises were really starting to get to me.

Dugas came to my CHU a little later to talk to me. His visits were starting to become more frequent. Initially, I was confused as to why he would share some of the information and concerns he had with me. Most of the discussions were about our mission. I think he needed to vent.

"Did you hear that gun run earlier?" he asked.

"Yeah, I did," I told him. "It scared the shit out of me. I wish they'd tell us before they started blasting shit around here."

Dugas laughed.

"We got a report that they killed six dudes on that run," he told me. "We're estimating that with this last one, we killed ten of those fuckers today, including that dumb-ass that blew himself up with that IED. So I guess we did some good today. Recon Platoon did BDA of that grape hut we shot up with that A-10 and pulled a body out of it. It took two body bags to get his ass back to Zangabad. That A-10 is a bad motherfucker."

I chuckled, knowing there was something in that grape hut despite not smelling any burning flesh.

"Why did we go to Route H instead of continuing with the mission as planned?" I asked Dugas, still wondering about his nerves.

"Look, man," he started. "This stuff out here is getting to be too much. We're going out here and taking contact every time we go out. I'm getting tired of this shit. I don't think most of what we're doing out here is making much of a difference. We've already lost Dumar and Martin, and we really can't afford to lose anyone else. We're getting spread thin, and what are we getting done? Look at what happened in

Lakani. They go out there and clear the village. They found about fifteen IEDs in that area, and that was just around the road itself. That doesn't include the ones they found in the fields and couldn't recover because it was too dangerous. That's a lot of IEDs, and then what do they do? They leave. They left the area and left no presence behind. Do you know what happens when you leave a little kid alone with a toy? He plays with it. If you tell him to stop playing with it and don't watch him, when you leave, he's gonna play with it again. We just left them out there to play, and no one's watching them."

I sat in silence. I wasn't sure if I should agree with him or not. He was making sense, but I still wanted to think what we were doing was making a difference. I didn't want to agree with him, but how could I not? Was I starting to question our mission?

"Look, man," he said. "I don't have a problem going out there every day. I don't mind if they shoot at us all day. I can handle the small arms fire. The IEDs are another story. We go out every day, and we get shot at. We talk to these farmers and villagers and try to get them to stop letting the Taliban set up in their fields and grape huts, but they don't give a shit. They just want to be left alone to harvest those fucking grapes. I'm sick of this shit. If these people don't care, why the fuck should we? We're here for them, and if they want to be left alone, we should leave them alone, man. Not one American life is worth a thousand of theirs. I don't want to lose another American fingernail to help these people. It's just not worth it."

I tried to think of an argument to counter what Dugas was saying, but I couldn't think of anything to say. I just sat there. I was trying to think of something to say, but I couldn't. I wanted to believe that what we were doing was worth it because we were protecting the locals, and we were defending American freedom, but Dugas was right, nothing was making sense. So I just sat there and let my platoon sergeant vent. I figured that was what he needed to do to justify being here. That's when it really hit me that Dugas wasn't scared, and if he was, he was scared for his men and their safety.

Around 1700 hours, a convoy from the company FOB showed up and dropped off a new 60 mm mortar man named Private First Class Douglas. Douglas was fresh, meaning he hadn't seen much action, but he came with good references. I was happy he was replacing Manley, who had lost his nerve after Martin got shot. Manley had come to me after that firefight outside Lakani and told me he needed a break. Because the mortar team fell under the realm of Weapons Squad, I was in charge of him and told him if he needed a break, he should get a break. There was no love lost between Manley and myself at the time, so when he left, I was glad he was gone, but the squad was bitter.

"This is bullshit," Schwartz said to me before he left. "That piece of shit is just scared because we got into a firefight? We get into firefights every fucking day. I need a break! Are you going to give me a break?"

"No, break for you, and I'm glad he's gone," I told him. "He never listened to a word I said, and he sucked at dropping rounds. Douglas is supposed to be better, so I'd rather have him than someone who won't listen."

Schwartz sat quietly for a minute, and I knew that I hadn't exactly convinced him.

"Look, Schwartz," I said. "What would you rather have a guy out there on the mortar who's scared, or someone who knows what they're doing? If he's scared, he's scared. And after Martin got shot, he was more than just scared. He was afraid. That's all there is to it. I don't want people out there that are too afraid to do their jobs."

"Well, it's still bullshit," Schwartz said as he stood up and walked away. I felt like the pressure was starting to get to a lot of the men in the platoon. Between our mortar man losing his nerve, my squad getting to voice their disdain, and Dugas telling me what was on his mind, I was wondering how long it would take before we all freak out. The pressure was building in me too.

Of course I was feeling all the strife and anger everyone else was feeling, but I was desperately trying to hold on to the belief that we were trying to make a difference. I didn't want to believe that people were losing their nerve or that we were spinning our wheels. I wanted to believe that when we went outside the wire, we were putting the fear of God or Allah into the hearts and minds of the Taliban. But were we? Was our enemy afraid of us at all? I was starting to hear questions similar to these racing through my mind. I didn't like what I was thinking.

There was this sense that the platoon was beginning to implode, and the thought terrified me. I reflected back before deployment when and all the fuss made by higher-ups, warning us not to go rogue. Apparently, a Stryker unit had gone rogue in a previous deployment and had killed innocent people for sport, and our battalion was determined not to let that happen. The briefings we had received were endless. But was that a possibility?

I looked around at the group of soldiers I was with and decided that no matter how bad things got, none of these men would get to the point where we would kill innocent people for any reason. Despite the dissatisfaction of the younger soldiers like Schwartz and the frustration of the seasoned soldiers like Dugas, I knew we would hold it together. I knew we would remain professional.

Unfortunately, it would get worse before it would get better. We had to start preparing for an upcoming mission around the Peshengan area—a mission we were expecting our battalion commander (BC) to go on. I was glad to hear he would be going out with us, and I wanted the BC to see what we were up against and hopefully give us more support.

What you want and what you get are two different things.

TEN

A PAINFUL REMINDER: IT'S STILL REAL

Some of you young men think that war is all glamour and
glory, but let me tell you, boys, it is all hell!
—General William T. Sherman

18 July 2011

We had a squad leader meeting with Lieutenant Labowski to talk about the upcoming company mission, and from the very start of it, I wasn't comfortable. Maybe it was because Dumar had just been blown up, and Martin had just been shot, but the whole thing just didn't seem to sit right with me. This was another one of those situations where, as an infantryman, I just had to keep my mouth shut and do my job.

The mission called for two squads, Second and Third Squads, to clear through villages north of Peshengan so our battalion commander and Kandahar's provincial governor (PG) could go into the area and hold a shura with the locals. Weapons Squad and an element from Fourth Platoon would provide blocking positions to the north and south. Weapons Squad was given the southern blocking position, where we would keep anything from moving in or out of the area of operations.

We originally planned on moving out at 0100 hours on 15 July, but that night, the weather turned sour, bringing in thick clouds, and the air turned "red." Red air meant we wouldn't have air support, so the mission was delayed until the weather cleared up. We waited for three days before the conditions were suitable. It was three days of anxiety.

Weapons Squad and Fourth Platoon's men stepped out at 0100 hours on the morning of 18 July. The goal was for the blocking positions to be set in before sunup, undetected if possible, so we could limit the traffic moving into and out of the objective prior to the arrival of main effort. Fourth Platoon left from the ANA gate on the west side of Palace, and my squad walked out the front gate. Alley led with the mine detector, and I was right behind him, navigating and pulling security. Behind me were Schwartz and Burke, followed by two mortar men and a man from First Squad, bringing our count to a seven-man element.

I'd planned the route several days before, and it seemed simple enough. Go eight hundred meters south on Route Q, turn west, and follow the grape fields to the intersection where we'd set up our blocking position. The reality of how it played out was far more difficult than the plan. To this day, I take full responsibility for the mistakes made on this movement. Again, what you plan for and what you get are more often two different things.

When my Garmin showed we'd gone eight hundred meters, we turned west into the grape fields. Alley was scanning for IEDs, and we were doing well for about two hundred meters when I looked up and saw a towering wall directly to our twelve o'clock. I stopped the movement because I remember seeing that wall on our outdated map.

"Alley, we're going to have to change course," I whispered. "I think we should go north until we hit a break in this wall, then we'll adjust our azimuth back on course."

Alley did as he was told and made a left turn through the grape field. We skirted the wall for about one hundred meters, and I was starting to get frustrated. We were climbing over grape walls, walking through mud, and it was pitch black. Even with the use of our night vision goggles (NVGs), the movement was slow and cumbersome. The compound wall seemed to have no end, and I was angry—angry at myself for messing up the route. I started to take it out on Alley.

"Fuck, Alley," I whispered harshly. "Why the fuck did you turn this way . . . What the fuck is taking so long . . . hurry the fuck up!"

Alley took the brunt of my tirades without saying a word. Finally, I had enough of skirting the wall and decided we needed to jump the wall before we got too far off course.

"Find a place where we can get over that wall," I said to Alley.

He turned west and found a low spot in the wall between some trees. As we got closer, Alley halted and slowly turned to me.

"Sergeant Wes, I just felt something across my face," he said.

"Something? Like what?"

"I don't know. I think it was a trip wire."

I tensed up and asked, "Are you sure?"

"No," he responded. "But there's something there."

I moved up to where he was and took the glove off of my right hand. Slowly, I felt the space in front of where Alley was standing. I didn't feel anything. No wires, no branches. Nothing.

"Are you sure it was a wire and not a spider web or something?" I whispered.

"I don't know," he whispered back. "It may have been a spider web, but something hit me across the face. There's no doubt about that."

Rather than take any chances, I took Alley's word for it and whispered back to the rest of the formation that we were turning around. We'd been moving for almost two hours at this point, and my frustration levels were climbing, but I wasn't ready to take any chances on tripping some Taliban booby trap. I told Alley he was doing a good job, and we lumbered on through the muddy grape field until we came to the next low spot in the wall.

Alley was the first one up to the wall, and he looked over. I asked what was on the other side, and he said it was a road. I was leery about walking on the roads as we'd done most of our movements through grape fields, and we'd been pretty lucky. But at this point, we were behind schedule, it was nearly 0300, and we didn't have much time before the sun was going to be up.

"Let's jump this wall, and we'll follow the road," I said to all the guys in the movement. I didn't get any complaints, and we started filing over the wall. When the last soldier was over the wall, we followed the road north for about one hundred and fifty meters before it turned left and headed west. Things were looking up, and we were making good progress now that we were out of the grape fields.

Using my night vision goggles in the infrared mode, I scanned for signs of fresh digging along the road that would be evidence an IED had been emplaced to snare us. I also looked toward the top of the walls bordering us on each side, making sure no one was waiting for us to trigger a command-detonated mine or ambush us with small arms. As we headed west, I noticed a Mosque less than one hundred meters in front of us and buildings to our left. Just as we scurried across a small bridge over a little stream, I heard an explosion, looked up, and approximately two hundred meters to our northwest, I could see a bright light coupled with what looked like fireworks flying into the air.

We all froze in our tracks and took a knee.

"Three-six, this is Three-four," I called on the radio. "We just heard an explosion about two hundred meters north of our position, how copy?"

I didn't get a response from the LT because by then, the reports from Fourth Platoon started rolling in. They'd hit an IED on their way to the northern blocking position and needed a medevac. I listened as they called in the first five lines of the nine-line, and when they called up the battle roster number, I wasn't sure who it could be. My first guess was one of their NCOs, but I couldn't be sure. Since I wasn't sure, I wasn't going to start rumors. When my men started asking questions, I told them to "shut the fuck up and stay in position."

Fear gripped me. I was terrified. I was more frightened than I had ever been in my life. My element was taking a knee on the road, and about two hundred meters away, one of my brothers may have been fighting for his life. The questions started running through my head: Should I keep moving? What if we turn around? Do they know we're on this road? Are we going to step on an IED?

I was trembling. I wanted to turn my guys around and go back to Palace, but I couldn't let myself do that. My squad was counting on me to be strong, and the rest of our elements were counting on us setting up the southern blocking position. About that time, Schwartz crept up behind me.

"Sergeant Wes, do you see where we are?" he asked, pointing to the buildings to our left. "That's the HME factory we searched a few weeks ago."

All I could think was, *Oh great!* but I pretended like I knew that the whole time and told him to "shut the fuck up and get back in position." I actually didn't want anyone too close to me at that point because I didn't want them to see me shaking.

As the Fourth Platoon kept calling back on the radio, trying to find a suitable HLZ, I decided we couldn't sit there any longer. We had to move, and there was no turning back. Fourth Platoon realized there was nowhere to land a bird, and they were going to have to carry their wounded soldier back to Palace. We had to keep moving and the longer we stayed there, the better chance we had of being detected, so I picked up my element, and we kept moving west.

We moved until we were due north of our blocking position and made a southern turn into the grape fields. We were still about four hundred meters away from the position, and it was nearly 0400. The sun would be up in about forty-five minutes, and we needed to make up some time. We cut through some grape fields and moved into an open field when Alley had to change the batteries in the mine detector. I was getting more nervous as we were stuck in an open field, chasing the night, and Alley was changing batteries.

We finally made it to a wall and were back on course when we located the road we needed on the other side of the wall. We were fifty meters north of the intersection we were set to block. It was still dark, but the sun was starting to light up in predawn fashion. I got the element over the wall and into the grape field on the other side of the road. I wanted to wait until we had sufficient light to see before we set in a position. The seven-man element spaced out the length of a grape row, and we waited. I called Lieutenant Labowski on the radio to tell him we had reached our position, and we would set in at daylight.

Then we waited.

At 0430, the first call for prayer came howling over Mosque speakers in all directions. The air was cold, we were wet from sweating, and the songs of Islamic prayer echoed eerily through the grape fields. I was shivering from being cold and wet, but those sounds only added to the tension of what was turning out to be a bad day. We'd already lost one man to an IED, and at this point, no one knew the severity of his wounds. Fourth Platoon was still carrying him back to Palace, and I hadn't heard the extent of his injuries. And now I had to listen to the Hajji prayers as they pierced my eardrums.

When the prayer finally ended, I grabbed Alley and told him to sweep along the wall to the south until we were in the corner on the intersection but still in the confines of the grape field. Alley picked up and started moving. I was right behind him, pulling security. When we got to the original position to set up, the metal detector started picking up hits. There was a lot of garbage on the ground, but there were also ominous-looking trees next to the wall running north and south, and I didn't feel good about it. I had Alley stop as I looked around for a different spot to set in our blocking position. We were at the T intersection where the north/south running road ran into an east/west running road. Just on the other side of the road to our south was a grape field which was bordered by a mud wall that wasn't very tall.

"Hey, Alley," I said in a hushed voice. "What do you say we get back out on the road and jump that wall there? We can bust down part of that wall and set the gun north facing up this road."

"I think that's a good idea," Alley said. "We're getting a lot of metal hits here. I'm not sure if it's just trash, but I don't like this. Not at all."

We headed back to where we'd left the rest of the squad, and I told them what we were going to do. The squad picked up, and we moved out onto the road and headed south. When we got to the intersection, I sent Alley across to scan for mines. He gave the thumbs-up, and one at a time, we rushed across the road, jumping into the field, and standing still long enough to be sure we hadn't been detected.

I set in security facing east and west. Schwartz had the squad hatchet and started smashing down a section of the wall so we could place the M240 in position to cover the road heading north. Once this was done, we waited. Now that we had time to relax a little bit, I started scanning our position. I quietly poked my head over the wall and noticed that the grape field we had just abandoned was the same grape field we had been in eleven days earlier. We were about three hundred meters from where Dumar had been blown up. It just felt creepy, like we'd returned to the scene of some crime.

This day was not going well. We'd already had one casualty and still didn't know his disposition. I had planned a terrible route: Instead of a distance of fifteen hundred meters as planned, we already walked more than three thousand meters through rough terrain. There were seven of us alone in a grape field. We were tired. I was on edge, and now we were within eyesight of where we lost one of our men just more than a week earlier.

At daybreak, the remainder of the company elements set out toward the villages they had been scheduled to search. Each compound was numbered, and the last compound, number fourteen, was a building just north of our position. The plan was for Second and Third Squads to search each compound, with Second Squad searching the final compound. From there, Weapons Squad would link up with Second, and we would head back to Palace together. They reached their first objective at about 0600, and I listened on the radio as they continued to progress.

"There's a kid pushing a wheelbarrow up the road," Burke whispered to me. "What should we do?"

Before I could respond, Burke jumped into the road with the M240 and stopped the kid. At this point, I had to go with the flow. I would have preferred to let the kid walk by, but since Burke committed himself, I had no choice but to back him up.

"Search the wheelbarrow and let him go," I told Schwartz, who also jumped onto the road. Covered by Burke, Schwartz searched the kid's load and found nothing of interest, so he waved the kid past.

"Dang, Sarnt," Burke said in his ghetto voice. "You see dat kid almost shit his pants? Man! I scared the shit outta him!"

Moments later, from the east, we could hear the sounds of a vehicle moving up. As far as I was concerned, our position had already been compromised, so I made the decision to stop the multicolored car and search it. Schwartz stopped the vehicle, and I stepped out of the grape field, pointing my M4 at the driver. I motioned for him to get out of the vehicle and raise the hood of his car. He quickly did what I had ordered him to do through wartime sign language. When you point a gun at someone, the language barrier disappears rather quickly. I covered the driver while Schwartz searched him for weapons. Once he was clear, Alley covered him while I conducted a search of his vehicle. I didn't find anything, and when I looked under the hood, I pulled out my knife and cut the wires leading to his horn to prevent him from honking his horn, which was an early warning system in Panjwei'i that alerted Taliban that US forces were in the area. When it was apparent we were wasting our time with him, we let him go. When I got back in the grape field, I laughed as I told the guys how I'd cut the horn wires.

"I'll bet that motherfucker is pushing his horn right now, saying, 'What? No horn?'" I said in my best Afghani-sounding voice. We all laughed, and the mood seemed to lighten up.

Over the radio, Second and Third Squads were calling off the building numbers they'd cleared, and things were going pretty good. I was silently urging them to keep pushing to number 14 so we could get out of there. I was still anxious only having seven people on our position. What if an IED got just one of us? It takes five men to carry the litter. What if two of us got hit? We'd be in deep shit, and we didn't have a medic. I started to think too much, and as I was looking south into the grape field, I started to get paranoid. Birds flying through the grape rows turned into Taliban with RPGs or AKs. I was getting nervous and scolded my squad members like little kids when it looked like they weren't pulling guard.

"Objective 7 . . . clear," came the call over the radio. It was nearly 0800. A few minutes after that call, a loud explosion rocked the earth as a plume of dust and smoke billowed about four hundred meters to our north. It was where our men were searching.

"What the fuck was that?" Burke asked.

"I don't know, Burke," I said, trying to stay calm. "Just stay put and keep your eyes open."

I listened over the radio to some frantic chatter going back and forth. The medic went into action, and I could hear Dugas calling up lines one through five of the nine-line. Someone had been hit. I heard a voice from COP Palace call and asked the disposition of the injury.

"He's missing both his legs," I heard Dugas calmly call back. I was shocked at how composed he was while relaying that message. My respect for Dugas's leadership skyrocketed because if I was there calling that up, I don't think I would have been that calm. Dugas had his shit wired tight. I relayed to my squad that someone had been hit. I didn't want to say too much because I didn't want to start a panic. When they asked who it was, I still didn't know. The battle roster was JBXXXX.

"Whose initials are JB?" I asked.

At that point, it could have been Jordan Blake, Josh Budd, or a lieutenant from our headquarters unit that had gone on the patrol. All three had the first initial "J," and I had no clue of any of their last four. We sat and waited.

"We probably won't know until we get back," I told them.

"Damn," Schwartz said. "I don't want it to be anyone, but I really hope it's not Budd. Or Blake. I guess that's fucked up that I would rather it be an officer than one of us."

"Yeah," I said. "I guess that's fucked up, but I guess I'd rather it be an officer too."

At that point, I heard Dugas come over the radio and say, "We need to send some guys out to pick up his SAW," and then it was obvious who had been hit. Blake carried an M4 and was a minesweeper. The lieutenant wasn't a SAW gunner. Budd was the M249 SAW gunner who had apparently just become a double amputee. A chill ran down my spine.

"It was Budd," I told my guys.

"Are you sure?" Schwartz asked.

"Well, I just heard Dugas say they have to recover a SAW. I'm pretty sure Budd was the only one with the initials 'JB' carrying a SAW," I said.

We all tensed up, and again, I was imagining Taliban forces raiding our position. I was on high alert and sure that at any moment, we would be hit. The car and motorcycle horns started sounding to our west; they knew we were there. I thought it was just a matter of time now. About twenty minutes later, the Blackhawk came in, hovered over a tree line, and landed at the HLZ to pick up Budd. A few minutes later, it lifted off, and it got quiet again. Over the radio, the company commander (CO), Captain Allred, insisted the mission continue. Weapons Squad continued to sit in the grape field and pull security in all directions.

"We need another medevac," Dugas said over the radio. "Battle roster JHXXXX is throwing up and is disoriented. He was really close to the blast. We need to get him out of here."

JH . . . Sgt. Jeff Hurst was the only one I knew with those initials. This day was getting worse. About twenty minutes later, the second medevac bird swooped in and picked up Sergeant Hurst.

"Charlie-six, this is Three-seven," Dugas said, calling the CO. "We're combat ineffective at this point. We need to rendezvous and exfil back to base."

"Roger," replied the CO.

"Three-three, this is Three-seven," Dugas said, calling Third Squad's leader. "Link up with Three-two at our position, and we'll head back, how copy?"

"That's a good copy," responded Third Squad as I waited for Dugas to call me and tell me to link up with them as well. Nothing came over the radio.

"Three-seven, this is Three-four," I called up. "What about us? What do you want us to do?"

"Three-four, this is Three-seven. Take your planned exfil route back to Route Q and head back to base."

Was he serious? We had seven guys, no medic, and no interpreter. It was broad daylight and there had already been two IED explosions that morning, resulting in three men having to be evacuated, and he wanted us—*seven dudes*—to get out of this area on our own? I was shocked and could feel the fear from earlier that morning creeping back up through my spine. Now I had to tell the six guys who followed me that morning that we somehow had to make it back through the grape fields to Route Q on our own.

"Are you fucking kidding me?" Schwartz asked.

Schwartz, Burke, and Alley stood in front of me. I didn't know what to say. There were only seven of us to begin with, and I didn't want to tread through hours of moving through grape fields to get back to Route Q.

"Look," I said, "we have to get back. There are too many IEDs between us and the rest of the platoon to link up with them. I say we have a choice, we can follow our planned exfil route, or we can take this road."

Alley wasted no time answering that question. "I say we take the fucking road."

I looked around and everyone seemed to agree. I have to admit I was glad they were thinking that way, but I needed to include a disclaimer.

"All right, we can take the road, but you all need to be aware that this is the same road we took back after Dumar got blown up. There's a good chance this road has IEDs on it, or they're watching it, waiting for us."

"I don't give a fuck," Alley blurted out. "Look, Sergeant, I promise I will do a kick-ass job sweeping. I don't wanna walk through any more fucking grape fields today."

I saw the look on the faces of my men, and I knew that was how we were getting out of there. We were taking the road.

"Fine," I said. "We'll take the road, but we need to haul ass. I don't want anyone fucking around. Let's get the fuck out of here, and, Alley, you'd better be spot on with that fucking minesweeper."

And so we went. Alley took the lead; I pulled security. Schwartz was behind me, then Burke. Our mortar team followed, and the attachment from First Squad pulled rear security. My legs were trembling with every step we took, constantly expecting the ground to open up and tear one of us, if not all of us, to pieces. And I worried about an ambush waiting for us along the same route we'd taken just eleven days earlier. I wasn't sure if taking this route was a good tactic or not, but I knew it was the fastest way out of the situation. My only hope was that I hadn't made a decision that we would pay for in the end.

We made it to Route Q in less than thirty minutes. We'd covered nearly a thousand meters and were on a paved road, and I have never felt so relieved. When we turned north, we were only about five hundred meters away from Palace. I was walking fast and breathing easy. Then Burke shouted, and I jumped.

"Sarnt Wes, is that a fucking bear?" he asked.

I looked over and saw a black four-legged animal walking across an open field. It was a cow. Laughing never felt so good.

When we got back to Palace, the rest of the platoon was filtering in through the ANA gate. I saw Blake and the lieutenant from HQ, so it only confirmed what we had suspected about Budd being the victim of the IED. The good news was that he didn't lose two legs; he lost his left leg as well as other minor injuries, if you can consider that good news.

I took off my gear, and Dugas came to my CHU to talk. We sat on the picnic table outside the front door and chain-smoked cigarettes. I let him know I was a little pissed about getting left out in that grape field alone, but he explained the danger of all the IEDs in the area made it too treacherous for us to link up with the rest of the platoon. I understood, and the conversation turned toward Budd.

Apparently, the scenery around this IED was similar to the one that got Dumar. Budd's squad was coming around a corner in the grape field near a thatch of trees. The first man came around the corner, and when the IED went off, Budd was in the blast area. Dugas said Sergeant Hurst was pretty close, but he seemed to think that seeing Budd lying on the ground was too much for him to handle. After Budd was medevaced, Dugas said Hurst started to vomit and seemed lost, which is when they had to call in the second bird. Hurst was later diagnosed with Traumatic Brain Injury (TBI), and in true infantry fashion, we gave him a hard time.

Fourth Platoon's injury was a PFC on the sniper team who had been a patrol with us before. He was well liked and respected, and it was a huge loss for Fourth Platoon. He stepped on a pressure plate, and the IED was a partial detonation which broke his ankle. They carried him back to Palace where he was transported by vehicle to FOB Zangabad and airlifted to KAF before making his way back to the States.

Just eleven days earlier, Budd had been one of the soldiers in the grape fields applying tourniquets to Dumar's wounds, and he helped carry him to the helicopter. Now Budd was lying on an operating room table at Kandahar Airfield, receiving surgery on his own wounds. Something about it just didn't seem right.

"That motherfucker is crazy," Dugas said of Budd, shaking his head while his eyes stared into nowhere. I know he was replaying the event of the explosion in his mind. "He was lying there on the ground with Doc working on him, and he tried to crawl onto the litter by himself. That's heart, man. This kind of stuff shouldn't happen to people like him. It shouldn't happen to any of us, but it sucks more when you lose someone who has heart like Budd."

I nodded and took another drag on my cigarette before I put it out. I knew how much Dugas cared about the platoon, and I didn't know what to say. Dugas sat quietly for a few more minutes before he got up and headed back to his CHU. I sat for a minute to gather my thoughts before I had to go give another speech to my squad. Again, I had to tell them to be strong while inside I felt weak.

I talked to Budd much later and asked if he would tell me what he remembered from that day, and this is the story he shared:

We had walked for about two hours when we were getting close to our objective. It was nearly 0600. We stopped one last time in a grape field before we were going to go into a village. I didn't realize at the time that my life would change forever in a few minutes.

I remember the area just as well as my own backyard. To the left of the grape field was a road that led to the village. In front and directly on the right of us was another grape field. Farther past the grape fields, there were tree lines and some mud huts. To our one o'clock (in front and slightly to the right), there was an empty field with nothing growing in it. There was a wadi on the side and then the road after the field. Our plan was to jump over the wall, run through the empty field across the wadi, and start going through the village.

Specialist Offutt went first with the mine detector, followed by Specialist Curtis, who was leading the patrol. It was my turn, and I took a deep breath, gripped my SAW with one hand, and jumped up on the wall leading with my right foot. The second my left foot touched the ground . . .

BOOM!

All of the sudden I was flying through the air and landed straight on my back. I didn't realize at that moment I was the one who stepped on the IED. I crawled back to the wall until Sergeant Hurst grabbed my plate carrier and pulled me behind the wall. As he was dragging me, I could feel my warm blood running down the back of my legs. That's when I realized my legs where fucked up.

Private First Class Smith, our medic, was over there in a few seconds, working on my legs, stopping the bleeding and giving me morphine, although I wasn't in pain. Someone cut my plate carrier off and stripped me down, making sure nothing else happened. I went in and out of consciousness a few times. I told Smith not to tell my mother because she would be mad, or as I put it, "Old lady gonna be pissed!"

Laying there, waiting for the bird, I never thought I was going to die. I knew I was in good hands. As I heard the bird come in to get me, I told my platoon sergeant and company commander not to pick me up and save their energy because I could do it myself.

As they carried me to the bird, my head hit the grape wall a couple times. I believe I called them all buddy fuckers for doing that to me.

As soon as the bird took off, I blacked out and woke up in Washington DC, missing my left leg above the knee and 80 to 90 percent of the muscle and tissue in the right leg.

ELEVEN

THE BEAT GOES ON

*I hate war as only a soldier who has lived it can; only as one
who has seen its brutality, its futility, its stupidity.*
— General Dwight D. Eisenhower

19-26 July 2011

After we lost Budd, morale started to take a deep plunge. No one was motivated
to go on patrols, and a lot of questions surfaced about whether what we were doing
in Afghanistan was worth the price we were paying. I'd already heard a lot of these
concerns from Dugas, but anxiety was spreading throughout the platoon. I began to
have questions of my own. They were not questions so much about our purpose, but
they were questions nonetheless. My concerns were more about my state of mind.

I was starting to realize that the harsh realities of living and fighting in a combat
zone at such a high tempo were starting to take its toll. It concerned me that my gut
reaction when I heard Budd's barrel roster number come across the radio was to an
empty sense of hoping it was an officer rather than Budd. It wasn't that I didn't like
the officer in question, nor did I wish him any harm or pain, but wouldn't it have
been better for Third Platoon to lose an officer from another platoon? When I saw
that officer walking back through the COP, I didn't have ill feelings toward him,
but I'd wished it was him rather than Budd. I felt sick inside for thinking that way. I
wasn't sure if it was even normal.

I was also jealous of Budd, Dumar, and Martin, and that worried me. I wasn't
envious that they lost limbs or had been shot, but I was jealous that they were out
of this fight. Though Martin would return, he wouldn't go out on any more patrols.
Dumar and Budd had both lost a leg and were struggling through a recovery that
would take months, maybe years. Why was I jealous of that? I wondered what it
would be like to not have the daily anxiety about the day-to-day patrols, where we

were constantly getting shot at or blown up with IEDs. I felt twisted inside when I found myself questioning if I wouldn't be happier trying on a prosthetic leg at an Army hospital back in the States.

My biggest concern was the fear I had on the road toward our objective after the IED exploded and took out the sniper from Fourth Platoon. I preached to my squad many times about the difference of being scared and being afraid. I always told them it was OK to be scared, but when it moves over into being afraid, it hinders your job performance. That morning, I was afraid. When the explosion that took out Budd went off, I was scared; but when we had to walk back to Route Q with seven guys, I was borderline afraid again. I was seriously concerned about my leadership abilities. Being a squad leader is a huge responsibility, and if I was going to lose my nerve at a crucial point, would I be able to do my job? Would I be able to lead my men if I was frightened to the point of being afraid? Needless to say, I had some issues.

Over the next couple of days, Palace was like a ghost town. I got out one afternoon to go to the porta-john, and if it hadn't been so bright outside, I might have heard crickets chirping. It wasn't unusual to see people out in the middle of the day, doing something, whether it was playing cards or darts or just sitting around talking. I checked the towers to make sure I hadn't slept through some Taliban attack that had overrun the COP, leaving me as the last man alive. The towers were manned, so I was safe, but something had changed at Palace. The fire was gone, and everyone had turned into hermits, grabbing as much sleep as they could before we had to start patrolling again.

We also lost Doc Smith due to a personnel change. I never learned the reasoning for it, but Smith was pulled out of Third Platoon and was replaced with Doc Bolin. The platoon took this as an insult. Though Smith wasn't *Mr. Personality*, we all loved and trusted him. He earned his pay under fire on more than one occasion, and we respected him. I didn't like Bolin because I didn't trust him. There was an occurrence during NTC in February where Bolin was bored on a training patrol and fired a shot from his truck. His errant shot "killed" Thompson, my gunner, after one of the NTC cadre called in the wasteful shot. After that, I despised this kid, and now he was our platoon medic. As luck would have it, the medic fell under the realm of Weapons Squad, so now he was in my squad. When he arrived, I walked over to his CHU as he was setting down his gear. He hadn't been at COP Palace for more than three minutes.

"Well, well, well," I said, looking at him like I wanted to choke him.

Bolin knew I hated him and told me later he didn't want to come to Third Platoon because he *knew* I hated his guts. He looked up at me as he was taking his kit off and mustered out a, "Good morning, Sergeant."

"Well, good morning to you too, motherfucker!" I yelled at him. "Get your kit back on. You've got tower guard in five minutes! Welcome to the Thunderdome, bitch!"

Dugas told me not to piss off the medic, but Bolin wasn't the first medic I ever pissed off on a deployment, and he hadn't proven himself to me. In my mind, Bolin was a turd, and I didn't want anything to do with him. The thing about Bolin is this: he's like a fungus, he grows on you. It wasn't an overnight transformation, but he did grow on me. I later learned that Bolin actually is a good guy. Over time, he became a friend, but it didn't happen overnight.

Sleep on a deployment is important to a soldier. It's not just a way to rebuild after a long mission or a way to recharge your batteries; it's a way to pass time. The idea behind sleeping as much as possible on a deployment is that when you're asleep, you spend less time deployed. It sounds silly, but if you have slept twelve hours a day for a year, you only have to live six months of it. The other half is spent in slumber. My problem is that I was much older than everyone else in the platoon, and I found it hard to sleep, but obviously, *Operation Sleep Away the Deployment* had kicked off. I just hadn't received the mission brief.

One highlight was that we were given Sgt. Travis Carden from First Platoon. Carden actually volunteered to come to Palace; he was friends with Moreton and Van Bockel. I didn't know him very well, but we did have a short history together.

Prior to the deployment, he would stand downstairs in our company area, and when a private would throw trash on the floor, we would jump their ass. One day, as Carden and I were eating some chips in the formation area, I decided to make my point to the group of privates in the area. I threw my empty chip bag on the floor in front of everyone in an animated fashion.

"You know I don't have to pick it up," I said, looking at Carden. "And since they don't care, why should I? I'll just do like the privates. I'll just throw my trash on the floor."

Travis laughed and added his own spin on it.

"Done with that!" he screamed as he threw his trash on the floor.

The rest of the time before the deployment, Carden and I would make a mess on the floor and justify it by saying, "Done with that!" I think it got through to the privates because the trash wasn't so bad after that.

I was glad to see Carden show up. We needed more NCOs, and he had a lot of experience. I'm sure later down the line he'd regret volunteering for this assignment.

20 July 2011

Patrols started back up on 20 July, and we took baby steps. At 0315, Lieutenant Labowski led a mounted patrol on the Strykers to Route H, and we sat in over-watch positions, trying to catch Taliban crossing into our AO from across the river that was our northern boundary. Nothing happened, and we knew nothing would. I think it was a way to get everyone eased back into the game. The next day, we set up outside Lakani trying to spot possible Taliban fighting positions; and again, we took no fire, and no one stepped on an IED. As commonplace as that might seem, it was a big deal for us, and our morale slowly started creeping back up.

23 July 2011

On 23 July, we were moving toward the village Kenai, west of Palace, near Peshengan. It was an afternoon movement, and it was hot. We dismounted from the trucks off of Route H, and we were about six hundred meters into the patrol when all movement stopped. I got a call on the radio to bring up Doc Bolin. I nagged him as we moved up to see what was happening, telling him he was a piece of shit, and he didn't deserve to be in Third Platoon.

"Doc Smith was a good medic," I said as we walked past the soldiers, taking a knee in the grape field. "I don't know why they gave us a shitbag to replace him. You'd better not kill whoever needs your help. I don't think we brought any body bags with us." Bolin just laughed and continued to laugh as I continued to berate him. It was his strategy.

We made it to the downed soldier. It was SPC Porter Curtis, and at first, it appeared he had a heat injury, possibly heat exhaustion. Bolin gave him an IV of fluids while I pretended to coach him, telling him not to "stick it all the way through Curtis's vein." Bolin just smiled. When Curtis could stand again, we turned the patrol around and headed back to the trucks. It turned out that Curtis hadn't fallen out as a heat casualty, but since he was so close to the explosion that took out Budd, he was diagnosed with TBI and sent to KAF for further evaluation. Curtis was our latest loss, but he would return.

After we got back to Palace that day, I got a new roommate. Moreton wasn't coming back to us, and his replacement as First Squad leader was S.Sgt. Derrick Fox. I decided to try to keep my distance from the new guy. I was starting to feel some detachment, and I figured if I knew the guy, I would take it harder if something happened to him. But Fox was too friendly to ignore. It didn't take long before I caught myself having long talks with him and getting to know him. Despite being a nice guy, I wasn't really impressed with Fox's military skill. My first clue came a few days after he arrived, and I was doing weapons inspections on the M240s because Thompson was complaining about his gun jamming. While we were cleaning the weapons, I was inspecting Thompson's barrel, and Fox, who had told me he's spent time in a weapons squad walked by, looked at the M240 barrel and said, "I've always hated cleaning the SAW." Wyscaver was standing in front of me, and our eyes met in disbelief. It's pretty easy to tell the difference between the barrel of an M240 and an M249. Wyscaver and I just laughed it off.

26 July 2011

Our first patrol with Fox came three days after he arrived. Weapons Squad and First Squad had the task of setting up in a remote location just northwest of Lakani. Once we got set, the rest of the platoon would enter a grape field from a wadi and try to draw fire while First and Weapons Squads would ambush the Taliban fighting position. I didn't like these plans for a couple reasons: First, I didn't like the idea of most of the platoon acting as bait; second, I didn't like not knowing where the Taliban would try to attack the bait. These missions had little, if any, positive results. This time, I would be going out with a new squad leader, and I wasn't sure how he would react under fire.

Fox took the lead on the movement after I had given him some advice on planning the route. I specifically mentioned that he should shy away from clusters of trees in the grape fields because the Taliban use them as IED markers, and I told him that when we got close to a compound on our route, we needed to move quickly. My advice fell on deaf ears. Private First Class Stroemer led out with the minesweeper, and Fox navigated the movement. I was the trail element for the movement, and I was getting frustrated at all the small groups of trees our squads kept passing. Several times, I had to tell Fox to move us away from the trees and avoid any more for the rest of the movement. We were moving slowly, and by the time we neared an inhabited compound on the route, it was starting to get light. Instead of moving quickly past it, Fox did a map check right next to the compound wall. I kept telling myself, *He's new. He's new.*

We finally made it to our objective, and as usual, it looked nothing like it did on our outdated aerial maps. Instead of a grape field, we ended up in a small sparsely covered field of overgrown brush. The only cover we had was a wall that was about twenty meters to our south and another wall directly to our east. The eastern wall had a hole in it, and we set up Burke and Schwartz at this position to cover any incoming fire when the platoon started moving across the grape field to our northeast. We couldn't get too close to the southern wall because if we moved through all the overgrown brush, it would have given our position away. Despite his minor mistakes, Fox got us to the objective undetected. Now all we had to do was wait for the rest of the platoon to play bait.

Our chaplain, Captain Olson, and his assistant, Specialist Roberts, were moving with the other elements of Third Platoon. I knew Captain Olson loved walking through the wadi, but I was pretty sure Roberts wasn't enjoying himself. The duo had been with us on a previous patrol where we had to cross a deep wadi, and Specialist Roberts was pissed. Later, when we had to cross the same stream from a different crossing point, he said some things I didn't expect from a chaplain's assistant. Specialist Roberts was a good guy. He just didn't like getting wet. Now while Weapons and First Squads waited in our dry location, the rest of the platoon was tromping through waist-high water to get to a release point just west of the Martin Tree Line, where it could enter the grape field and achieve some measure of surprise.

We waited in our position for a couple hours, the whole time listening to the radio traffic of the platoon and tracking their slow, encumbered movement. When they finally reached a point where they could exit the wadi into a grape field, I told Burke and Schwartz to get ready in case they took fire from the trees. I kept hearing

Dugas cussing over the radio to the Third Squad leader to "get the fuck out of the wadi!"

Meanwhile, I sat in my dry position and waited.

It didn't take long before the enemy took the bait. The Martin Tree Line opened up, and we had rounds landing on the ground near our position. I called in that we were taking fire but realized rather quickly that those rounds weren't meant for us. Due to the position of the rest of the platoon and the position of the Taliban fire, we couldn't return fire from our position without firing over the heads of our brothers. I made the call not to fire. I wanted to avoid any fratricide. As I was calling this information on the radio to Dugas, an enemy position opened fire just south of our position. We were too out in the open to return fire, and since we hadn't been detected moving in, I didn't want to give our position away, but I had to do something. Fox was close to me, and I moved up to him.

"Who's your 320 gunner?" I could tell his blood was pumping, and I didn't blame him. It was his first patrol, and he was already getting a taste of our Panjwei'i madness.

"My 320 gunner is . . . ," he paused, trying to remember the name. "It's Stroemer."

"Get him to drop an HE (high explosive) round into that tree where that fire is coming from."

Fox pulled Stroemer to our position, and I had to point out where to fire the 40 mm grenade. Stroemer aimed his first round and fired. There's no telling where that round landed, and it was obvious that it was Stroemer's first time firing this weapon in combat.

"What the fuck was that?" I asked Stroemer. "You need to aim down. I think that one went about five hundred meters too far. Aim down and hit that tree line."

I'd hoped he hadn't given us away. Rounds kept streaming from that tree line, so I assumed he hadn't compromised our position. His second shot was dead-on. When the HE round hit the tree, it exploded, sending shrapnel and pieces of tree raining down. All fire from the southern tree line stopped. We never did BDA, but I'm sure if Stroemer didn't kill anyone, he definitely scared the shit out of whoever was shooting from that position.

When the fires from the north slowed down, we got instructions from Dugas to move northwest and link up with the rest of the platoon on the other side of the wadi. I wasn't thrilled about crossing this small river, but I kept my mouth shut. Using my map, I gave Fox the area where we wanted to go, reminding him to stay away from clumps of trees. He led us to the wadi, and then he led us *into* the wadi. I was probably bitching worse than Specialist Roberts. We had stayed dry the whole time, and now we were getting soaked. The drop off into the stream was at least ten feet on either side, and once we were in it, Fox had a hard time finding a way to get out.

After we'd moved about twenty meters west through the water and passed at least two spots I saw where we could get out, I was getting frustrated. Schwartz was right behind me, and Burke was pulling up the rear. The rest of the platoon was already across the wadi and radioing for our progress. I kept telling Dugas we were looking for a way over the north end of the stream. Then the platoon took fire again. Directly to our east, we could see the Martin Tree Line, and we were pretty sure that was where the fire was coming from; but we didn't have positive identification, and I damn sure didn't want to give away our position in the death trap we were stuck in.

"They're right behind us," Burke said with some angst in his voice. "I think they're coming toward us."

The firefight was nowhere near us, but being in the tiny valley we were in, the echoes of the bullets reverberated through our bodies, making it seem a lot closer than it was in reality. Burke was getting nervous, and his anxiety fueled Schwartz to get more than a little excited.

"Sergeant Wes," Schwartz said. "They're right behind us. Let's open up before they hit us."

"Relax, Schwartz . . . and you too, Burke," I said, trying to stay calm. "They're not that close. It just sounds like it because it's echoing off these walls. Don't fire back. We just need to get out of this wadi."

"No, Sarge," Burke argued. "They right there. They're coming up behind us. I can hear it."

I yelled up to Fox to hurry and find a way out of the wadi. Burke stood, holding his M240 at the ready in case someone came up behind us. Fox finally found an exit point, and we started to climb out of the dale. It was taking a while to get twelve men up the wall. Every minute that went by, Burke got more and more worked up. He was convinced they were right behind us, and Schwartz started to panic. As I was getting ready to climb the steep wall, and before I knew what was going on, Burke opened up with the gun. Schwartz followed suit with his M4. My ears were ringing with all the sound bouncing off the walls of the wadi. Burke got off nearly fifty rounds, and Schwartz probably emptied a magazine before I finally got them to cease fire.

"What the fuck are you two doing?" I yelled. "Those assholes are about four hundred meters away, and now you just gave away our position. Don't fire another fucking round unless you see someone with a weapon. Let's get the fuck out of here and quick!"

Though I trusted my squad members in a firefight, I knew Burke wasn't in the mind-set to make the decision to return fire, especially since we were in a deep canyon, and all he was doing was compromising our position.

"But, Sarge," Burke argued, "they was right there. I could tell!"

"Damn, Burke!" I spat back. "It sounds like they're right there because of the echo. They aren't anywhere near us. Don't fire another shot. We just need to get the fuck out of here."

We finally pulled ourselves out of the water and were only about two hundred meters southeast of Zangabad. The rest of the platoon had made it to the north gate of the FOB, and I called Dugas to tell him we would be entering Zangabad through the south gate. The whole rest of the walk, I ribbed Burke and Schwartz.

"They're right behind us . . . They're moving in on us . . . They're coming up right behind us!" I said, feigning panic in a high-pitched voice. They both just walked in silence. I should have been pissed, but it was all I could do to not laugh. I would later refer to this as a Burke-and-Schwartz bitch moment, but it wouldn't be long before we all had our own bitch moments to look back on.

TWELVE

A Bend in the Road

> *No bastard ever won a war by dying for his country. He won*
> *it by making the other poor dumb bastard die for his country.*
> —General George Patton

31 July 2011

We were at the point where we thought we were spinning our wheels. We had lost a lot of guys, some due to noncombat related injuries, but several to IEDs, whether it was amputations or TBI, and one to gunshot wounds. The only time we heard of any Taliban deaths we caused was through ICOM from Taliban radio operators. We weren't sure if we were making a difference. We were starting to get disheartened and needed something to boost our morale.

There was a big patrol coming up. I was giving my squad the mission brief the day prior to the patrol. I was only allowed one gun team, and I asked my gun teams who wanted to volunteer to go. Gun Team 1, Schwartz and Burke, were quick to volunteer; next were Gun Two, Thompson and Wyscaver.

"Thompson just got back from leave, and Wyscaver ain't done shit," Schwartz said. "We need a fucking break. Let those two take this one."

"You two need a break?" I asked. "What about me? I don't get a fucking break! When am I gonna get a break?"

"Take a break then," Burke said. "Have Sergeant Dugas go out for you."

"Sergeant Dugas is already staying back on this one," I informed them. "I don't get a fucking break. Fine bitches. Thompson and Wyscaver, get your shit ready. Schwartz and Burke need *a break*."

About 2330 hours on the night of 30 July, we loaded the Strykers and rode the one mile south to FOB Zangabad. We unloaded by the south gate. Third Squad was leading the patrol that would take us south of Lakani. Third Platoon was being supplemented by about fifteen soldiers from Fourth Platoon since our numbers had diminished from the losses we'd suffered, in addition to leaving a contingent of men back at Palace for force protection. The strategy for this patrol was for Fourth Platoon and our First Squad to get into position in two separate grape huts south of Lakani while Weapons Squad, along with Lieutenant Labowski, would travel another five hundred meters east of those two positions and overtake a compound. From each position, we hoped we could oversee the movement of the Taliban into Lakani. The patrol was based on some intelligence we had received regarding known Taliban infiltration routes. We would observe their movements which would shape future missions in the area.

I always hated when Third Squad led the movements because we were sure to take the longest routes and most likely through muddy terrain. I knew the mud wasn't Third Squad's fault, but as coincidence would have it, this movement was typical of this squad. We traveled for hours, walking through grape fields and constantly changing directions. We climbed over walls, walked through mud, and crossed roads. At one point, we crossed a road and climbed a wall on the opposite side of the road. On the other side of the wall was a thick wall of trees which hindered the movement, slowing down the patrol. I was last man in Third Platoon, and the Fourth Platoon element was behind me. After the thick trees, we walked nearly one hundred meters through thick mud that, at some points, was almost knee deep. I finally got out of the mud and was ready to climb over the next wall when a call came over the radio.

"This is Three-three. I need everyone to look around and see if you see a LAW lying on the ground."

Someone dropped a Light Anti-tank Weapon, a shoulder-fired rocket that weighs more than ten pounds and didn't realize it? I thought this was a joke. But it wasn't. So we sat in position for almost thirty minutes while Third Squad tried to account for their missing weapon. The squad leader eventually came from the front of the position to the rear where he rummaged through the trees by the road and recovered the missing rocket.

"Did you find it?" I asked him on his way back.

"Yeah," he answered. "It was in those trees by the road."

"How the fuck do you not realize you lost a LAW?" I asked with sarcasm in my voice. "When do you realize you're missing that weight?"

He didn't answer, so all I could do was roll my eyes in the dark.

I was tired and frustrated but relieved our missing gear had been recovered. The movement resumed. We kept moving for hours through grape fields, muddy grape rows, open fields, marijuana fields, and every other type of terrain the area had to offer. I didn't think this movement would ever end. At one point I was walking one direction down a grape row, and when I looked over to my right, I could see IR chemlights on the helmets of soldiers going the opposite direction in the very next row over. I was getting pissed and wanted to just jump the wall right there.

At 0400 hours, we climbed another wall, and I could see a road on the other side of a small wadi. After I got over the wall and crossed through the cold, smelly water of the wadi, I got on the road and pulled security for the rest of the elements coming across. Lieutenant Labowski came up to me and said, "We have a Frago," he said, meaning a change to the mission. "We're going to stay here while Fourth Platoon and First Squad move on to their positions. We won't make it to our compound before daylight, and we'll be compromised."

Finally, I felt like we were starting to think before we acted. The movement took much longer than we'd expected, and now we had to change the mission, and I was actually happy about it. Third Squad set up security on the road facing north. After Padilla swept for mines further south on the road, I set up Thompson and Wyscaver facing south to pull security. It was still dark, but I knew we'd be here for a while, so I sat against the wall on the east side of the road and took off my NVGs. Third Squad, Weapons Squad, and the LT waited on the road while First Squad and Fourth Platoon moved to their position.

Not long after Fourth Platoon radioed that they were in position, First Squad called back that they were getting multiple metal hits with their minesweeper. Lieutenant Labowski advised them to move back to the road, and we all waited for our guys to return. After the sun came up, Fourth Platoon's leader called the LT and said they'd been compromised and were also moving back to the road.

While waiting for Fourth Platoon to return to the road, we were at the southernmost position on the road. About forty meters in front of us, the road curved to the left, and we couldn't see beyond the curve because of the mud wall that had been built along the side of the road. That kind of wall was typical in this area. Suddenly, I heard the faint sound of a motorcycle. It sounded like it was moving north on the road we were on. Carden moved up to me and asked if I heard it. I nodded, and we stood on the road with our M4s pointed south. A motorcycle came around the corner with two men on it. The driver almost tipped the bike over when he saw us, two American soldiers aiming their weapons at him less than thirty meters away. Needless to say, he stopped, and the two men quickly dismounted with their hands in the air. The passenger threw a pile of blankets on the ground as he got off the bike. My first thought was that there would be weapons in the blankets because we'd been told that the Taliban cover their weapons with blankets when they move to hide their rifles from helicopters flying overhead. I was excited to search this wad of blankets.

I pulled security for Carden while he searched the two men. He emptied all their pockets and dug through the blankets. We found nothing. The blankets weren't obscuring any weapons or explosives. The look on the faces of these two men was of utter terror. They were shaking and nervous. I felt pretty sure these two were not Taliban, but just a couple of guys headed to work in the grape fields. They were going to be late for work though because we held them on the side of the road, and they weren't going anywhere until we left. We didn't want them to tip off anyone of our location. I offered them bottles of water as they squatted facing the wall.

As I was giving one a bottle of water, I heard another motorcycle heading our way from the same direction. Carden and I lined up again on the road, and just before this bike came around the corner, it started blaring its horn. Again, when the motorcycle came around the curve, the driver nearly lost control when he saw two men aiming weapons at him. He regained control, stopped the bike, then dismounted, and walked toward us with a smile on his face. He was a little too smug for me.

Again, I pulled security while Carden searched him. One thing I liked about Carden is that he didn't put up with any shit. At one point he was pulling stuff out of the guy's pocket, and the guy reached down to grab something away from Carden, at which point Carden just slapped his hand like he was a little child reaching for a light socket. I had to laugh. Then Carden tossed me a small green book that looked like a passport.

"What the fuck is this?" I asked.

"I don't know, but I've never seen one before," Carden replied. "He doesn't have anything else, but there's something about this guy. I don't like him."

"Well, put him against the wall with those other two," I said. "Make sure they don't talk to each other."

Lieutenant Labowski came up to me, and I showed him the passport Carden had gotten off the latest guy. He looked through it and then looked up.

"The next motorcycle that comes up that road honking its horn, shoot it," he ordered.

"Are you sure about that, sir?" I asked.

"Look, horn honking is an early warning system," he explained. "The next time someone comes around that corner honking, we're gonna shoot 'em."

"Yes, sir," I said and chuckled a little under my breath as I relayed that message to Sergeant Carden, who was coming back from putting the latest catch against the wall.

"Is he serious?" Carden asked.

"Yes, he's serious. So if someone comes up this road honking their horn, we're gonna fuck 'em up," I said.

"Fuck yeah," Carden said.

Less than ten minutes later, a third motorcycle started approaching our position. Carden and I moved closer to the curve in the road, and Lieutenant Labowski moved up with us. I was in the center, Carden was on my left, and the LT was on my right. Right before the motorcycle hit the curve, its horn started blaring. Without a word being said, all three of us moved our M4 selector switches from safe to semi at the same time. It sounded like one loud click. I know it was only a few seconds later, but it seemed like a long time before the bike rounded the corner. In that time, I had several thoughts running through my head, including, *I hope there aren't any kids on this motorcycle*, and *I hope we have enough time to tell*.

The bike came around the corner, and we were close enough to see the look of panic on the driver's face, but it was too late. We all three opened up on the motorcycle, each of us firing twelve to fifteen rounds. The next events happened in slow motion, like you'd see in a movie, but this was real.

A cloud of dust kicked up around the motorcycle, and it flipped rear over front, launching the three riders through the air. The bike toppled to the ground, and the three passengers came to a thud, two on the road and one just east in the grass. The rider in the rear was wearing a loose garment, and as he was flying through the air, it looked as if he was wearing a burka, and I thought we'd just shot a woman. We all sat, weapons at the ready, waiting to see what would happen next.

As the dust settled, we could hear a moan coming from the wreckage. At least one of them was still alive. We called up the medic who came up, and Lieutenant Labowski and I pulled security on the crash site while Sergeant Carden moved up and started to search for weapons with Doc Bolin in tow. I was feeling a little guilty because I was afraid we'd just killed these guys because they were honking their horn. What if they were honking to let people know they were coming around the corner? I know the honking was an early warning system, but it made sense to use the horn as a warning that they were just driving around a blind spot in the road. I was starting to second guess my actions.

"We got an ICOM radio," Carden called back. "And an AK! Here's another AK and a bayonet."

All my trepidations vanished. We had actually just shot three Taliban fighters from a distance of less than twenty meters. I looked over at the last guy that had come around the corner honking. His head was hung, and he looked like a leader who had just lost three of his men. There was no longer any doubt that this guy was Taliban too. Lieutenant Labowski made the decision right there that this guy was now officially a detainee and someone put some flex cuffs on him.

Carden finished clearing the three men in the road, and I walked up. Doc had already assessed the injuries and determined the first guy in the road had only seconds to live and wasn't worth wasting time on. The second had been shot in the arm and the leg and lay still on the road just looking toward the sky but still breathing. The third, the one who had been thrown off the road, was moaning. He had multiple gunshots in his chest, arms, and legs. His right hand was partially amputated and was hanging by some skin, probably from hitting the ground after the bike tossed him in the air. He was in bad shape, and Doc was patching him up.

I looked down at the first guy and watched as he took one last breath. I could see his chest rise and fall, and it was almost like you could see him give up the ghost. It's a weird feeling seeing someone die and know you were right there at their last breath.

It was decision time. Word came over the radio that the battalion commander ordered us to bring back any dead bodies. It was clear that if we waited long enough, the third man would die. We had one dead body already, and no one was going to willingly carry this carcass back. And how were we going to get back? Would we travel down the road another click to the desert and get picked up by our trucks? And how long would that take? Or would we go back the way we came, lugging at least one dead body, carrying two injured Taliban, and escorting one detainee over walls and through muddy grape fields? How many hours would that take?

Lieutenant Labowski assessed the situation. We all looked at the map of the area and decided to spin up the trucks, and we'd carry the dead and escort the detainee from there. Now it was up to Doc to make a decision.

"Is that guy going to make it?" the LT asked Doc.

"I've got his bleeding stopped," Doc explained. "If we can get him to a hospital soon, I think he might make it. But it would have to be soon because he's pretty fucked up."

The LT looked at me and Sergeant Carden and asked what we thought. Carden wanted to dump the two remaining bodies into the wadi and head back. The LT and I both knew that was the wrong idea. I think Carden was just talking shit anyway.

"We're going to have to call a medevac," I told the LT. "If Doc got the bleeding stopped and he might live, we have to do it. And maybe we can put that dead body on the bird too so we don't have to lug it back."

The LT thought for a moment, got on the radio, and came back to where Carden and I were standing.

"We're going to medevac these two injured, but we can't put the body on the bird," he said. "We can only medevac wounded personnel. We're going to have to carry the body back."

"What the fuck," I said. "I don't wanna carry that dead motherfucker back. Why don't we just leave it here? This is bullshit."

The LT agreed, but we had our orders, and we were bound by those orders to bring this dead Taliban fighter back to FOB Zangabad. How we were going to do it was still up in the air. Carden called in the information for the nine-line, and then we waited for what seemed like a long time. While we were waiting, we did some more thorough searching of the dead Taliban and the one who just lay there without a sound. The one who was still alive was already missing his right hand and his right eye was missing as well. His previous injuries were obviously caused by some kind of explosive blast, which indicated that he likely made a mistake at one time building or emplacing an IED. I had no sympathy for him.

After some time, we heard the sounds of the incoming bird. I had a soldier throw a green smoke grenade onto the HLZ, which had already been cleared by our minesweepers. The green smoke billowed and dissipated. The bird kept flying. It wasn't our medevac. So we waited a little longer. I was glad the medics didn't take this long when it was Dumar or Budd lying in the fields. We heard a second helicopter, and this time it was confirmed to be our medevac. I had the same soldier throw another green smoke. We could reasonably predict we would take some incoming fire this time since our position had been revealed with the previous green smoke. We all lined up against the wall to receive any incoming small arms fire from the north from Lakani. It was no surprise that when the aircraft made its descent from the east, gunfire from Lakani opened up on the medevac bird. I thought it was ironic and wondered if it ever occurred to them that we were evacuating two of *their* men. I wondered if they would have even cared.

We suppressed the gunfire while several of our soldiers helped load the injured Taliban onto the helicopter. After the bird took off, I remembered that we still had the first two men that we held up. I also saw that there were several people stopped from Third Squad's position on the north end of the road. In addition to our two men, there were several small children and an old man held up on the side of the road. After the bird left, Lieutenant Labowski gave us permission to let the civilians go and said we were going to drag the dead body south to the desert. When we let the locals go, an old man that Third Squad had stopped took off, leaving behind a wheelbarrow that he'd been pushing. Someone made the suggestion that we load the body onto the wheelbarrow and push it back to the trucks, which should be at the desert by the time we got there. I thought it was a great idea. Then someone suggested we make our detainee push the wheelbarrow. Everyone agreed, even me, until I thought about it a little more.

"I don't think we can make him push the wheelbarrow," I said to Lieutenant Labowski. "That might be considered some kind of cruel and unusual punishment. We could get into some deep shit."

Lieutenant Labowski thought for a second and looked up.

"Sergeant Wes is right," he said. "We can't do that. Load up the weapons and all the stuff we got off these guys and put the body on top of it. We'll push it back to the desert. It's not that far."

We put the detainee toward the front of the formation, and the wheelbarrow was toward the middle as we slowly made our movement south toward the desert. Several times the wheelbarrow fell over, tossing the body and the weapons onto the ground and drawing some laughter. After nearly thirty minutes of walking, we made it to the desert, and Dugas was waiting with two Strykers and the MRAP-All Terrain Vehicle (MATV). The body was thrown into the back of the MATV, and the weapons were put on one of the Strykers.

The ride back was bumpy, and I was exhausted. There were several times I caught myself dozing off. Eventually, we made it back to FOB Zangabad and dismounted the trucks. I had assumed we would drop the body and the detainee off and head back to Palace. I was wrong. Now it was time to answer for what we had done, and according to the LT, "It can go either way."

"What does that mean?" I asked.

"It all depends."

"On what?"

"On how this all gets perceived by battalion."

Sergeant Carden, Lieutenant Labowski, and I dropped our kit at the truck and headed toward the battalion Tactical Operations Center (TOC). Now I was worried. I wondered if we'd get in trouble for killing those guys. Surely we'd be OK. We found weapons and a radio on them. They were undoubtedly Taliban. Why would we get in trouble?

When we walked into the TOC, people were patting us on the back like we were heroes. It felt good, and it looked like battalion perceived our action as a good thing. I felt better. We answered a boatload of questions and filled out sworn statements regarding the man we detained. We told the story over and over to different people and had to point out where it all took place on the map. It seemed endless. I was still exhausted, and I just wanted to go back to Palace and get some sleep.

Then we had to go with a civilian contractor as he searched the dead body for more intelligence. I was amazed at how much we had missed when we searched the body, but when we did, we weren't looking so much for information, but weapons. When the civilian was done searching, we had to determine which pieces of what he found and what we brought back belonged to which of the three men we had gunned down.

Following that ordeal, we had to write more statements and answer more questions. I wondered if it was worth killing anyone if it was going to be this much of a pain in the ass. I'll bet they didn't have to do all this in Vietnam. After several hours, we were done, and we loaded up the trucks to go back to Palace. I couldn't wait to climb into bed and get some sleep.

We learned later that the two men we medevaced to KAF both died, making them two more confirmed kills. These were the first three confirmed kills in the battalion. Additionally, the detainee we brought back was named Esa Khan and was number 5 on the battalion's most wanted list. We had done well.

When we got back, we all had to tell the story to the guys that didn't go. Schwartz and Burke were pissed, but I had to laugh and say, "You guys wanted *a break*!" A lot of people were saying we should have killed the other two, or we should have just pushed the bodies into the wadi and kept going. But I think we did the right thing. Lieutenant Labowski made some good decisions, and what we did was by the book. I felt no guilt for anything we'd done because I felt like we'd followed the rules.

Later, we would have to answer questions about why we opened fire on the third motorcycle when we were able to stop the first two. Brigade Legal was questioning our Escalation of Force (EOF) procedures. But the fact of the matter was that by the time that third motorcycle had come around the corner, it was too close for us to stop because each time a bike came around that corner, we'd moved closer to the bend in the road until it was impossible to stop it using EOF procedures. Again, we were justified, and the questioning ended.

What troubled me at this point was how much we were actually questioned about the event. The guys we killed had AK-47s, enemy radios, and a slew of intelligence. If we had stopped them, what would have kept them from turning those weapons on us? We should have been considered heroes, but we were questioned like we were criminals. Something was definitely wrong with how we were fighting this war. This should have been a warning to me, but I didn't take it as such.

THIRTEEN

FULL MOON REPRIEVE

Safeguarding the rights of others is the most noble and beautiful end of a human being.

—Kahlil Gibran

02 August 2011

I'm not sure what got into Lieutenant Labowski after we killed those guys. It could have been a taste for blood, but I think it was more a vision of opportunity. Regardless, our platoon leader decided that waiting on the side of a road to ambush unsuspecting Taliban was our new plan of attack. It made sense because it had worked once, but I wondered if the LT wasn't putting too much stock into the idea. I thought we got lucky—once.

We'd been sitting around by the gate for a while, and by 2330 hours, we were finally leaving the south gate at Zangabad. As I stepped foot outside the gate, I felt the sudden urge to take a shit. I was a little pissed at the timing of it, but I couldn't do anything, so I figured I'd just have to try to hold it until we got back. We got into the grape field south of the FOB, and about two hundred meters into it, the urge turned into bubble guts, and I knew I wouldn't be able to hold it. I was the last man in the element, and Doc Bolin was directly in front of me. I still hadn't made nice with him, but when the movement halted, I needed a favor.

"Doc," I whispered. "I need you to do something."

Doc came back to where I was, and I turned my back to him.

"I need you to get into the outside pocket of my assault pack and get my baby wipes," I said over my shoulder. One thing I learned a long time ago was to never go out to the field or on a mission without something to wipe with. Doc gingerly reached into my pack, trying to be very quiet, and pulled out the pack of wipes.

I put my weapon on the ground and took off my gloves. After telling Bolin to warn me when we start moving again, I started unbuckling my belt, and I pulled my pants down to my knees. I would have taken them down to my ankles, but I was wearing knee pads, and I was running out of time. My bowels weren't going to even wait for me to take my assault pack off. Then Bolin turned around to watch.

"Dude," I said to him. "You might not want to watch this."

"Are you taking a shit?" he asked.

"Duh, motherfucker! Quit watching me! What are you, some kind of faggot?" I whispered at him, trying not to laugh.

As he turned around, it all came out in one loud burp. By the time Bolin turned back around to look at me, I was already wiping my ass.

"That was it?" he asked.

"What do you want?" I replied. "Should we make a full production out of this? I don't have the time!"

I was trying not to laugh too loud. I put all my gear back on and pulled my night vision goggles down to look at my work. My version of NVGs had infrared, and behind me was a glowing orange streak about three feet long. I had to laugh, telling Bolin he should look at it. Unfortunately for him, his NVGs didn't have infrared capability, and the poop didn't glow in the dark. And then the smell crept in. I wished we'd move, but we weren't so lucky. We were stuck there for a little while, and I thought Bolin was going to puke. I thought *I* was going to puke.

We were about two hundred meters into the movement when Fox said he saw three men standing outside a grape hut. I stood on a grape wall looking toward the grape hut with my NVGs. I didn't see a thing. Since we were on our way to set up an ambush, Lieutenant Labowski thought it would be best to check it out rather than risk being compromised. He took three men with him and they made their way to the grape hut. When they got there, it was empty. Fox swore he saw something, but I didn't believe him.

That investigation took forever. It was now well after 0200, and we still had a long way to go before we hit our ambush site. The sun would come up at about 0430, and if we weren't in place before dawn, we would probably be seen setting up. I wanted to scrap the mission and go back.

"Sir," I whispered as I walked up to the LT. "It's almost 0230, and we have a long way to go. Do you want to just bag this thing, and we can try again tomorrow?"

"We have time," he responded, turned around, and started moving back to his position in the formation. There was no getting out of it.

We began to move quickly. Our objective was the same road south of Lakani, where we shot the three Taliban guys just a few days before, but we would be further north. Knowing that time was of the essence, we didn't mess around. We made it to the release point just before 0400, and the sun was starting to make its predawn glow in the eastern sky. We dropped off First Squad at a grape hut, and Weapons Squad, along with a handful of attachments, moved toward the tree line to set in the ambush.

We made it and were undetected. The LT and I did a quick recon of the site and left security while we went back for the rest of our ambush element. We set in quickly and started to wait. The position that we chose was ideal for an ambush. We were off the road and just inside a small dry wadi which concealed our position. Lieutenant Labowski was in the furthest position south. Thompson was next to him. Wyscaver was just north of Thompson, and I was a little further north of Wyscaver. Schwartz and a few guys from other squads were north of me. We sat quietly, trying not to fall asleep, and we waited.

A little traffic made its way up and down the road. It was mostly people walking or pushing wheelbarrows. There were a few motorcycles, but none were honking so we remained quiet. Lieutenant Labowski called Fox on the radio about 0615 and told him to shoot some small pen flares to try to rustle up the Taliban. Fox shot two flares and nothing happened. At about 0700, the LT told Fox to drop a 320 round into an open field to try again. The flares weren't big enough, but an HE round in an open field should get something going. Fox cautiously picked out a field, double- and triple-checking to make sure no civilians were in the area, and dropped the HE round. The ICOM chatter picked up. They knew we were in the area but didn't know where.

We continued waiting next to the road, and sometime after 0800, we decided we wouldn't have any luck ambushing anyone. The LT and I planned our withdrawal, and I went up and down the line, explaining that we'd be pulling out one at a time and moving back toward our release point. Before I got to the far northern position, I heard a motorcycle coming up the road from south to north with its horn honking. I quickly made it back to my position and placed my selector switch from safe to semi and waited. My heart was pounding. Since the bike was coming from the LT's position, he would initiate. If he didn't fire, no one would fire.

I could feel the veins in my body pulsing with adrenaline. It seemed like it took forever for this motorcycle to make it to our position, and I was convinced we would open up on the driver. My hands were shaking, and I was trying to make eye contact with Thompson and Wyscaver to make sure they knew not to fire unless Lieutenant Labowski initiated. As the bike made it past the LT's position, I poised ready to fire. In a split second decision, the LT let the bike go by with the horn blaring. When it passed my position, I knew why. The driver was just a child—a young boy of maybe twelve years of age. I let out a sigh of relief and was thankful that Lieutenant Labowski was calm enough to show some restraint. We later decided that the Taliban knew we were in the area and were using this kid as a decoy, hoping we'd shoot at him. Thankfully, Lieutenant Labowski was too steady to fall for the trick.

We pulled out of the position and headed back to Zangabad. It was uncomfortably hot, walking through the grape fields, and we were just south of Lakani. I was pretty confident we would get hit, but we didn't. We made it back to Zangabad, then Palace, without incident. It was one of the few patrols I'd go on where we didn't have some kind of enemy engagement.

03 August 2011

I slept most of the day, or at least as much as I could, and at about 2230 hours that night, we set back out to try another ambush south of Lakani. Lieutenant Labowski called this a deception mission. I called it stupid. A gun team from Weapons Squad, along with Dugas, Padilla, Doc Bolin, and me, were inserted from the desert side, southeast of Lakani. We were supposed to set into an ambush position alongside a north-/south-running road. Once we got set in, First and Third Squads would follow in behind us. When it got light, they would move through the grape fields and try to instigate Taliban movement along the road so Weapons Squad could kill them.

After we got off the trucks at 0245, Padilla set out with the minesweeper, and I was right behind him. Schwartz was right behind me, followed by Burke, PFC Nick Sepeda, Doc Bolin, and Dugas pulling rear security. We moved pretty quickly through the fields since it was such a small element. We were walking past a grape hut when I noticed someone standing next to a grape wall. He was glowing bright orange through my NVGs, and he was so still. I stopped the movement and called Dugas over the radio.

"There's a man standing next to the grape wall to my eleven o'clock," I whispered into my hand mic.

"Did he see us?" Dugas asked back.

"I don't think so," I replied. "He's just standing really still. What do you want to do?"

"We have to keep moving," Dugas said. "Let's snatch him up and take him with us so he doesn't alert anyone that we're out here."

"Roger," I said, moving up to Padilla to tell him what we were going to do. As I moved up, I got a better look at the "man" that was standing next to the grape wall. It wasn't a man. It was a large grape root. It was facing east and must have absorbed a lot of heat from the previous day's sunlight and was still glowing through my NVGs in the shape of a small man. I felt pretty dumb.

"Disregard," I called back to Dugas.

"Did he see us? Did he run off?" Dugas asked.

"Negative," I said, trying to think of an excuse. I couldn't. "It was just the root of a grape plant. It looked like a man through my NVGs."

"You are a dumb-ass," Dugas said. "I guess we can't be too paranoid, though, so let's move out, turd."

We moved to within one hundred meters of where we planned to set up the ambush. Dugas and I took Padilla to scout out the area, leaving Schwartz, Burke, and Sepeda to pull security. We moved up to a tall wall, probably eight feet high. There was a small ledge about halfway up the wall, and I told Padilla to sweep the area for IEDs and to take a look over the wall. He climbed onto the ledge, and his M4 racked against the side of the wall.

"What the fuck was that, Padilla?" I whispered in an angry voice. "We're trying to set in a fucking ambush. Do you think you can make any more fucking noise?"

Padilla apologized and swept the area. When it was clear, I climbed onto the ledge, and my M4 smashed against the side of the wall, making the same noise Padilla did when he climbed up the wall. For the second time on this patrol, I felt pretty dumb. It turned out the ledge was only about two feet wide, and when we both climbed onto it with our weapons slung, they hit the wall. We all froze for a few minutes to make sure we hadn't been compromised, and when we felt confident we were good, I apologized to Padilla and looked over the wall. There was a good view of the road, but just on the other side of the road was an inhabited compound that posed a threat to civilians if we had to open up from this position. Additionally, if we stood on this ledge, we would be exposed from our rear. This was not a good place for an ambush.

I climbed down and walked up to Dugas.

"What do you think?" he asked as Padilla moved off the wall.

"I don't think this is a good place," I explained. "There's a civilian compound on the other side, and I don't think we can cover our rear if we're standing on that wall. We'd be better off climbing over the wall and getting on the road, but I can't tell if we'd have cover if we were actually on the road."

I expected Dugas to tell me to drive on with the mission. I knew he was cautious, but I figured he'd want to continue setting up the ambush. He surprised me when he said no. We moved up and down the wall in both directions and decided there was no place to safely set in an ambush. Dugas called Lieutenant Labowski on the radio to tell him what we found. The LT was less accommodating than Dugas.

"When you get set in, let us know. We're about to dismount the trucks now," Lieutenant Labowski called to Dugas.

"Sir," Dugas called back. "This is not a good place for an ambush. We are going to pull back."

"Look for a different spot."

"We did. There is no place we can effectively set in an ambush. We're going to pull out of here."

I could tell in the sound of Lieutenant Labowski's voice that he didn't believe us. I hoped that he would just scrap the whole thing, and we'd go back to Palace and regroup. No such luck. Lieutenant Labowski argued with Dugas about setting up the ambush. Dugas stood fast to his position. We would not set up an ambush here, but Lieutenant Labowski made the decision to carry on the mission with a movement to contact.

"What do you want to do?" I asked Dugas.

"Set a course to the east, and we'll push back," he said. "If we get far enough out there, we can link up with the trucks after the other squads push past us."

I could tell Dugas was pissed. It was obvious Lieutenant Labowski didn't trust his judgment and was planning to continue on with the mission anyway. I was there, and I helped Dugas come to his conclusion, so I felt a little put out as well.

We gathered the rest of the squad and started pushing east. We were making good time, and our intent was to push far enough east so that the other squads would bypass us on their movement north toward Lakani. We jumped walls, crossed open fields, and weaved in and out of grape fields until we came to a spot in a weed-infested grape field and sat down against a large mud wall. Dugas called the LT and told him we were at a halt position and asked for his status. Lieutenant Labowski came back over the radio and gave an eight-digit grid location. I heard this and looked at my GPS watch. I couldn't believe what I was seeing.

"Are you fucking kidding me?" I said, looking at Dugas, who was sitting right next to me. "They are only one hundred meters south of us right now, and they're moving right toward us! This is unbelievable."

"The LT is gonna make us go with him," Dugas said with a hint of anger.

So much for our little hide site. Dugas called in our position to avoid anyone jumping the wall just south of us and shooting us on sight. Lieutenant Labowski was pleased, probably thinking we'd planned this location to link up with him. It didn't take long before the first soldier jumped over the wall and walked less than fifty meters in front of us. When their last man walked past us, we picked up and followed behind them. We were heading to Lakani.

Our movement halted about four hundred meters south of Lakani. The LT left my gun team and a few others behind, including Sergeant Keelslice, to pull security for the rest of the platoon to move into the center of town. We hadn't had much luck getting into Lakani, and I was happy to stay put while the rest of the platoon moved out. It was actually pretty quiet, and even though the sun was starting to move up, it wasn't very hot. We watched the platoon's movement toward Lakani and scanned the fields and surrounding grape huts in case any Taliban fighters decided to be brave. Things remained quiet until the platoon crossed a tall mud wall into Lakani. From our position, we heard the first shots from an enemy machine gun and the return fires from Third Platoon. Keelslice coordinated air assets to our position, and I relayed his messages to Lieutenant Labowski from my position.

The firefight didn't last long. This was the first time the platoon had made contact where I wasn't directly involved. Oddly enough, I felt a little left out. When everything had calmed down, Dugas called me over the radio and told me to move into the village. We tried to follow the route the rest of the platoon followed. Padilla still swept for IEDs, and eventually, we made it into Lakani to the scene of two men sitting on the side of the road in flex cuffs and a burning motorcycle. There were no casualties, and when everyone was accounted for, we moved east toward the desert with our detainees.

We made it back to Palace after bringing the detainees to Zangabad. They didn't stay long and were soon released. I never learned why, and I didn't care. We had obviously wasted our time, but at least we made it into Lakani.

06 August 2011

We were moving into another ambush, but this time, things were a little different. First, Lieutenant Labowski was with me instead of Dugas. I can't be sure, and he'd probably deny it, but I felt like the LT didn't trust Dugas after the last botched ambush site. Another difference was the amount of light while we were moving. Our movement started at about 0200, but the moon was starting to get full, and it was almost light enough to see without NVGs.

Private First Class Stroemer, a soldier on loan to Weapons Squad from First Squad, led the formation with the minesweeper. I followed close behind Stroemer to navigate the movement. Behind me were Schwartz, Burke, Thompson, and Wyscaver. Somewhere in the mix was Lieutenant Labowski, Doc Bolin, and an interpreter. I was happy about all the ambient light provided by the moon, but I didn't feel very comfortable. If we could see in the dark without NVGs, so could the Taliban.

We moved quickly, and Stroemer did a great job for his first time running the Vallon. We moved to the release point ahead of schedule. From there I followed Stroemer, and Lieutenant Labowski got in behind me as we moved into the ambush site. This time we were setting up an ambush in the Martin Tree Line, almost right where Martin had hit the IED. Needless to say, no one was comfortable with this mission. I even thought about what I would have to tell Stroemer's wife if he hit an IED. I can't speak for anyone else on this patrol, but my nerves were on edge.

When we found a good spot to set up the ambush, Lieutenant Labowski signaled to Schwartz with three IR flashes of his NVGs. The signal brought in the rest of our ambush element. We set in place and waited for the sun to come up and the rest of the platoon to bait out the Taliban fighters by walking through the grape fields south of the tree line.

We waited for movement and soon heard the early warning horns honking from Lakani. The ambush line started to get a little tense, and Dugas was relaying his location over the radio. Lieutenant Labowski was at the far eastern position of the ambush line, and I was at the far western point. It was up to either one of us to initiate the ambush, depending on which end of the ambush the enemy entered the kill zone. At about 0630, I heard a creaking sound coming from the east. I could see a young Afghani man pushing a wheelbarrow up the road, and everyone tried to burrow deeper into position to avoid being seen. Everyone except Lieutenant Labowski, that is. When the man was directly in front of the LT, he stood up and pointed his rifle at the would-be target. I jumped up to cover Lieutenant Labowski, wondering why he made that move. The man was obviously surprised, and I think he may have shit his pants. Luckily, the LT again showed restraint and didn't blast the guy. But we had been seen, and all we could do at that point was pull the guy to our position and keep him quiet. We searched him, found no weapons, and put him behind us while Bolin guarded him and made sure he stayed quiet.

Twenty minutes passed with no sign of movement on the road when a man walked out of what we thought was an abandoned compound about seventy-five meters to our east. He turned and went back into the compound. Nobody moved; I wondered if he saw us. A few minutes later, he emerged from the compound again, turned in our direction, and spotted us. His eyes opened up wide, and he ran away to the east. Lieutenant Labowski jumped up and started to chase him. I followed to provide security for him, but it was too late. The guy got away and we had been compromised.

Lieutenant Labowski called Dugas and told him to head back to Zangabad, and we would link up with him there. We grabbed the kid that we'd snatched and took him into the grape field. When we were about one hundred fifty meters away from the tree line, we started asking the young man questions. He was frightened and said through our interpreter that he was afraid that the Taliban would see him with us and cut off his head. We tried to explain that we had pulled him this far into the grape fields so no one would see him with us, but he was too scared to answer any of our questions. I was starting to get frustrated. No matter how much we tried to convince him we could protect him if he told us where the Taliban were hiding, he gave us nothing.

"Sir, this is bullshit," I said to the LT. "He's not gonna say anything. We need to just kick him off and get back. We've wasted too much time on this asshole."

Lieutenant Labowski tried for a few more minutes, but the kid wasn't talking. Finally, the LT made the decision to let him go, and we moved out from there. Our interpreter told him to go away, and we started our movement back to Zangabad. When we made it about three hundred meters away, I heard a single shot from the tree line. Everyone turned and poised for a firefight.

"What the fuck was that?" Lieutenant Labowski asked.

"Well, sir, if you ask me, I think the Taliban just whacked that guy," I said. I heard some laughing around me, and I couldn't help but chuckle myself. "That motherfucker should have told us something. At least then he would have died for something."

I didn't say much else as we moved back toward Zangabad. I wondered if I should have felt guilty if my assessment was correct. I didn't, though. As far as I was concerned, that guy had a chance to give us some information. We probably could have taken him back with us to protect him, but he was more afraid of the Taliban than he was of us. I guess he had good reason. I guess I didn't give a shit. The kid didn't tell us anything even though we could have protected him, so I could have cared less if the Taliban blew his brains out. I guess I was starting to get a little too thick-skinned.

Lieutenant Labowski wanted to keep conducting ambushes, but as the month was progressing, so was the full moon. Thankfully, we were able to convince him that it was not in our best interest to travel at night during a full moon. There were times in the middle of the night that the moon was so bright it almost looked like daytime. Lieutenant Labowski gave in, and we delayed any more night movements until the moon started to wane. The moon had provided us with a reprieve from night movements; I would finally start to get some more sleep. I even prayed every night to have a few more nights of full moon. I was tired of moving through the grape fields at night. I felt our luck was wearing thin.

A few days later, Lieutenant Labowski, Carden, and I were called to Masum Ghar to talk to brigade legal about shooting the men on that road. We had to explain again why we hadn't used escalation of force. While talking to one of the legal officers, we learned that we were not allowed to conduct any offensive operations in our AO without the consent of the brigade commander. That meant no more ambushes. Apparently, we were allowed to sit on a road and conduct an interdiction patrol, but an ambush was an offensive operation, and the brigade commander would have to sign off on it. We were told that likely wouldn't happen.

I was relieved that our ambush days were over, but I had to wonder what kind of war we were fighting at this point. No offensive operations meant we were expected to go out on patrols and wait to get shot at before we could do anything. Did they really expect us to do this? We had to be reactive rather than proactive. How could we ever win this war fighting like that? I couldn't believe it.

I was starting to lose the heart for our fight in Afghanistan. Dugas had complained to me in my CHU so many times, and I had defended what we were doing. After hearing this news, I stopped defending our actions. The politics of this fight were starting to show, and we were walking around with our hands tied behind our backs, at least until someone tried to kill us.

A squad photo taken at a makeshift range at FOB Zangabad. From left to right, Schwartz, Burke (kneeling), Alley, Me, Hendrick, Wyscaver, and Thompson (kneeling and covering his face). (Photographer unknown)

I stood near Dugas while we were waiting for EOD to detonate what we thought was an IED. It turned out not to be an IED, but we felt it was better to be safe than sorry. We also got to see our favorite Air Force EOD operator. (Photo by Will Schwartz)

At COP Palace, one of the tower guards called over the radio that he had possibly seen someone emplacing an IED about two hundred meters from our south wall. When the alert sounded, most people didn't have time to get into full uniform. Schwartz (left) and Burke (right) were two of the first soldiers up to the tower. This tower was built on top of my CHU and is the same tower Zisha killed himself. (Photo by Casey Westenrieder)

While manning a random traffic control point, I came across this pleasant Afghan civilian. He was the happiest civilian I met the entire time I was in Afghanistan and was he friendly with us, despite the fact that we were delaying him. (Photo by Will Schwartz)

Dugas takes a knee outside a village during the air assault mission we performed the day we moved to COP Palace. Water was scarce, and we were trying to rest up and let the day cool down before we walked back to FOB Zangabad. On that walk back, we received fire from an automatic weapon, marking the first time our whole platoon took fire. (Photo by Casey Westenrieder)

During a firefight in Gharandai, Burke takes aim at a grape hut while Dugas (left) tries to guide in the air assets with hand and arm signals. We couldn't reach the helicopters on the radio until one of the pilots dropped an empty water bottle with his radio frequency from his cockpit. Schwartz (right) was retrieving more ammo for the gun. (Photo by Casey Westenrieder)

I was constantly made fun of because of my age. Not long after arriving in Afghanistan, Dumar (right) walked into the tent with his pants pulled up like an old man and started to make old jokes. I played along. (Photo by Will Schwartz)

On a patrol, Staff Sergeant Van Bockel rests during a halt in the movement. Van Bockel was Second Squad's squad leader. Despite the two us having some disagreements, he became a good friend of mine after the trials were over. (Photo by Casey Westenrieder)

In the village of Shapozai, Dumar squats against a mud structure while Lieutenant Labowski talked to some villagers. This picture was taken within hours of Dumar losing his leg from an IED explosion. (Photo by Casey Westenrieder)

Although in this photograph, Curtis looks angry, he was one of the most trusted soldiers and one of the funniest people I knew while deployed. He is also one of the few people I invited to my home after we got back. He will always be one of my lifelong friends. (Photo by Casey Westenrieder)

During a patrol near Route H, I found an eggplant growing in the grape fields. I picked it up and tried to lift everyone's spirits by hanging it out of my crotch. The fun ended when Keelslice smashed the eggplant against a wall. (Photo by Will Schwartz)

Schwartz kneels in the road on a patrol and shows off the new trick he just taught one of the local kids. Burke stands in the background watching. (Photo by Casey Westenrieder)

In a field just northwest of Lakani, Weapons Squad and First Squad waited for the rest of Third Platoon to cross a grape field to draw out the Taliban. This is me in the field, watching for signs of the platoon. (Photo by Will Schwartz)

Christiansen became part of Weapons Squad soon after we arrived in theater. Though Christiansen didn't go on many patrols, he played an important role as a member of the squad. (Photo by Casey Westenrieder)

During the only air assault mission Third Platoon executed, Weapons Squad took over a compound in an area code-named Tiger North. Burke overwatched the southern side of the compound from the rooftop. (Photo by Casey Westenrieder)

On a patrol with the Canadians, Schwartz is shown here in our blocking position. It was the first patrol where Third Platoon was in charge. I knew as soon as I met Schwartz he would be a loyal, hardworking member of Weapons Squad. He didn't disappoint me. (Photo by Casey Westenrieder)

It was an honor to patrol with Doc Smith. He is shown here inside the compound we overtook during our air assault mission. Smith saved a lot of soldier's lives while in Afghanistan, including Sergeant Dumar's. He earned the Bronze Star with Valor for courage. (Photo by Casey Westenrieder)

Van Bockel was in front of me on the first patrol we made into Lakani with the Canadians. Since we had just come from Alaska, the heat was more than we expected, and it was a real eye-opener. Shown here, Van Bockel is taking a breather as we halted while moving into Lakani. (Photo by Casey Westenrieder)

Schwartz (right) was known for his witty comebacks. They didn't always come out like he wanted them to, but he was always making people laugh. Here he had just made a remark to someone good enough for Wyscaver (center), and Dugas (left) to laugh. (Photo by Casey Westenrieder)

Schwartz (left) and Doc Bolin stand outside COP Palace during a routine traffic control point. When Bolin replaced Smith as the platoon medic, I made his life really hard. He ended up growing on me and proved himself to be a great medic and a great friend. (Photo by Casey Westenrieder)

Specialist Green in a photo with his mother, Suni Chabrow. Green was the company RTO before he was hit with an RPG on August 28, 2011. He was the second Charlie Company KIA. (Photo provided by the Douglas J. Green Memorial Foundation)

PFC Brandon Mullins takes a break in the back of a Stryker to eat. Though Mullins was in First Platoon, he had many friends in Third Platoon, and he often referred to himself as the Kentucky Gangsta. On August 25, 2011, Mullins was the first Charlie Company KIA. (Photo provided by Cathy Mullins)

FOURTEEN

PESHENGAN . . . AGAIN

> *Sure, we want to go home. We want this war over with. The quickest way to get it over with is to go get the bastards who started it. The quicker they are whipped, the quicker we can go home.*
>
> —General George S. Patton

11 August 2011

I wouldn't see Lakani again. After the last patrol, we switched gears and started patrolling west of Palace. Although we didn't go into Peshengan, when we headed into the area, we always referred to them as Peshengan Patrols. There were actually several small villages in the area with names I can't spell or don't remember . . . or both.

Somewhere along the line, we compiled a running count of how many patrols we had been on where we *didn't* receive contact. We had made it to five. Leaving Palace at 0445 that morning, I was hoping we'd make it to six, and since we were dismounting the Strykers on Route H and leaving them on the road to cover our movement, it seemed like we had a chance.

We got off the trucks and started moving east toward Peshengan. We had no intention of actually getting into the village, but rather scouting the area to get a feel for the enemy presence in the area. It wasn't the first time we'd been there, but it had been a while, and it was looking like we would be spending some time there over the next few weeks.

After moving more than eight hundred meters through the grape and marijuana fields, Sepeda twisted his ankle, climbing over a wall. It was Karma coming back on him because the day before he had ribbed one of his peers for twisting an ankle on an earlier patrol. Rather than continue the route, we doubled back on the route we had already taken. We had never done that before because it was our standard operating procedure to never take the same route twice. Truthfully, the route was changed up a little on the way back because we took different grape rows. We were setting a new precedent in our patrolling procedures, and I felt comfortable that we were doing something different by tracking back through different grape rows. I believed it was unlikely the Taliban would have had time to set up in the area through which we have just recently walked.

Dugas disagreed.

"They're going to hit us when we get close to the trucks," he confided to me after the platoon was turned around.

"You're crazy," I told him. "We're going to hit number six today. You're either crazy or paranoid or both!"

"Nope," he said. "They'll hit us when we get close to the trucks, then they'll hit us again when we're loading the trucks."

"Why would you say that shit?" I asked. "Can't you just let us get back to Palace without getting hit? You're gonna jinx us. You shouldn't say that."

"I'll tell you why they're going to," he explained. "If it was me, that's what I would do."

I think I rolled my eyes and started moving. Now Dugas was in the mind of the Taliban? He had to be paranoid. I was convinced Dugas was nuts.

We got to within 250 meters east of the trucks, and I was feeling pretty good. I was last in the order of movement pulling rear security, and Schwartz was right in front of me. Burke was in front of Schwartz, and Dugas was ahead of Burke. I watched Dugas climb to the top of a grape wall and scurry about ten meters to the south before jumping into a small open field. Burke was always trying to show off his athleticism, so while Dugas did it because it was the infantry thing to do, Burke did it because he was athletic and able. Schwartz did it because Dugas did it. I wasn't going to do it. I was too old.

I watched Schwartz start to move and hustle the distance to the field. I climbed up to the top of the wall and took my time. As soon as I got to the top of the wall and made my left turn, shots rang out from behind me. These were the shots that you could hear cracking as they whipped past your head. These shots were not only snapping by my head, they were also being fired from a nearby location. Now I wished I had hurried, but it was too late for that. I dropped to the ground and got as flat as I could. I heard the round whizzing past my head, and I was afraid to even lift a finger up. I was about to have my bitch moment when Dugas came to the edge of the wall.

"Where's that coming from?" he yelled.

I was too scared to look back. I just knew it was close, and I also knew the general direction.

"It's coming from right behind me!" I squealed in a voice sounding much like a little girl. I didn't realize it at the time, but that line would be the butt of many jokes for some time to come. I could see Dugas roll his eyes at me.

"Get the fuck off this wall, you turd!" he yelled. "I need to know where it's coming from."

I contorted my body into a kidney shape, still lying as flat as I could so I could see behind me. I saw a grape hut less than a hundred meters to the north and just to the east of it was a tree line.

"It's coming from that grape hut," I squeaked in the same girly voice. "It might be from that tree line right by it!"

"Well, get your ass over here before you get shot!" Dugas yelled.

I started to low crawl. If you've never low crawled, you need to understand that this is a dreaded movement. There actually isn't any *crawling* to it. It should be called "stay low while you drag yourself across the ground" then while lying on your stomach with your head turned to one side, you push yourself forward with a knee while pulling the ground with both hands and dragging your face through the dirt. It sounds easy, but it's not. It's even more difficult when you're wearing about eighty pounds of body armor, ammunition, hand grenades, and dragging an M4. I think I made it about three feet when I said, "Fuck it. I'm too old to low crawl."

I got up on my hands and knees and did what the Army calls a high crawl, which is nothing more than crawling like a baby. And I was feeling a lot like a baby as I was crying out, "I'm gonna get shot in the ass. I'm gonna get shot in the ass." The whole time, Dugas, Schwartz, and Burke were giggling at me. When I got to the point where I could enter the field with the rest of the platoon, I rolled off the wall and turned to face the grape hut.

Wyscaver and Thompson were ahead of me in the formation, and when I hit the ground, I heard them open up with the M240. Burke moved up right next to me and started spraying the grape hut with his gun. It took a few minutes, but soon both guns were talking and peppering the grape hut with pretty accurate fire. I was still shaking at this point and just leaned against the grape wall while my gun teams did their jobs.

We ceased fire and sat in the field for about thirty minutes. Our air support rolled in, and we started moving again. I was about one hundred meters from the Strykers. Part of the platoon had already started mounting the trucks, and I started thinking about what Dugas said.

"Shows us how much you know," I called up Dugas. "So you called the fact that we'd get hit, but we're about to get on the trucks, and we haven't been hit. You were only half right."

"We ain't on the trucks yet, old man," he said smugly. I think I rolled my eyes just as a single round was fired from a tree line to our south. I hit the ground again and realized we were taking fire from the south and the north. The Strykers opened up with the .50 caliber machine guns, and the firefight was over almost as fast as it started. But Dugas had called it. It was almost like he'd planned it. I never doubted him again.

15 August 2011

We hadn't had a patrol in a few days due to a day for a planning meeting and platoon equipment layout for accountability. We got started a little later than we had planned, and at 0600, we were dismounting the trucks on Route H not far from where we had been a few days earlier. Again, we had no plans of getting into Peshengan but to conduct a movement to contact patrol in the area northwest of the village.

When we had gone nearly eight hundred meters, we stopped, and Lieutenant Labowski was talking to a local national in the grape field. We were in a holding pattern for a while, and Schwartz said he heard some movement in a tree line just west of our position. He wanted to shoot into it, but I told him to hold his horses, and we started moving again. Schwartz was directly in front of me and behind Burke. In front of Burke was our terp, who was carrying the radio that intercepted the enemy communications. As we turned west to head back toward Route H, Abdul, the interpreter, started translating the messages he was receiving over the radio.

"They see us, and they are watching us," Abdul said. A few moments later, he reported, "They said in two minutes they will attack."

Experience had taught me not to put a lot of stock in what was said over the ICOM radio. The Taliban knew we intercepted their communication and many times would send false information to mislead us or to change our direction of movement. I called up what Abdul had intercepted to Dugas and looked at my watch. It was 0811, and I kept walking.

I walked past a tree line and looked into it. There was a trail that ran between a grape wall and deep into the thick grove of trees. It looked like it would be a good fighting position since there were clear fields of fire, and it was covered overhead, shielding it from view from any overhead aircraft. I didn't see any movement in the trees, so I just kept moving.

Again, I was pulling rear security. The report that we were getting hit in two minutes made some people nervous. I jumped over a grape wall into a grape field and saw Schwartz and Burke looking anxious. It was 0812.

"What are you worried about?" I asked them loudly with a smile on my face. "We still have one more minute!"

Burke turned and looked at me. He may have had the best sense of humor in the platoon, but he didn't think that was funny. He turned around and kept walking, and I looked at my watch waiting for the two-minute mark to come. When it showed 0813, I called out, "It's just about go time."

Silence. Silence. BLAM!

I couldn't believe it! The ICOM chatter was dead-on! The Taliban hit us two minutes from when they said they would. And these guys weren't playing around.

We got hit from the tree line I had looked into, from a southern grape hut, and from a grape hut to the northeast. It seemed like it was coming from all directions all at once.

We dug down deep into the grape field, and I was watching the rear. I didn't see any muzzle flashes or any movement, but I could hear the rounds coming from the tree line, and it was less than one hundred meters away. I called up Burke on the gun, and he opened up. I took aim, pulled the trigger, and CLICK! I misfired.

"Are you fucking kidding me?" I said out loud, wondering if I had even charged my weapon before the patrol began. Burke saw I had misfired and said, "Sergeant, get back."

Burke opened up with the M240, and I got my weapon into action. I stood up and fired about seven rounds into the tree line. Burke was scaring me with the gun. He loved to shoulder fire the M240, which isn't easy to do. And I could see him aiming it in a direction that was fairly close to my position. I warned him I was there, and he told me to get down. I may have been his squad leader, but I wasn't going to argue with him.

To our north there was a wall about seventy meters away that had an area cut out of it. I was worried about someone jumping over that wall, so I called Bolin over to pull security on it while I kept watching the east. Bullets were flying in so many directions that it was hard to tell where they were coming from and who they belonged to. The gunshots coming from the east were close. After a short lull, the rounds started firing again, and I got nervous. I could tell they had moved in closer, and I was certain they were in the field with us. I pulled out a hand grenade and just waited to see a head pop up over a grape wall so I could drop it in. When nothing happened, I turned to Bolin and handed him the grenade. I didn't want to set it down and forget it, but I didn't have time to put it away and still maintain control of my weapon should I have to fire it again.

The ICOM chatter continued during the firefight, and Abdul was closer to Schwartz who acted as an intercom system for all the incoming messages.

"They're trying to pin us down!" Schwartz yelled.

"Well, no shit!" I yelled back. "I don't need ICOM chatter for that!"

The exchange got pretty heated, and I opened up on the tree line again, emptying the magazine that was in my weapon. I got down, reloaded my weapon while Burke took up my fire. I was trying to call in the information I had while giving commands to the gun team and the soldiers around me.

"I've got a pop up," Bolin said, and I assumed he was talking about the grape hut to the northeast.

"Well, shoot him," I said, and Bolin didn't respond. A few minutes later, I asked, "Was he in that grape hut?"

"No," Bolin said. "He was on the other side of that wall."

"Which wall?" I asked.

"That wall right there," Bolin said, pointing at the wall I'd told him to cover.

"Holy shit!" I said. "Why didn't you tell me it was that close?"

Bolin didn't respond, and before anything else could be said, Schwartz yelled out the latest intercept, "They're not going to let us go!" and a few moments later, he screamed in a very scared voice, "They got a mortar!" It was another bitch moment that would haunt Schwartz.

"They don't have no goddamn mortar!" I yelled. I was getting tired of Schwartz getting people worked up by relaying the ICOM chatter. "Hey! You guys calm the fuck down! You're listening to that ICOM chatter shit, and it's freaking you the fuck out!"

After ten minutes, some air force A-10s came on station, and the drama ended for a little while. I got a call over the radio to put out my VS17 panel to mark our position. After I placed it over the top of a grape wall and called it in, the LT said that there would be an A-10 gun run in less than a minute. About five seconds later, the bird opened up on the tree line to our south, scaring the shit out of everyone in the field. We all laughed about it, and seconds later, another airplane opened up. Having the air force support us with the A-10s was always a mood lifter. We sat in the field laughing and joking for about twenty more minutes before we picked up and made it back to the trucks without further incident.

19 August 2011

I tried to keep my birthday a secret because the infantry has a tradition that the whole platoon gives you a pink belly on your special day. Burke got onto Facebook and found my birthday, and when it got out, I swore I wouldn't patrol on my birthday. Two days earlier, we made an attempt at a sloppy ambush that produced nothing and made it back without any enemy engagement. There was a single shot fired from a tree line from a great distance away. No one even turned to look.

The night before my birthday, Lieutenant Labowski made arrangements for Fourth Platoon to drive the Mobile Gun System (MGS) trucks in support of our mission the next day. The plan was to burn down the fighting position we'd passed on the 15 August and hopefully take fire from the southern tree line. When that happened, we would call in the MGSs, and they'd fire their 105 mm rounds into the tree line.

After hearing this plan, I changed my mind. birthday or not, a herd of wild goats couldn't keep me from going out. It was going to be the best birthday ever!

We moved into the grape fields and traveled about eight hundred meters to the east, turned south, and cut right through the tree line that we planned on burning down. It was a risky move because the Taliban are notorious for setting in IEDs where they fight. We already learned that at the Martin Tree Line. After the entire platoon made it through the tree line, Sergeant Carden and Stroemer threw two incendiary grenades into the fighting position. Everyone waited for the tree line to go up in flames. Our hopes were dashed when nothing happened. Apparently, the trees were too green or too wet. Since our real purpose was to incite a firefight, I yelled for Carden and Stroemer to throw two fragmentation grenades into the same area. They did, and still, nothing happened.

We moved forward and waited longer, still nothing happened. We finally made it back to the trucks, and we finally made it to our sixth patrol without trading shots with the enemy. Thanks a lot, Taliban, for fucking up my birthday!

20 August 2011

It didn't work the first time, so we thought we'd try it again, and back we went. The MGS trucks were staged at Palace in case we needed them. The day before, the trucks stayed about a mile east of our position, and we thought we may have been compromised. On this patrol, we weren't going to waste time trying to burn up fighting positions with incendiary grenades. Our goal: Try to pick a fight and then call in the MGS trucks to wreak havoc with their 105 mm rounds.

We made it all the way to the farthest point of our planned route and were heading back before we even picked up any ICOM chatter. I figured by the time we were halfway back, we'd get hit, but nothing happened. The closer we got to Route H, the more the ICOM chatter picked up. The ICOM chatter was coming from our southeast—a grape hut that had several small children standing outside of it. There was no way we were going to shoot at that, and the Taliban knew it.

The peculiar thing was that there was one young male, probably about sixteen years old, standing in the grape field watching us. He would get down, stand back up, and then get back down. When I passed him, he was about thirty meters from my position, and the movement had slowed to almost a halt as the platoon was climbing over a tall mud wall. I started to suspect this guy as a spotter, and I aimed my M4 at him, looking through my ACOG to see if I could see a radio or a cell phone in his hand. As I had him in my sights, a shot rang out from the west of me. It made me jump, but the kid slumped and fell to the ground. Lieutenant Labowski took him out.

My first reaction was that it was a bad call. I didn't see a cell phone or a radio in the kid's hands. I didn't think shooting this young man was the appropriate course of action, and I was almost pissed off. But oddly enough, all the ICOM chatter stopped. Apparently, the kid was spotting for someone in the grape field and would duck down when he had information about our position or movement to relay to them. The information would then be sent over the ICOM radio. Lieutenant Labowski knew this because he was standing next to the interpreter with the ICOM radio, and as he was crossing the wall, the intercepted message described him. He looked around, and the only one he saw in that area was the same kid I had in my sights. That was the last time I doubted Lieutenant Labowski.

I don't know that it counts that Lieutenant Labowski fired his weapon, but if you don't count it, we made it to our seventh patrol without getting into a firefight or getting hit by an IED. Oddly enough, it was the second day in a row. My hope was that we were nearing the end of the fighting season. The only other possible explanation was that the Taliban knew about the MGS trucks waiting at Palace for us to get hit.

21 August 2011

We realized that we were being watched and kept an ICOM radio running most of the time that was manned by one of our interpreters. This day we picked up a transmission that described movement of trucks into Palace. Dugas grabbed a flare, and shot it into the air in the direction he thought the transmission was originating. A man stood up and ran away, and the ICOM chatter went crazy, confirming that the Taliban had spotters reporting on what was going on in Palace. This explained why we hadn't been hit on our patrols where we had MGS trucks waiting in the wings. They were watching us, so there was little doubt that they were setting up fighting positions, emplacing IEDs, and who knows what else.

The scary thing was that we had spent so much time patrolling and fighting in the area west of Palace that we didn't do enough to keep the bad guys at bay. I didn't feel comfortable at Palace anymore. I wanted to start running patrols into the surrounding area, and I wanted to fortify our positions. I wanted to do a lot of things. The fighting season wasn't over yet. Not by a long shot.

22 August 2011

Instead of patrolling around Palace, Lieutenant Labowski had bigger plans that, in all reality, had the potential to change the momentum in our AO. I thought we spent too much time patrolling the Peshengan area, but we were going back to Peshengan again. This time, however, we were bringing friends.

The LT made arrangements for an engineer unit to join us on patrol with the intention of blowing down a tree line where there were known fighting positions. It was the same tree line that we had been shot at every time we were in the area. This was a good day to bring a video camera on patrol.

About 0600, we dismounted the trucks and only pushed about one hundred meters into the grape fields east of Route H. I was at the end of the platoon, pulling rear security with Burke and Schwartz. Stroemer was hanging back with me to give us a little more security while the rest of the platoon moved toward the tree line with the engineers.

We waited in the field for more than an hour while the sappers wired the tree line with C-4 explosives. When they returned to our position, we all took cover behind a grape wall in anticipation of this huge series of explosions that would topple about one hundred meters of tree line. Fox had the audacity to ask me what we were going to do with the trees when they came down.

"I think we'll just leave them there unless you want to gather up a bunch of firewood," I said, thinking he was kidding.

"But if we leave them there, they can use them as cover to fire behind," he said. He was serious.

"Look, Fox," I told him. "The reason we're blowing this tree line is because there are known fighting positions in there, and we keep taking fire from it. They're already using the trees as cover. But if the trees are up, the birds can't see them when they fly over. If we knock the trees down, they can still use them for cover, but they won't have overhead cover."

I liked Fox. He was a really nice guy, but when it came to military savvy, he lacked something.

We hunkered down waiting for the boom when someone got the bright idea that we should call up to battalion to let them know we were about to destroy this tree line. I knew that wasn't a good idea. Within ten minutes, we had reported our intentions, been denied, and set up security while the sappers returned to the tree line to retrieve the explosives they'd spent more than an hour carefully emplacing.

I know it had to be a kick in the balls for the engineers because those guys love blowing shit up. But the real disappointment was the reason we were denied. The story I was told was that if we brought ANA with us, our battalion commander would have let us blow the tree line. Could that be true? Whether there is truth to that story or not, I felt there was no reasonable answer anyone could have given me for denying us and the sappers permission to blow the tree line down. This was a dangerous area well known for the fighting positions in this particular tree line. By not allowing us to blow it down, the message sent by battalion was that our safety was not a priority. Our battalion commander was supposed to come to Palace and give us an explanation, but he didn't.

I didn't care. I wrote in my journal that night, our colonel could "lick my balls." My priority from that point forward was solely for the safety of my men. If the battalion-level leadership didn't care for our safety, then I didn't care about their missions.

We stopped patrolling the Peshengan area for a while after that. In fact, that was my last patrol into the Peshengan area. My leave was coming up, and I would only do one more mission in the Peshengan area. There was no love lost between me and Peshengan.

That same tree line that our BC refused to let us blow became a launching point for several RPG attacks and the most likely site for IED detonations in that area. Several men were killed in this area, and even more were injured. Right after we stopped patrolling this area, this stretch of Route H became an IED hot spot. And things were about to get a lot worse.

FIFTEEN

THE LAST FULL MEASURE

But no one laughs,
'Cause there ain't nothin' funny when a soldier cries.
And I just wipe my eyes . . .
—from "Letters from Home"
by John Michael Montgomery

25 August 2011

The final planning meeting for the company mission was scheduled for later in the day, so we were trying to relax and stay out of the heat as much as possible. I was in my CHU, daydreaming about my upcoming leave and how nice it would be to get away from the heat, the bugs, the shooting, the IEDs, and just the plain misery of being in Afghanistan. Schwartz came to my door around 1400 and said we had been spun up for a Quick Reaction Force (QRF) mission.

I jumped up, threw on my uniform, and started making sure the guys in my squad were getting ready before I went to find the LT or Dugas to find out what was going on. The details were vague, but a Stryker just north of us had been attacked by rocket propelled grenades and small arms fire. They had sustained some casualties and needed to have a vehicle towed and help with security in the area.

I gave Dugas my list of who I was taking with us. We all rushed to our trucks and headed toward Route H. When we got there, we dismounted, and I realized it was the same area we had been patrolling for the past few weeks . . . just outside Peshengan. We had obviously ruffled some Taliban feathers, so this action may possibly have been in retaliation for our patrols. I walked over to a culvert by the tree line we were denied permission to destroy, and there was a sergeant first class standing by the side of the road, talking to Lieutenant Labowski. As I listened in on the conversation, I got the gist of what happened.

Their group had been sweeping for mines and emplacing metal engineering stakes around the opening of the culvert so they could string concertina wire around the hole in hopes of thwarting Taliban IEDs from ending up in the culvert. Two RPGs were fired, and one struck their vehicle, disabling it. When the small arms fire started, their lieutenant was shot in the pelvic area and went down. The medic was working on him when this SFC walked up and saw the LTs head resting on the rock.

"I decided I needed to move the rock out from under his head because I figured it wasn't very comfortable," he explained to Lieutenant Labowski. "So I reached down and lifted the LT's head and pulled out the rock. But it wasn't a rock. It was a jug of homemade explosives!"

As I was picking my jaw up off the hot pavement from hearing that story, Lieutenant Labowski told me to get our guys together so we could go investigate a burning grape hut that had been hit with a Hellfire missile from an Apache gunship. We formed up and got in a line to move into the grape field toward the hut. I took up the rear and we moved out. As we were moving into the field, I saw Manley in the line. In my mind, I was running through the list of names I had given Dugas, and Manley was not on it. In fact, I had asked Dugas before we left if we needed mortars, and he had said no.

"What the fuck are you doing out here? You were supposed to stay at Palace," I said to Manley in my most irritated voice.

"Lieutenant Labowski told me to get on the truck," he replied.

"Well, I'm your squad leader, not the LT," I said in frustration. "You shouldn't have come out here. You were supposed to stay back!"

I couldn't do anything about it at the time, so I just had to adapt to the extra personnel on the ground.

"There's nothing we can do about it now," I said. "Just get your ass in line and move out."

When we made it to the grape hut, it was still on fire, and we weren't able to go inside to do any battle damage assessment. Pieces of the thatch roof were falling from the burning roof.

We moved from the hut, back to the road, then we headed further north to a set of ruins where the enemy fire may have originated. The ruins were an old Mosque, and we decided not to make any waves by entering the building.

We turned east and started moving toward an open field, and Wyscaver, who was right in front of me, turned to me and said, "Manley's only got one bottle of water."

"You're kidding me," I said.

"No, Sergeant," Wyscaver said, almost laughing. "He's only got one bottle of water, and he left his camel back on the truck."

I couldn't believe it. It was nearly 1400 hours, and according to my watch, it was 143 degrees in the grape field, and Manley only had one bottle of water.

"I hope he falls out," I said to Wyscaver. "Pass it up to him that when we get back, I'm going to take care of this."

We crossed the open field to a small compound that was nearly one hundred meters north of the road. Lieutenant Labowski took a squad inside the building while I stayed outside with the rest of the platoon. While the LT and the squad were searching this compound, I laid into Manley.

"Where's your camel back?" I asked.

"I left it in the truck," he replied.

"Do you realize how stupid that is?" I asked rhetorically, and the question tirade continued. "Do you have any idea how hot it is out here? What are your chances of survival without water? Do you expect to get water from someone else? What the fuck were you thinking? You're an idiot. I hope you fall out on the way back. Trust me when I say this is your last patrol with Third Platoon. We'll take care of this when we get back to Palace."

The LT came out of the compound, and of course, no one inside the compound saw anything or knew the source of the enemy fire. I'm pretty sure they knew, but no one was talking, so we headed back to the trucks.

The movement back to the road took a long time because we were crossing an open field, and we were deliberately trying to exercise some semblance of a tactical movement. After all, we had experienced our share of being shot at while crossing open areas. Since I was in the rear, I was the last one across the field. After I got to the road, Schwartz walked up to me.

"First Platoon got hit," he said. "I think they had a KIA."

"Oh shit," I said. "Where did you hear this?"

"It was on the company net," he told me. "I just heard about it when I got back to the truck. I heard it was Mullins who got hit."

I didn't know Mullins very well, but I knew he was member of First Platoon's Weapons Squad, and I knew he and Schwartz were friends. I didn't want things to get too emotional out there on the road and worked to neutralize it and refocus attention to the mission.

"Don't believe everything you hear, Schwartz," I said. "That could just be talk over the radio, and it may not have been Mullins. Don't stress right now. We'll find out more when we get back to Palace."

We continued to pull security on the road until the wrecker was able to load the damaged Stryker onto a flatbed truck, and then we headed back to Palace. When we got there, it was confirmed that it was Mullins who had been hit. Obviously, I wasn't there, so I can't give a true account of what happened, but the medic on site, Specialist Alamillo, shared the story with me.

We made it about six hundred meters outside the gate when it happened. It was as though I had been slapped on both ears. I remember looking out through the windshield, and somehow nothing made sense.

Then it went dark, for the first few seconds, I don't know if I passed out or if it was just dark because of the blast and the thick dust cloud outside.

My ears were ringing for a bit, and then all the sound returned at once. My heart was pounding; I could feel pain in my leg, my shoulder, but most of all, my head. I could hear someone yelling for a head count. Then looking up, I saw what looked like antifreeze start leaking down. I panicked, but tried to stay calm.

"Is everyone OK?" I kept hearing someone say.

The smell of fuel followed and with that were thoughts of roasting alive in that truck. I reached for the door handle. I had flipped though my leg was still caught on something. I remember feeling it and thinking, *Motherfucker! That bitch is broken!* I didn't care. I wanted out.

Then the truck began to make crunching sounds, and a new way of dying from being crushed came to my mind. I pulled the door handle with everything I had. My arm hurt, my leg hurt, and my head was pounding.

"Alamillo! You all right?!"

It was Sergeant E. I looked him up and down and subconsciously did a quick blood sweep over my own face.

"I'm stuck, but I'm all right, Sergeant. Are you all right?" I asked, and he nodded. I could see he looked dazed, but I'm sure we all did.

After I freed myself, Sergeant R came running up. He grabbed me by the shoulders and looked into my face.

"Doc, you all right?" he asked, and the words seemed to echo through my head.

"I'm good, Sergeant! We need to get the others out . . ."

He looked at me and said to me, "Doc, go to the truck!"

I shook my head and said, "The others . . . we need to get them out . . ."

"Doc, we'll bring them to you! Go to the truck!" he ordered.

I hobbled to the second truck, trying to keep my head from spinning too hard. I sat on the ramp, and the pain in my shoulder started to kick my ass, and I knew something was wrong. I just wanted to sit there and not move. I didn't want to do anything.

Sergeant R came to me, and I knew just by looking at him that something was wrong.

"I can't get a pulse, Doc," he said. I could see the weariness in his face, the fear of the worst. I jumped out as best as I could and moved back to the Stryker.

I could not make heads or tails of the position Private First Class Mullins was in. I saw his pale hand and took it in my own. His hand was cold; my heart was racing which forced fear and pain away. I pushed Mullins's sleeve up and tried to take a radial pulse. I felt nothing. I dug around until I found his neck. The carotid vein is the final vein to lose blood. The body has mechanisms to keep as much blood flow to the organs and the head. I felt no pulse, felt no breath, and the realization hit me. I remember almost falling back. Someone grabbed me, and I broke free. We needed to get him out. I began yanking on the cage, tried to force the door open, and even cut my fingers trying to rip the metal off to no avail. It was so frustrating to not be able to do anything for my own brother, to not be able to help him.

Sergeant R grabbed me by the plate carrier and pulled me to face him. "Doc, help the others, and we'll get him out!

Moments later, our company commander, Cpt. Sean Allred, was on the scene. He provided the following statement about what happened after Alamillo was taken back to the COP:

We were on the scene within fifteen minutes of the call over the radio, which was blindingly fast considering the normal trip out there could span close to a half hour of just driving. When we reached the First Platoon element now separated by a massive hole in the pavement, I dismounted my vehicle and immediately ran toward the flipped MATV, where I was met by the First Platoon sergeant, who confirmed to me quietly that Mullins was still trapped in the vehicle and was already dead.

Upon inspection of the vehicle, it was clear that Private First Class Mullins suffered severe head trauma as his neck appeared broken, and his head was pinned underneath his helmet by a radio mount that had been crushed inward wedging his swollen skull to the door jamb of the MATV. The brigade surgeon was on the scene along with the deputy commanding officer who had accompanied the special recovery team. The recovery team was able to cut the seat out of the back of the capsized vehicle and roll it out of the truck while I simultaneously wrapped my arms underneath Private First Class Mullins's armpits and carefully pulled him out of the vehicle and lay him to rest on the pavement.

The surgeon began to work on him first by cutting a tracheotomy hole in Private First Class Mullins's neck and beginning lifesaving actions. Upon approach, they took over packaging Private First Class Mullins for hoist extraction since there was no feasible place to land a helicopter due to the grape rows and trees.

The helicopter had to hover at fifteen feet with its rotor blades almost smacking branches as they hoisted Private First Class Mullins off-site. The Air Force PJs (Pararescue Jumpers) believed that Private First Class Mullins had regained a pulse, but having been trapped in the vehicle for that long, I thought that the possibility was more like wishful thinking.

I was able to find a small brown command pull string which was used to initiate the device, and I traced it by pulling it back to the grape hut where it was fired. There was no indication in the area that the enemy had left their firing position, and often, enemy forces would remain on scene to engage us further or film their actions.

I had my Mobile Gun System (MGS) platoon leader maneuver his MGS and engage the grape hut. The MGS fired eight rounds into the structure and was able to level one of its four sides. I assembled a small element and led them to the grape hut to conduct BDA inside of the structure.

I was not able to find any enemy forces within the grape hut and determined that they had slipped away immediately after firing the IED.

We continued to work into the late evening, cleaning up the site and collecting all of the debris and equipment. I later received the final confirmation that Private First Class Mullins was pronounced dead. I gathered the 1SG and went to COP Nejat to deliver the final word to First Platoon.

On 25 August 2011, PFC Brandon S. Mullins was our company's first KIA of the deployment.

27 August 2011

I had a choice to stay at COP Palace or go to Mullins's memorial service. Since I didn't know Mullins very well, I would have given up my seat to someone who had known him better, but as it turned out, there was room. I felt that even though I didn't know Mullins well, a lot of the guys from Third Platoon did, and if nothing else, I needed to be there to support them.

The ceremony was well planned and in very good taste. Our chaplain, Captain Olson, did a great job putting together a slide show of Mullins and finding the perfect scriptures to go with the service. It's difficult to watch a soldier cry. It's even more difficult to be the soldier with tears rolling down your face. Though I barely knew Mullins, I stood in the formation, watching the service with tears burning my cheeks. Mullins had been the company's first KIA, and it stabbed me like a knife. I could only imagine how his close friends must have felt. I saw Schwartz, Sepeda, and Hendrick take it the hardest.

The ceremony wound down, and we all paid our respects to the M4 rifle and the pair of combat boots. We loaded our Strykers and moved out of Sperwan Ghar in silence. After we returned to Palace, the mood was somber and quiet.

28 August 2011

I slept in. The memorial service, coupled with a sergeant of the guard (SOG) shift really zapped me. Around 1300, Dugas came to my CHU and said he had a task for Weapons Squad.

I dragged myself out of bed and got my guys together. Dugas was always looking for new ways to improve the security on the COP, and he wanted a heavier gate at the entry control point. Our task was to get the scrap material left by the Canadians and try to make the front gate more secure. It wasn't working out very well.

I walked back to the kitchen tent to get some water, and there were a couple guys sitting outside on the couch. One of them told me that the company command element had just been hit by an RPG, and our company RTO, Specialist Green, had been medevaced to KAF.

I had just seen Green the day before at the memorial service for Mullins. If there is one guy in every unit that has nothing but positive things to say, ours was Green. He was always the guy who had something quick to say and could get just offensive enough to make you laugh but not make you angry. Green was just a fun guy to know and be around. Knowing he was a great guy made it more difficult to hear that he was wounded.

Hurley was Green's best friend, and he was sitting on the couch, looking worried.

"If something happened to him, I'll have to call his mom," Hurley told me. "I don't want to have to do that."

I couldn't imagine the stress he was feeling.

"Think positive," I told him. "We haven't heard anything yet, so that's good. No news is good news."

I left him sitting on the couch and went back out to the gate to supervise the work. Thompson, Wyscaver, Christiansen, and Schwartz were doing their best to rig up a gate. It wasn't going well, and a rumor started circulating that the battalion commander was going to visit. Someone from the tower called down that a convoy was coming up. Our uniform standard at COP Palace was a little relaxed when we had down time, but we had to make sure we were in the proper uniform when other units came through—especially if the other unit came from battalion.

I ran through the platoon area to alert everyone about the incoming convoy and to get in the proper uniform. I ran to my CHU and got out of my civilian T-shirt and into an Army gray physical fitness shirt. By the time I got outside, our sergeant major was on site. We gathered all the soldiers on the COP that weren't on guard duty to listen to what he had to say.

According to the sergeant major, Captain Allred was on a mounted patrol just outside Sperwan Ghar. He stopped the trucks to inspect a culvert and took Green with him. They were hit by an RPG, and the commander was injured and sent to KAF. The sergeant major didn't know much about his condition, but then he dropped a bomb on us all.

"Specialist Green was hit too," he said. He paused before continuing, "He didn't make it."

I felt like I had been punched in the stomach. Even though Hurley told me earlier about Green getting hit, the confirmation of Green's death took my breath away. How could someone you just saw a day earlier be gone? And as bad as I felt, I knew that I didn't even know Green very well. Hurley was sitting ten feet away from me. When the news came out of the sergeant major's mouth, I looked up and watched his face tense. Green and Hurley had gone to basic training together, been stationed in Alaska together, been through one deployment together, and both were scheduled to get out of the Army together in just a few months. Both of them were scheduled to fly back to Alaska in less than six weeks to separate from the Army at the completion of their enlistment. They were both short timers, and both had actually volunteered to go on this deployment.

I walked up to Hurley and put my hand on his shoulder. He had tears rolling down his face. I didn't know what to say. I couldn't find the words. There simply are no words. I can't imagine losing my best friend in such a tragic way. I was speechless. I walked away to let Hurley mourn.

I later got the story from Captain Allred about what happened that day on the road. This is what he told me:

The situation along Route B was growing more challenging as the enemy sought to limit our ability to maneuver. I learned later after the memorial service for Private First Class Mullins that the enemy was attempting to emplace an IED inside of a massive culvert that had a culvert denial system emplaced. Knowing that I would have to lead my command element to FOB Zangabad the next day to pick up an officer who was conducting an investigation into my order for the MGS to engage an enemy fighting position on the day the Private First Class Mullins was killed, I devised a simple plan and assessed levels of risk with the course of action.

The biggest risk it seemed was the possibility of an IED a quarter mile up the road in the culvert. There was a great risk and probability of recoilless rifle attack or RPG attack, but there was no avoiding the immediate threat of the IED and the catastrophic effect it would have on my small convoy.

I devised a plan to dismount approximately two hundred meters south of the bridge and dismount into a deep ditch and follow it up to the creek where I could be covered and concealed and use my rifle optics to clear the culvert from a safer distance. I understood the risk associated with this course of action and had originally planned to just do it by myself and get it done without drawing too much attention since my TAC element only had a few dismounts. My MGS platoon leader implored me not to go at it alone. I thought about it and agreed that a buddy team would be safer on the ground and conceded the point.

On approach, nothing seemed out of the ordinary to tip us off that an attack was imminent. People were still out, working their fields and behaving normally. We reached the dismount point, and as I was moving to the back of the Stryker ramp, I turned, in my usual matter of fact way, to which Green and I would joke, and asked Specialist Green, who was my radio telephone operator and had been at my side on every mission, if he wouldn't mind joining me. He shrugged his shoulders, sighed, and said, "No problem, sir," in a manner consistent with his normal feigned annoyance whenever I would ask him to get up from a comfortable position and go do something.

With that last little conversation, the ramp was already lifting, and we were down into the deep ditch in a matter of seconds. This long ditch was about four to six feet deep and had been dug by the Canadians to limit east-west movement of the locals. It didn't do anything more than annoy them, but it was a ready-made covered route to our objective that none of our soldiers had patrolled previously, making the threat of IEDs very low.

I led with Specialist Green close behind me, keeping our heads down and moving quietly up to a small embankment where the creek flowed on the other side. This position was good with tall grass across the stream and some concrete barriers strewn about that could provide excellent cover from any small arms fire if the occasion should arise. I slowly pulled my head up over the berm, looking down at the creek and its bank and then over at the culvert in question. Since there was a trail breaking into the woods directly parallel to the stream, I would have been exposed from behind when I crossed the shallow berm to stand next to the creek and peer down into the culvert. I realized I was glad that Specialist Green was there to cover my back. I turned to him where he had instinctively already taken up security from behind one of the concrete barriers down the path. I asked him if he had me. Without turning around, he replied, "I got you, sir."

I climbed lowly over the berm and down to the bank and moved forward about ten feet from where Specialist Green was positioned. I used my ACOG and verified that the culvert was clear, and while rising to my feet, I called over the radio for the TAC vehicles to move up on the road to our position so they could pick us up, and we could continue movement.

I remember looking back and seeing my vehicles coming up the road, and then within an instant, I was flat on my side and forward of where I had been. My head was ringing, and when my vision became less clouded, I was able to see down into the culvert where all around was a shower of falling concrete and dirt landing all around me and splashing like raindrops into the creek that I was now partially hanging over. I instantly realized that we had just been hit by something but really couldn't hear anything. I looked down to see if my legs were still there and noticed they were attached and looked all right. I reached inside the fist-sized hole in my right pant leg at the knee to see if it was still there. I could feel this sopping feeling around my ankle and foot and looked down to find a hole in my boot and noticed my sock was starting to sink in. I figured that I must have been barely touched by whatever had struck us.

I stood up amid the cloud of grey and brown dust and called out for Specialist Green. While calling to him, I moved back toward where he had been, noticing first that all of the concrete barriers had been knocked over, and the one closest to where I was standing had been split in half. I then noticed the smoke trail leading back through the thick grass and upward, I immediately returned fire and began suppressing the enemy position, knowing now that we had been hit by an RPG and that perhaps the enemy would reengage us or attempt to take us. As the dust cleared, I found Specialist Green as he rolled down the berm to my feet. He let out a long low guttural moan as blood escaped his mouth and pooled onto the freshly disturbed moon dust. I realized from the sound that he was making, a noise I had become familiar with when enemy fighters were letting out their death moan, that it wouldn't be long.

As I pulled Specialist Green closer to me and rolled him over, I first noticed his left arm had been torn apart much like someone would expect a wound from a grizzly bear paw with long deep lacerations running the length of his left arm. After that half second taking in his arm, I then saw the gaping hole in his left side which seemed to stretch from his hip up to his chest and as far over as his sternum. I must have been yelling over the radio for a medic since I couldn't hear anything, and the ear bud to my radio had been blown out of my ear. I had no idea how loud I was at the time since it seemed everything was underwater.

It felt like zero time at all that my TAC dismounts arrived at my position where the highest-ranking soldier was an SPC who immediately moved to Specialist Green's previous position to take security while Doc Smith moved to where Specialist Green and I were positioned. The entire event had only lasted about two minutes before Doc was with us and began an attempt to treat Green. I held a mask over Green's mouth and nose in an attempt to assist his labored breathing. I held his head as his chest rose with gasps and called his name over and over again. He was dying, but his body hadn't given up yet. As I noticed his insides on the ground, Doc just gave me a helpless look, but we continued to try and patch him back together while a PFC was placing a litter down so that we could move him.

The RPG had torn straight through Green's front plate and blown his side plate and rear plate completely out of his vest. It had also severed his M4 barrel at the slip rings, and we were not able to recover that part of his weapon.

As I attempted to lift Specialist Green on the litter to move him up to the road and into the back of the awaiting Stryker, my right leg gave out and I fell completely over into the creek. The wide open gap in my lower leg would not allow me to stand with the extra weight and move backward. I then realized I was missing a bit more than I thought originally. It was a tough fight just to get the litter upright and prevent Specialist Green from falling into the creek with me. I stood in waist deep water, trying to press the litter so that it wouldn't slide in with me while the PFC and Doc Smith got control of it and began moving.

They were under way, and I climbed out of the creek and moved up to the road while continuing to return fire into the enemy position as we were now more exposed in the open on the road. I waited until the Stryker Specialist Green was loaded on left before I had my driver drop the ramp, and I climbed in.

The base and its aid station were only a quarter of a mile away, and a medevac from there would have been quicker than attempting one on the ground. The event in its entirety took less than ten minutes from point of injury to when we were loaded up and on our way back to the FOB. Once we made it back on the FOB, I dismounted and hobbled/ran over to the aid station, stripping off my equipment outside the door and moving inside to see the solemn faces and Specialist Green's lifeless body being bagged and packaged for the medevac bird that was minutes away.

Doc Smith was Third Platoon's original medic. This is his recollection of the event:

We heard a boom. Smoke and dirt filled the air and the truck I was in pulled forward. I had them drop the rear hatch so I could get out and brought another soldier with me. We jumped out of the back hatch as we heard the commander screaming for a medic.

That may have been the scariest moment of my life. I was sure I was going to die as I ran the 150 meters to reach Green and Captain Allred. I heard the CO scream, "He's dying, and we need to get him out of here!" or something along those lines.

I got to Green and was blown away by his injuries. At this point in my deployment, I had already seen a lot, but this was by far the worst. His arm was badly damaged. So was his leg as well as the side of his face. The worst part was that his side was split open, and all his insides where falling out.

I checked his pulse, and I thought I could feel one, so pulled out a BVM (bag valve mask used for resuscitation) and tried rescue breathing. I handed it off to the commander while I started to treat his wounds. My first thoughts were, *I do not have anything big enough to try and cover and seal up this wound!* I was horrified.

The CO and I got very little treatment done before someone came back with a litter. We needed to move Green so we could try to get him back to the aid station that was just up the hill. We started moving over some rough terrain, me carrying the head side of the litter and the PFC and Captain Allred on the other end.

Almost immediately, Captain Allred's leg gave out, and the litter almost tipped over. Green rolled toward the CO. There was no way Captain Allred was going to be able to help us carry the litter.

We got Green back to the Stryker, and we rushed to the aid station where a team of medics, and the company first sergeant were there to help me get him in. The helicopters were called, and we treated him for as long we could, trying to make sure everything we could do was done until our senior medic had to call it. Green didn't make it.

I just broke down and had to walk away. I had to cry. It was a long day. Chaplain Olson, who happened to be visiting for Mullins's memorial ceremony, helped me get it together enough to try to be calm.

On 28 August 2011, Douglas J. Green became Charlie Company's second and last KIA.

Green's memorial service was on 31 August 2011. There wasn't a dry eye at Sperwan Ghar that day.

SIXTEEN

FINAL MISSIONS

The final test of a leader is that he leaves behind him in other
men the conviction and the will to carry on.

—Walter Lippmann

29 August 2011

I thought, or at least hoped, that Green's death would delay any patrols for a couple days at least. No such luck.

A company-sized mission was scheduled to take place the day after Green died. We had been planning the mission for some time, and it was another one of those missions that just didn't add up in my head. At the leaders meeting several days prior to the mission, the company commander had promised "no dry holes," meaning each platoon would find something at each of their objectives.

The mission was planned to leave out of First Platoon's area of operations. The whole company would leave at the same time, and at certain designated points, each platoon would peel off and get into place by a certain time, then at a designated time, each platoon would hit its objective simultaneously. And of course, we were all guaranteed to find something.

Originally, I had planned on bringing only one gun team, but the day prior to starting the mission, I talked with Lieutenant Labowski and Dugas about the personnel we would need. Lieutenant Labowski left it up to me. Burke was on his midtour leave, so the only other person I could trust to carry the M240 was his assistant gunner, Schwartz, but he had planned to do this mission carrying an M4. He wasn't going to be happy.

I assembled Weapons Squad to do a squad briefing, and at the end of the brief, I turned to Schwartz.

"I've got good news and bad news," I said to him. His eyes widened. "What do you want first?"

"Give me the bad news," he said slowly.

"The bad news is you've got to carry the gun on the mission," I said, trying not laugh.

"Son. Of. A. Bitch!" he yelled. "What's the fucking good news?"

"The good news?" I asked. "I lied. There is no good news. This mission is gonna suck."

Schwartz was so disappointed. He had planned on carrying a light load, and now he was stuck carrying a machine gun and all the rounds of ammunition that went with that weapon.

"Whose idea was this?" he asked.

How was I going to tell him it was my decision? It was all I could do to keep from laughing at his fit as it was.

"It was that damn Lieutenant Labowski," I said with a smile.

"You're so full of shit," he said. "Whose idea was it, really?"

"OK, it was mine," I admitted.

Schwartz scowled at me and walked off, grumbling something under his breath.

"Hey, we need more firepower out there," I called to him as he was storming off to his CHU. "Quit acting like a bitch and load up about seven hundred rounds of 7.62!"

I knew he was pissed, but he'd get over it.

The movement to Third Platoon's objective was roughly about six kilometers, so it was much too far to take Christiansen. I needed an extra man to carry ammo for the guns, and about a week earlier, we had gotten a replacement. His name was Degan Berhe, and he had a bit of an attitude. He was assigned to Third Squad so I asked his squad leader, Staff Sergeant Holt, if I could take him along as an attachment to Weapons Squad. Holt had no problem with it, so I scooped the new kid up.

Berhe was not a small kid, and when I told him what we were going to do, he seemed enthusiastic. The day of the mission, I loaded all my gear and told Schwartz to load Berhe down with as much ammo as he could carry. When it was all said and done, Berhe had twelve hundred rounds of 7.62 mm ammunition and all the water he could carry. It was going to be a long night for the new kid.

On the evening of 29 August, we left Palace at 1800. We stopped at Sperwan Ghar to pick up additional people and ended up staying there for about two hours. While we were there, our breach team found a team of engineers and asked how much C-4 explosives we would need to breach the wall we were planning on blowing up. The engineers looked at what we had and laughed. They ended up stringing together eight and a half pounds of plastic explosive for us and gave a quick lesson on how best to breach the wall.

On the way to First Platoon's COP, one of our trucks got stuck in the mud, and we had to tow it out with another Stryker. This mission was really getting off to a bad start. It took about forty-five minutes to get going again, and by the time we got to First Platoon's COP, it was almost 2200 hours. We were originally supposed to start the mission at 2100.

Finally at 2300, we started the movement. Third Platoon fell in behind First Platoon, and we started walking. It seemed like the walk that would never end. I had put Berhe in front of me since he was new, and I wanted to keep an eye on him. It was dark, and through my night vision goggles, I watched several times as he teetered from one side to the other before catching his balance, but he never went down.

At 0100, we were still more than a thousand meters away from our assault point, and the no-later-than time was 0130. It wasn't going to happen on schedule. We finally reached our assault point at 0150 and got set in place.

But something wasn't right. Holt led the movement to this objective, and after we'd set in the breach team and the security, I started looking around. What I saw didn't quite match up with the imagery that we'd looked at in preparation for this mission. This was another one of those times that I maybe should have said something, but I kept my mouth shut. I believed that if we were in the wrong place Holt would have known better, and Lieutenant Labowski would have caught it.

Because of our late departure, the hit time was pushed back to 0215. Third Squad was our breach squad, and First Squad was set to clear the first objective. When the courtyard in this compound was cleared, it was Weapon Squad's job to get on the roof of the second objective and pull security while the rest of the compound was cleared.

That was the plan.

Third Squad advanced to the wall and set in the explosives. First Squad and my gun team, consisting of Schwartz and Berhe, took cover behind a mud wall and waited for the fireworks. Over the radio, I heard the breach team announce the fuse had been lit and the countdown began.

When eight and a half pounds of explosives goes off, it's not quiet. The ground shook and for a brief moment; night turned to day. First Squad ran in behind Third, and the explosives show continued with fragmentation grenades and bullets flying. It was a classic case of what the infantry calls violence of action.

The call came out that the courtyard was clear. I ran up with my gun team into the courtyard, and immediately, I knew something was wrong. None of the buildings in the compound were where they should have been, and the landmarks we had seen on the imagery were not there. Fox walked up to me in the darkness.

"I think we breached too far south," he said.

"I think we breached the wrong compound," I said back.

Lieutenant Labowski was pissed. He called all the squad leaders together, and we did a quick map recon. We had breached the wrong compound and in doing so completely destroyed a huge section of some *innocent* Afghani farmer's wall, used up all of our explosives, and we had totally lost the element of surprise.

Our actual objective was only about one hundred meters east of our position, so we withdrew from the wrong compound and didn't even leave a note. I left wondering what this farmer would think in the morning when he discovered a huge section of his compound wall was missing. I actually chuckled at the thought.

We went up the road and found our *real* objective. There was no way to breach the wall, so we had to go through the big iron door. After pushing and prying on the door, an opening big enough to crawl through was made, and two soldiers slid their way into the compound and opened the door.

First and Third Squads cleared this compound again with guns blazing. When it was time for the gun team to move in, we hurried into the compound, and finally, things looked like they were supposed to look. We rushed over to the building we were supposed to get on top of and quickly jumped onto a mud wall next to the house and helped each other get on top of the building. We cleared the roof for IEDs and set in the gun to pull security.

The assault teams kept moving through the compound, and I was standing up on the roof, pulling security, when three explosions went off on the other side of the wall directly in front of me. In the darkness, the explosions looked like flowers, and I didn't know what had just happened. Schwartz was laughing at me because apparently, I did a little "dance in place" before I sank down on top of the roof and got on the radio.

"What the fuck just happened?" I hissed over the radio. "Did we just hit an IED?"

Someone called back that they were flash bangs or stun grenades.

"Well, shit!" I said back. "It would have been nice if someone had radioed up what was going on! I think I shit my pants!"

The assault teams continued to clear the compound. It was a dry hole, and the reasons for that could have been anything: it may have been dry to begin with; the Taliban may have been tipped off that we were coming; they may have heard the explosion we set off and ran before we had a chance to get there. Whatever the reason, it was dry, and at 0430, we set off back to First Platoon's COP empty-handed.

When we got back, everyone was completely exhausted. We had traveled more than ten thousand meters carrying all our gear through unforgiving terrain in the dark. After a short breather, we ate breakfast with First Platoon and loaded our trucks to head back to Sperwan Ghar and then finally back home to Palace.

On the way to Sperwan Ghar, we got stuck behind a route clearance team that was searching culverts for IEDs. I was in the MATV with Dugas and Schwartz, and Padilla was driving. We didn't have gunner in the turret, but the hatch for the turret was open to let air circulate through the truck. I can't say how long the trip to Sperwan Ghar actually took because I know I was struggling to stay awake, but we finally made the stop and rested at Sperwan Ghar for about an hour.

The fifteen-minute drive back to Palace was delayed once again by the route clearance team. Waiting behind these guys was mind numbing. We would move up a few meters at a time then wait and wait . . . and wait. When we finally got moving, I looked from the backseat of the Tumbler through the windshield to see if we had passed the route clearance team. As I looked forward, the Stryker directly in front of us hit an IED. The asphalt road opened up and blasted chunks of rock and other debris into the air. Our truck was about fifty meters behind that truck, and with the turret hatch open, debris rained down inside the small MATV.

Luckily, the IED wasn't a direct hit. It went off just a few meters to the right of the Stryker's front wheel; otherwise, there would have been some serious damage and likely some injuries. Because of the blast, we had to call out EOD and have them exploit the site. It only took about two hours for them to get there, follow a command wire to the other side of a wall, then leave. I was so tired that when we finally made it back to Palace, I rolled into my bunk and slept with my smelly uniform on.

Berhe had impressed me on that mission, and I wanted him in Weapons Squad. Thompson was really starting to act strange, and after talking to Dugas about some of the crazy things he was saying, we both agreed that Thompson needed a change of scenery.

I swapped Thompson for Berhe and made Wyscaver the gunner for Gun Team 2. Berhe was his new assistant gunner. Thompson wasn't as upset as I thought he would be. He went to Third Squad where he was made a rifleman and was trained as a squad sniper. There was no love lost. I missed having Thompson, but it was for the good of Third Platoon and Weapons Squad.

02-03 September 2011

I was getting close to going on leave, and I was getting more and more paranoid about not making it that far. I decided that when I was a week out from leaving Palace for my midtour leave, I wasn't going out anymore. Of course, that's when the new mission came down that we would be spending three days in sector.

The plan called for Second Squad to act as a Small Kill Team (SKT) in a grape hut just off of Route H to watch for Taliban IED emplacement teams. The IED threat along this route had increased, as had the RPG threat. While Second Squad was set in their position, the rest of the platoon was going to take over compounds near an area we dubbed the Ghars because of the small mountains that seemed to jut out of the earth for no reason. There were two Ghars, and we called them Big Ghar and Little Ghar because . . . well, one was big and one was little. We didn't always put a lot of thought into stuff like that. We didn't really have to.

We had done patrols in this area before, and we knew there were some compounds in the area that we could occupy with little resistance from the locals while we patrolled the area, searching for any Taliban activity.

We left Palace around 0300 on the morning of 02 September and stopped the Stryker convoy several times along Route H to give the impression that we were doing a mounted patrol in case we were being observed. At a designated stop, Second Squad dismounted their Stryker, consolidated, and moved out toward their position. I have to admit it went off without a hitch. Van Bockel was awesome.

Further down Route H, the Strykers stopped again, and the rest of the platoon dismounted the Strykers along with an element of ANA soldiers. We moved quietly through the grape fields and made it to our first strong point early Friday morning. The owner of the compound was friendly and opened his doors to us; it all seemed too easy.

Weapons Squad took a position on top of the roof of one of the buildings in the compound while Third Squad and Lieutenant Labowski conducted a small patrol into the nearby village. While the patrol was out, we picked up several transmissions over the ICOM. There were no confrontations, but there were obviously Taliban in the area.

When the patrol returned to the compound, Lieutenant Labowski said we would stay in this compound until the following morning when we would move to a different location. I think I was still in denial that we were actually staying out in sector overnight and lost a lot of my motivation that morning.

I'd spent several hours on the roof, and when it started to get hot, I moved down the mud steps into the courtyard of the small compound. I found some shade against one of the buildings, took off my equipment, and sat down to try to relax. I don't know what it was about this compound, but I couldn't relax. Maybe it wasn't the compound; maybe it was the heat. Or maybe it was the ants crawling all over me. Or maybe it was just that I was getting sick of being in Afghanistan. Or maybe it was the fact that I was going on leave soon, and I didn't want to get killed before I got on that plane. Whatever it was, I could tell I wouldn't relax while I was in that compound.

The building we were huddled up against only had two rooms. The Afghan soldiers took the larger room and crammed themselves in like sardines. The other room was much smaller. It was maybe the size of a large walk-in closet. In the smaller room were two large piles of marijuana seeds. By large piles I mean roughly four feet tall and about four feet in diameter. There was no mistaking what kind of seeds they were. The smell of marijuana permeated the air.

A lot of the guys in the platoon were sleeping in this room, and if it hadn't been so cool in there, I would have made them leave. The last thing we needed was to get wrapped up with some Afghan National about us stealing his pot seeds.

The day was uneventful until about 2100, when Dugas came over the radio and said that he and Second Squad had been compromised. Trucks from Palace spun up and went to collect the squad. The entire time I was listening to the conversation on the radio, I was just bitter. Second Squad was getting to sleep in their own beds while the rest of the platoon was pulling guard or sleeping on a concretelike slab.

"Assholes," was all I could mumble before I tried to get a few hours of sleep.

The night was miserable. I used my assault pack as a pillow and covered my face with a *shemagh*, an Arab headdress, to hide from the mosquitoes and the ants. But the shemagh made me sweat, and when I took it off my face to cool down, the mosquitoes and ants swarmed me. At about 0330, I couldn't take any more, so I sat up and chain-smoked cigarettes and felt sorry for myself.

At 0430, we started getting everyone up so we could move out by 0530. Also at 0430, Second Squad, along with Dugas, was reinserted into the grape field not far from where they had originally been emplaced. This time, they didn't take over a grape hut but stayed in the grape field to keep eyes on Route H.

When the platoon was ready, we left Third Squad behind to pull security from on top of the Ghar while we moved east to a large compound and set in a large L-shaped firing line across the compound walls facing east and south. Lieutenant Labowski wanted to make our presence known in hopes that the Taliban would see us in the area and emplace IEDs that evening on Route H, and when they did, Second Squad would hit them.

I leaned against the wall and ate an MRE. The ANA soldiers were loud and obnoxious; it seemed like a joke for them to be out there. But then again, at this point, it seemed like a joke for us to be out here too. We were not allowed to conduct any offensive operations unless it was authorized by the brigade commander, so basically we were conducting movement-to-contact operations until we got shot at or blown up. Then we could defend ourselves. It was getting ridiculous.

We sat in that position for more than an hour. My body ached from lying on the hard ground the night before, and I wanted to go back to Palace to get some real sleep. At that point, I couldn't imagine being out for one more night. When the LT gave word to move out, I took up my position as the last man in the order of movement.

We were heading back to the compound we stayed in the night before to pick up Third Squad and move on to our next objective, which was a grape hut about two hundred meters south of Route H. As we were moving out, something caught my eye. Lying on the ground was a small plastic sealable bag. It was one of the bags that came in an MRE that you would use to mix a drink powder. We had been stressing to the soldiers not to leave trash in the fields because it only alerted the Taliban to where we had been, so I bent over to pick up the trash. The bag wasn't empty.

The bottom of the bag was filled with marijuana seeds, which had obviously come from the compound we stayed in that night. My first notion was that someone was going to take these seeds back to Palace and start a garden. My thoughts went back to when we'd first arrived in country and sergeant major warned us against doing just that. I stuffed the bag of seeds into my assault pack and planned on holding a bitch session when we got back to Palace.

We linked back up with Third Squad and moved north toward Route H. The movement wasn't very far, and we kept an easy pace. When we got to the grape hut we were going to set up in, we realized we were not alone. The farmers who worked the grape field were inside, hanging grapes to let them dry into raisins. There were four men and several children working in the hut. Lieutenant Labowski decided to turn it into a little shura. This time, I got involved.

I was very intent on making these people understand that they needed to stand up for themselves. I argued many points to them: They live in fear, they *can* stand up to the Taliban, they need their freedom . . . and on and on. For every argument I had in their favor, they had an excuse why they couldn't fight: no weapons, small numbers, they need to work the fields . . . and on and on. I finally got tired of it. It was very obvious that I wasn't trained to do a civil affairs job with these people, and at one point, I even wondered how many of these men, if not all of them, were actually Taliban themselves.

During this mini shura, Second Squad called over the radio that they had been compromised again. Our conversation with the farmers was going nowhere, and I turned to Lieutenant Labowski and told him we needed to stop wasting our time.

The trucks from Palace were on their way to get Second Squad, and I was agitated. Of course, they'd been compromised; and of course, they were going back.

Before the trucks made it to the pick-up point on Route H to pick up Second Squad, an explosion went off in the vicinity of where that squad was. I ran outside of the grape hut to look in that direction. After all, they were only a few hundred meters to our east. There were several small children playing outside the grape hut, so I shuffled them inside to keep them from getting hurt if, for some reason, a firefight erupted in our area. We could hear a loud blast of a .50 cal machine gun blaring in the direction of where Second Squad was located.

Lieutenant Labowski called Dugas on the radio to make sure they were all right. Dugas called back that an ANA truck had hit an IED, and they just started blasting into the grape fields. Later, Dugas recounted the events of their two days in the grape fields. Here's what he said:

> We inserted early on the morning of 02 September. We wanted in before daylight because we suspected that the Taliban were emplacing IEDs in the early morning. We set up in a grape hut less than a hundred meters off Route H. Once we cleared the hut, we set up our security, which was basically Offutt at the door.
>
> Throughout the day, the locals passed by the hut. There was a dirt road east of the hut, and some of the locals rode motorcycles on the road. Some of them actually leaned their bikes against the hut that we were in. We could see them through the holes in the hut, and I have no idea how they did not see us. Van Bockel could have reached through the holes and grabbed some of them if he wanted to.
>
> As the day went on, the locals came out and began to farm the grapes and sunflowers in the field next to the grape hut. Children played in the field and next to the hut. There was no solid door, so they could easily see

into the hut. I guess the only reason they could not see us is because of the difference in the light between the dark hut and the bright sun in the field.

Toward the latter part of the day, we could hear more locals around the hut. One of the children in the area stopped and looked inside the hut and saw us. We were compromised. The kid left, and we could hear him raise the alarm. Soon, we began to hear more and more people in area, and I made the decision to leave.

I radioed the Strykers to come and pick us up. As we were loading up in the trucks, I looked back to see approximately twenty people in the area. They weren't doing anything threatening; they were more shocked at the dumb Americans leaving their hut.

On the second day, we did not occupy a grape hut. After being seen in one, we figured the huts would be booby trapped. We occupied a grape row about fifty meters south of Route H. We locked down each end of the row with soldiers pulling security.

Throughout the morning, we could see A-10s and a C-130 gunship in the sky above us. I, being the paranoid person that I am, pulled out my VS17 panel to mark our location. Before lunch, a convoy of MRAPs and HUMVEEs drove by. As the last vehicle passed our position, the vehicles toward the front of the convoy were hit by an IED. After the explosion happened, the convoy did a Death Blossom, firing their weapons blindly into the grape field.

When the firing started, we hit the ground. Several rounds of small arms fire, and .50 cal flew over our heads. I made contact with the COP and told them the situation. I instructed the SOG to find out through company what unit was hit and if we could help. The SOG said that it wasn't a US convoy; rather, it was an ANA convoy. The convoy didn't sustain any casualties and moved out. I figured that I didn't want to push our luck and radioed for the trucks. We mounted up and went back to the COP.

After I heard Dugas and Second Squad were leaving, my mind started to race. I couldn't believe how lucky they were and that they would be going back to Palace . . . again. But then I remembered *our* purpose for being out there. If Second Squad wasn't out to see IED emplacement, then why should we be out in these fields?

"Sir," I said to Lieutenant Labowski, "we've argued with these people long enough. I'm somewhat certain that some, if not all of them, are Taliban anyway. We need to get out of here. And if Second Squad is going in, we should probably go back to Palace too."

I didn't think it would work, but it was worth a shot. Lieutenant Labowski got on his radio and called up to company headquarters, telling them that we were going in. After a brief pause, he told me to call Palace and have the trucks come pick us up.

Surprise quickly turned to relief as I pressed the button on my microphone to tell the SOG to send in the trucks. I wanted to say, "And hurry before someone changes their mind," but I didn't. I guess I figured if I said it, it would jinx it.

When we got back to Palace, I went into my CHU, fell on my bed, and slipped into a coma. As ratty as those beds were, I never felt more comfortable. I don't remember how long I slept. It wasn't too long, and when I got up, I took a shower and felt terrific.

On 04 September, Lieutenant Labowski said we were going to have a planning meeting that night for a patrol that would take us back into the area we were just in, accompanied by a group of ANA. I looked at the LT and made a joke. Well, maybe it wasn't a joke but more of a suggestion.

"I'm going on leave soon, and Schwartz is going to take over as Weapons Squad leader while I'm gone," I said. "I think I'll stay back and let him lead the squad on this patrol."

Lieutenant Labowski laughed, and for some reason, his smirk changed that suggestion into a fact. I went to the Weapons Squad CHU and found my little protégé.

"Get up, Schwartz," I said to him. "You need to go to the planning meeting tonight because you're taking over as Weapons Squad leader starting tomorrow."

"When are you leaving?" he asked.

"In about a week," I responded. "But I need you to be ready to take over as squad leader while I'm gone, so you need to get prepared now, and I need to get used to not going on patrols."

"You've got to be kidding me," Schwartz said. "Do you think they're going to let you stay back and let me run the squad while you're still here? That won't fly."

"Look here, smart-ass!" I grumbled at him. "You let me worry about making this fly. You just do what I told you and get ready for this planning meeting."

Schwartz laughed, but he got up and started getting ready. I went to the planning meeting with Schwartz, and when Dugas asked why he was there, I told him he had to start getting used to running my squad while I was on leave.

"You're going to leave a PFC in charge of Weapons Squad?" Dugas asked, knowing full well that I intended to leave Schwartz in charge.

"Hell yeah," I answered back. "So from now on, you don't refer to him as Schwartz. This is Three-four . . . Weapons Squad leader!"

Schwartz started to squirm, and Dugas turned on him.

"If I hear anyone call you Three-four or Weapons Squad leader, I'm gonna smoke your ass. Do you hear me?" Dugas said.

"Roger, Sergeant," Schwartz said with wide eyes.

After the meeting was over, I pulled an SOG shift, worked out, and went to bed. I had put my foot down and was dead set that I would not leave COP Palace again until I left for leave on 12 September. Lieutenant Labowski made many comments about how I was going out, but I referred him to my *squad leader*.

"Take it up with Three-four, sir," I would tell him. He would laugh and walk away.

On 05 September, Schwartz became Weapons Squad leader for Third Platoon. I tracked his progress for the rest of the time I was there and felt confident that I'd left my squad in capable hands. He made some minor mistakes early on, but he learned quickly. He would be fine. After all, it was only temporary.

SEVENTEEN

SHENANIGANS

It is difficult to judge the decisions I made so long ago under circumstances so different from the present. I do know, however, that I am not always comfortable with them.
—From *Once a Warrior King: Memories of An Officer in Vietnam* by David Donovan

The days at Palace started to run together. It was hard to remember if something happened yesterday, the day before yesterday, or even a week ago. There were times when something would happen in the morning, and later that day, we would refer to that event as something that happened several days ago. It's hard to explain that kind of phenomenon, and I guess that's what it would be like to serve time in prison.

As the time went by, I started feeling bad for myself and for the platoon. I can't say it was me feeling sorry for myself or others, but I didn't think we should have been subjected to some of the stuff we had seen and done. I particularly felt bad for the younger soldiers. Many of these kids, some even younger than my oldest son, were seeing and doing things that most people their age didn't have to see or do. It turns a boy into a man in a big hurry, and I found it somewhat sad.

I'm not trying to say that we had the worst living conditions in history. I'm sure there were other places in Afghanistan where soldiers were living without electricity, hot water, and hot meals. I won't even try to imagine what it was like in Vietnam during that war. But the constant high tempo of our area of operations was really draining us all. We needed a break, and all the talk of rotating guys to KAF for weekend getaways was nothing but talk. We couldn't afford to lose the manpower.

Despite the day-to-day drudgery of the whole thing, we did manage to have some good times and make some crazy memories. I guess it only makes sense that if you put a handful of infantryman together in one place with nothing to do but patrol, some crazy things are going to come out of it. Some of the things we got into were completely legal and were necessary to pass time. Some of the things we got into were borderline. Some of the things we got into would come back to haunt us later.

Dart Losers

The dart board became the center of attention for a handful of us in the early hours and later in the evening when it wasn't so hot outside. The darts had plastic tips, and the original six darts didn't last long. An old friend of mine, Jake "the Snake" Jegelewicz, sent bags full of plastic dart tips and another big bag full of darts, so we were back in business.

Typically, if you were at a bar playing darts, the stakes might be buying the next round or even putting up money. We weren't allowed to drink in Afghanistan so that was out of the question, and none of us were good enough to feel comfortable about putting up monetary wagers, so we had to come up with something else to bet. Gambling was illegal in the Army anyway. It turned into . . . a humiliation.

I know it's childish, but one day, while throwing darts with Burke, I decided the loser would have to run from the dart board to our snack tent about seventy meters with their pants around their ankles, and it had to be videotaped.

Yes, it was my idea. And yes, I lost.

So I dropped my shorts to my ankles and ran all the way to the end just trying not to fall over. Burke thought it was the funniest thing as he ran alongside me with the video camera. The guys from the platoon that were outside their CHUs had no idea what was going on. The interpreters were in shock.

In all, I ended up with seventeen videos of people, including myself, running with shorts around their ankles. There were a few that didn't get recorded. Some people chose not to throw darts because they were afraid to *bare it* if they lost. Some got bold and played without a shirt. Dugas would throw, but he made it clear that if he lost, he wasn't running, and who was going to argue with him? After a while, it was so commonplace to see someone running across Palace with their pants around their ankles that no one even bothered to look up.

Dead Man's Candy

On 31 July, the day we shot the three men on the motorcycle, we were waiting for the helicopters to come pick the wounded Taliban men up. I was standing on the road talking to Fox when Carden came up to me and asked me if I wanted some candy.

He held up a small piece of candy that was wrapped in a foil wrapper. It looked like a piece of saltwater taffy, which wasn't exactly my preferred choice of candy. I declined it.

"Come on," Carden said. "You gotta have some of this. It's really good."

"I don't want any candy, dude, but thanks," I answered back.

"Hey. You shot these guys, so you have to have some of their candy."

It took a second for that statement to register.

"Where did you get that candy?" I asked.

"It came out of that dead guy's jacket," Carden said, laughing as he spoke.

"That's fucking gross," I said, trying not to laugh. "I'm not eating that shit!"

"Come on," Carden pled with me. "I ate some. The LT ate some. It's our new tradition. You have to eat the candy of the guys you shoot."

"The LT really ate some?" I asked.

"Yes," Carden replied. "You *have* to eat some too!"

I didn't want to be the guy to break a brand new tradition, so I caved.

"Give me the fucking candy," I said to Carden and snatched the toffee out of his hand. I unwrapped the chewy piece of toffee, gingerly put it in my mouth, and chewed it until it was all gone.

"Are you happy now?" I asked Carden, who walked away laughing.

The new joke after that was "We're Third Platoon. We'll kill you . . . then eat your fucking candy."

Pink Belly

I mentioned earlier that it was an Army tradition to pink belly someone on their birthday. A pink belly involves the birthday boy getting held down and his belly exposed while the rest of the platoon takes turns smacking his belly until it turns pink, hence the name pink belly. Sometimes they turned into black-and-blue belly, and I didn't want any part of that on my birthday.

On the morning of 19 August, I pulled out a KA-BAR knife that a friend had given me on my first deployment, and I made it obvious that I was willing and ready to use it in the event someone got the idea of giving me my birthday present.

The day went by without incident, and later that evening, I was in the radio shack filling out a sworn statement for an officer that was doing some kind of investigation on our platoon. It was dark outside, and when I opened the door to find that officer and give him my statement, it was already too late. Before I knew what was going on, Wyscaver and Bedient had jumped me from behind and tackled me to the ground. I was furious. I reached for my knife, and I fully intended to stab someone . . . anyone. In my mind, I was thinking, *We have a medic here, so it'll be OK!*

As my hand made a fist around the hilt of the knife, Bedient wrapped his hand around mine, making it impossible for me to unsheathe the blade! I was bucking and screaming and trying to throw these guys off of me. I looked up, and someone was trying to grab my feet to keep me still. I hiked my knee and kicked out, making contact with Schwartz's face. I was screaming and cussing at everyone. I was also dipping, and I was spitting tobacco juice at people who came up to attempt a smack on my belly. Burke was the only one that made an attempt, and he went easy on me.

When no one else gathered the nerve to smack me, my attackers decided to let me go. I heard the countdown. "Three . . . Two . . . One," and they released me! I jumped up as fast as I could, but they had all scattered in different directions. I quickly calmed down and laughed about it with everyone else afterward.

The Generator Repair Debacle

On 24 August, it started out to be a pretty quiet day because we weren't running any patrols. We had to send a handful of people to Sperwan Ghar for a class, and several people were involved in an upcoming planning meeting for a company mission. I knew from my experience working with our company commander, it wasn't going to be a fun mission because he usually found a way to make things worse than they really had to be.

Somehow I got out of doing any of that, and I stayed behind at Palace. I got a little bored, so I took my watch, which had a thermometer on it, and set it outside. It actually gives a decently accurate reading if it's not affected by body heat. It was about 1135, and after about ten minutes, I retrieved my watch . . . 135 degrees. It was going to be a hot day.

I was watching movies and pulling an SOG shift when our interpreter came to my CHU to tell me a generator mechanic was there, so I went out to talk to the guy.

It was a local national who had been hired to hook up a second generator that had been delivered to Palace a few days prior. I asked him what he needed to do, and through translations, he explained that he was going to hook up part of our power needs through one generator and leave the rest on the old generator, essentially relieving a lot of the burden on the single generator we had in use at the time. I told him to go ahead and do the work.

I went back to my CHU, and about an hour later, the interpreter came back to tell me the generator would be turned off momentarily while the guy working on it switched over the power from one generator to the next. So the lights went out, and I waited for the power to come back on. When it did, it was on for less than five seconds before an enormous pop hit the corner of my CHU. It was so loud I hit the floor, and at first I thought someone had shot at my CHU. Then I could smell burning electrical wires. I looked up in the corner with a flashlight to where the popping noise came from and found that the breakers were tripped in the breaker box. I stormed out the door, grabbed the interpreter, and found the generator mechanic to find out what had happened.

"He say he hook up power, and it on 220 volts . . . not 110 volts," the interpreter translated to me. "He say he have to get part to make this generator run on 110 volts. He not have part now."

I'm sure my eyes rolled to the back of my head.

"You tell this guy he needs to hook everything back up the way it was before he got here," I told the terp. "Tell him he's not leaving here until all the power is back on, and it's hooked up the way it was. He can get his part and be back here whenever, but we can't be without power."

The translation from my words into Pashto hit the mechanic, and he just nodded and rambled off a bunch of words I couldn't understand. The terp looked at me and just said, "He say, 'OK.'"

I went back to my CHU and was in there for about twenty minutes when the temperature started to rise on the inside to near unbearable levels. Since the power was out, so were all the air conditioners on the COP.

I went back out, and as I was leaving, the interpreter showed up with the mechanic and said, "He say he can't hook up new generator. He need part and be back in few days."

"Well, he needs to hook the old generator back up before he leaves," I said.

The interpreter turned to the mechanic and said something in Pashto, and the mechanic said something back before the translation came that, "he see what he can do."

Was he serious? I felt like we had already had this conversation. I was already hot because the inside temperature in my CHU almost matched the levels of the summer heat outside, but when I heard *that*, my blood started to boil. *He'll see what he can do?*

"Look here," I said in my best calm, stern voice. "You tell this guy that if he tries to leave here without hooking that generator back up, I am going to shoot him in his ass."

The interpreter laughed, and as the laugh turned into a half smile, he saw that there was no joking look on my face.

"I'm not kidding," I told him, which wiped the smile completely off of his face. He turned to the mechanic, said something to him in their language, and the mechanic looked nervously at me before he hurried off to work on the generator. Within twenty minutes, my air conditioner was back on.

I really wouldn't have shot the guy, but who comes out to an American COP, burns up a generator, then leaves without returning the power . . . and then expect to walk away like nothing happened?

Despite the generator running again, the spike in the power caused by his faulty wiring job caused damage to some equipment on the COP. Several of the air conditioners no longer worked, and electrical items plugged in without a surge suppressor were fried. My AC worked, but I lost a power strip, and the only thing that was burned up in my CHU was my hair trimmers, which normally wouldn't have been a big deal, but it was getting close to my leave date and I was in need of some *manscaping*, so I wasn't too thrilled about that.

Later, when the rest of the platoon returned from Sperwan Ghar, I was not very popular for letting some mechanic blow up about two-thirds of the air conditioners. Everyone living in a CHU with no air-conditioning had to move into CHUs that still had air. Dugas moved into mine, and it would be a couple days before the AC guy from Zangabad would be able to come and fix or replace the units that burned up.

Smoking Joes

I've never been into smoking dudes when they got out of line. I've never been opposed either, but I usually try a different method first. If being reasonable doesn't work I had little choice but to smoke a joe.

In Afghanistan that year, I lightly smoked a couple guys for doing something I thought was stupid. One was taking his iPod to tower duty. The other threw an empty water bottle on top of the Hesco Barrier at Zangabad.

Three soldiers got serious smoke sessions from me.

Christiansen and Opie

Christiansen was on guard duty with another soldier, who we'll call Opie. Both were in Tower 1, and both of them fell asleep. Hurst was on SOG that night and caught them. Since they were both in my squad, he just woke them up. He knew my policy about other NCOs smoking my soldiers, so it was with great pride the next morning he told me what he'd found.

"Guess who I caught sleeping on guard duty last night," he gloated. "Christiansen and Opie. Both of them were in Tower 1, and both of them were crashed the fuck out. It's not the first time I've caught either one of them asleep, but they were both asleep at the same time in the same tower. What are you gonna do about it?"

He cocked his head to the side as his eyebrows went up, and he smiled his evil Samsquanch smile. I had no choice. I had to smoke them.

After a half hour of push-ups, flutter kicks, sprints, and various other forms of exercise, I told them both that if one of them would throw up, I'd be done. Christiansen tried to stick his finger down his throat, but he couldn't make himself puke.

I finally got tired of smoking. I made them pull all the chairs out of all of the towers, then had them sit outside and write a one-thousand-word report about the dangers of falling asleep while in a combat zone. Additionally, they had to run to every tower at the top of each hour and make sure the guards were awake.

Manley

When Manley went out on that QRF mission that he wasn't supposed to go on and did it with only one bottle of water, I told him I would take care of him when we got back to Palace.

I started to smoke him in front of the CHUs, and Dugas made me stop and take him behind the CHUs so he wouldn't be humiliated in front of the rest of the platoon.

I took Manley out back, and after the same routine I'd used on Christiansen and Opie, I gave Manley the same offer.

"If you throw up, I'll be done," I said.

Manley bent over and gave it everything he had to try to puke, but he had no luck.

"I can't throw up, Sergeant," Manley said between breaths. "I haven't eaten since yesterday at lunch."

It just got better! Not only had he gone out on a patrol he wasn't supposed to go on, he did it with insufficient water and no food in his stomach. All I could think of was the fallout patrol we'd done out of Zangabad and the reason they had fallen out was because they'd skipped meals.

"I know you're kidding," I blurted out. "You went out with no water and no fuel in your body? You really are a retard. I'm not smoking you anymore, but you need an IV."

I called Doc Bolin over and had him stick Manley, who took two bags of fluids. Additionally, Manley spent the rest of his time at Palace pulling a guard shift on and a guard shift off. That lasted for a few days before his replacement showed up from Sperwan Ghar.

Infrared Chemlight Golf

Dugas came back from a trip to Sperwan Ghar yielding a new toy. Someone at the company headquarters had giving him a one-wood golf club, and the games were about to begin.

I was sitting in my CHU one evening, and Dugas came into my room with his helmet on and night vision goggles mounted.

"Get your helmet and mount your NVGs," he instructed me, so I stood up and did as I was told.

"We're not going on patrol, are we?" I asked.

"No," he said. "This is much better!"

It was dark outside, and when we got outside, I saw that Dugas had a small collection of infrared chemlights piled on the table next to the golf club he'd brought back from Sperwan Ghar. I was trying to put two and two together, but it wasn't adding up.

We went to the drive-up ramp on the southeast side of the COP and stood at the top near the wall. Dugas pulled out a chemlight, bent it to break the glass module inside of it, and started to shake it. I put my helmet on and dropped my NODs so I could watch it glow.

"What are you doing?" I asked.

"You're gonna love this," he responded as he pressed the chemlight into the hard dirt so it stood on end. With his night vision goggles over his eyes, he stepped back, pulled the golf club over his shoulder, and swung like he was teeing off at Pebble Beach.

When the head of the club made contact with the chemlight, the plastic stick exploded and sprayed over the wall of COP Palace and into the grape field. I exploded in laughter.

"That's the coolest thing I've ever seen," I squeaked out between laughs.

"Your turn," he said as he tossed me a chemlight and handed me the driver.

I busted the chemlight, set it up in the dirt, and pulled the club back. Hitting chemlight with a golf club in the middle of the night wearing NVGs was harder than Dugas made it look. I missed and hit the ground short of the target. That was enough to make us both laugh even more.

I hit in on the second swing and watched the chemicals spray over the wall. It was hilarious, and we'd found a new game. I was really surprised that Dugas had come up with this game because he was very adamant that no one could stand on the walls of the COP unless they were in full kit. But I didn't care. He was loosening up a little, and we were having a blast.

I guess it's the simple things that make you happy.

Alcohol and Hand Grenades

General Order Number 1 is a long list of what soldiers on deployment can and cannot do. The two things that stand out to most deployed soldiers are the prohibition of pornography and the ban on possessing and consuming alcohol. We all knew these rules existed, but it wasn't uncommon for both of these rules to be broken.

Sometime toward the end of August, I got a package in the mail. It was a small pillow crammed into a box. Inside the pillow was a liter of cheap vodka. Since the bottle was plastic, the heat from Afghanistan had somehow caused the bottle to compress, and more than half the bottle had leaked into the pillow it was wrapped in. But there was still nearly half a bottle left, and I could barely contain myself.

I hid the bottle away, and that night, after an SOG shift, I grabbed a Sprite out of the snack tent and mixed a few drinks using an empty water bottle. I felt warm and tingly inside and slowly drifted off to sleep.

At about 1700 on 08 September, I was sitting in our picnic area eating dinner when the ANA compound attached to us came under fire. This was becoming more common, so I kept eating. But when the bullets started flying through the trees on the west side of the COP and landing inside our compound, it became a little more serious.

Dugas started yelling, "Everyone . . . get in your CHUs!"

I was pissed. I just wanted to eat the lousy dinner Miller had cooked, but I grabbed my plate and headed for my CHU. When I got inside, I cussed to myself and finished eating my meal. When I finished eating, I threw my plate in the trash and sat in on my bunk. I didn't want to go outside because I didn't feel like getting shot by a stray bullet despite the fact that the shooting had stopped.

At about 1730, Dugas came into my CHU, and I could see a worried look on his face.

"This is fucked up," he said. "Those rounds were landing *inside* our walls. We have to do something."

"We can't do anything about that," I told him. "They weren't even aiming at us. Those were just stray rounds meant for the ANA. They just happened to get lucky enough to put some in our direction. You need to relax."

"Relax? How in the fuck am I supposed to relax after that?" he snarled at me. "I'm telling you. We need to start building up our COP defense, or we're going to get overrun."

"I know how you can relax," I said as I reached for that bottle of vodka. It was a risk showing this contraband to the platoon sergeant, but I felt like it would calm him down. I pulled out the bottle, held it up, and pointed at it. Dugas's eyes widened. He looked out the door behind him, shut the door, and nodded.

We put a movie into my computer and started watching it as we mixed drinks. There wasn't much left in the bottle, so when it was all said and done, I had one drink and Dugas had two. It wasn't enough to get drunk, but it was enough to help calm his nerves.

When the movie was over, we sat in my CHU and talked about what we were doing there and how we both thought we could change things to make our situation better. It was almost 2200, and as we were talking, a huge explosion went off outside the COP. I'm not sure how far away it was, but it was enough to rattle the walls of my iron CHU. Dugas started to freak out again.

"We need to do something," he said. "We need to throw a flash bang (stun grenade) over the wall!"

"Dugas, I don't even have any flash bangs," I said, then smiled. "I do have a frag, though."

"No," he quickly responded. "We can't do that."

There was a short pause in the conversation.

"Fuck it," he said. "Throw the frag over the wall."

"Are you sure?"

"Yes!"

And he left. I assumed he was going to let everyone know what was going on, so I grabbed a fragmentation grenade from a shelf in my CHU and walked outside. No one was around, and I assessed the situation. I wanted to make sure I threw the grenade high enough to get it over the wall and not let it come back in on me. I also wanted to make sure I got it far enough over the wall that the kid in the guard tower over my CHU wouldn't get hurt. I knew there were thick grape walls about fifteen meters on the other side of the wall, so I just had to make sure I threw it hard enough to get it into the field.

I pulled the pin, held the grenade for a few seconds, and contemplated replacing the pin. I have a friend who once told me, "It's a fun place where once the bell is rung. But once it is rung, it cannot be unrung." Again, I thought about disarming the grenade.

I felt like I was feeding into Dugas's paranoia. But he told me to throw it, and who would pass up a chance to throw a live hand grenade?

I cocked back and threw the frag as high and as far as I could, saying "frag out" in a moderate tone. I ran underneath the overhead tent area of my CHU and waited for the explosion. A few minutes after it detonated, Dugas came back to my CHU.

"No more frags," he said.

"Why?" I asked. "Are we in trouble?"

"Yeah," he grumbled. "The LT is pissed."

I looked up and saw Lieutenant Labowski marching toward us, so I went inside my CHU and sat down on one of the folding chairs and waited for the upcoming ass chewing.

"Who threw that fucking hand grenade?" Lieutenant Labowski asked as he barged into my room.

I sat there for a second and raised my hand.

"What the fuck do you think you're doing?" he yelled, and he proceeded to *verbally counsel* me, explaining that I had done that with no warning and how I was an idiot for "playing with explosives while consuming alcohol." I had no idea how he knew we'd been drinking, and I wanted to argue that I wasn't drunk, but I just sat there and endured his rage. I could tell he was disappointed in the decision to throw the grenade.

Despite the fact that I was several years older than Lieutenant Labowski, I felt ashamed that I had let him down, and I would never throw another hand grenade in Afghanistan again. Later that night, Dugas and I were hitting chemlights over the wall, and I was still feeling stupid for throwing the grenade.

"Why didn't you tell Lieutenant Labowski that you'd told me to throw that grenade?" I asked him.

"Oh, don't worry about it," he responded. "It's all been taken care of."

I didn't know what that meant, but I still didn't feel good about it. In fact, I had a bad feeling about the whole thing.

This chapter covers just a few of the things we got into at COP Palace to pass time and make things more interesting. The stories are really quite endless, ranging from simple football games to raising and slaughtering farm animals for food. I thought it was best not to give away too many stories because some of the things I've mentioned already caused enough trouble further down the line. It was like we got a handful of shit and threw it into a spinning fan, and no one saw it coming.

EIGHTEEN

MIKEY ZISHA

In no other profession are the penalties for employing untrained
personnel so appalling or so irrevocable as in the military.
—General Douglas MacArthur

20 August 2011

I was working out in our "prison" gym when a convoy pulled in, stayed for a few minutes, and then left. I didn't know why they had come, and I didn't care. The closer my leave date came, the more my enthusiasm was starting to decline. I finished working out, and as it was getting dark, I walked from my CHU to the CP. On my way there, I noticed an unfamiliar face. It was getting dark, but I was pretty sure we didn't have any Asian soldiers in our platoon at the time.

"Who the fuck are you?" I asked the new face—a question I asked all the new faces on the COP. When you see the same thirty faces every day, a new one stands out.

"Private Zisha, Sergeant," the squeaky voice responded.

"What the fuck are you doing here?" I asked.

"I'm new," he said. "This is my first day here."

It hit me that the convoy had dropped this kid off when I was working out. I started asking him the usual questions, such as where he was from (New York), how old he was (nineteen), and where he was stationed for his last duty station.

"Fort Benning," he responded.

"Were you in Third Infantry?"

"No, Sergeant. I was in Basic Training."

"You have got to be shitting me," I gasped. "You just got out of Basic, and they sent you here? Un-fucking-believable! Well, welcome to the Thunderdome, bitch! This is the shittiest place in the entire battalion. You'll have your CIB in no time, kid."

I walked off, shaking my head. Who in their right mind would send a kid straight out of Basic Training to Palace, of all places? This had to be a screw up.

I was headed back to my CHU, and I saw Carden telling the new kid he had guard duty in twenty minutes. Carden rattled off a list of things Zisha would need for his shift, and he warned him not to be late. Zisha scurried off, and I walked up to Carden.

"Hey, that kid is straight out of Basic Training," I said. "Who's the idiot that sent him here?"

"I don't know," Carden said. "But he's got guard duty in about twenty minutes, and I told him not to be late. You wanna bet he's late?"

"I'm not taking that bet," I said and headed to my room.

About twenty-five minutes later, I walked out, and Carden was smoking Zisha because he was late. He made him do some push-ups while in full kit, and Zisha was able to do about ten push-ups before he was smoked. I remember thinking, *That's pretty weak.*

Carden stood him up and, as SOG, inspected his uniform and equipment. Zisha had all his gear, but his night vision goggles were not mounted to his helmet.

"Mount your NVGs," Carden instructed our new soldier. "How the fuck are you gonna see in the dark on guard duty without your NVGs on your helmet?"

Zisha pulled out his NVGs and fumbled with them. He looked like a caveman trying to turn on a computer.

"You don't know how to mount your NVGs?" Carden asked. "What the fuck did they teach you in Basic?"

Zisha just stood there, so Carden grabbed his helmet, snapped on the rhino mount, and clicked on Zisha's NVGs and sent him to the tower for his guard shift.

"Do you believe this shit?" Carden asked me. "He was late for his shift, and he didn't even know how to mount his NVGs. That kid couldn't even do more than ten push-ups! What is wrong with the Army anymore?"

I just laughed. I was as shocked as he was, but I chalked it up to Zisha being nervous. I headed back to my CHU and didn't give it another thought.

In the Army and other branches of military service, no doubt there's a period of time when all new personnel go through some sort of indoctrination. It's not uncommon to be referred to as a cherry or the FNG (Fucking New Guy). This tradition has probably been around since the dawn of organized military. I'm sure the Spartans or Roman Army had some sort of rite of passage. And for Zisha, it was no different. The downside for Zisha was when he arrived, mid-deployment, the platoon was established. These men trained together and had grown to trust one another. We were familiar with the surrounding area and the type of enemy we were fighting. Zisha was inexperienced, but it wasn't his fault. He was just a victim of circumstance.

Over the next few weeks, I would see Zisha getting smoked for various reasons. I never witnessed any of his infractions, but I had no reason to doubt the NCO that was administering the discipline. After all, as hot as it was out there, no one wanted to waste their time smoking anyone when they could have been in an air-conditioned CHU. And none of our leadership was vindictive in my opinion.

When I'd walk by Zisha doing push-ups or flutter kicks, I'd ask, "What did he do this time?" and the most common responses were "We caught him asleep on guard duty" or "He went to the tower without any water." There were a few other reasons, but for the most part, his punishments seemed justifiable to me. Falling asleep on guard duty is a court-martial offense and not having water on guard duty was just asinine.

So I'd see Zisha getting smoked and just continue on my way. It wasn't uncommon for a soldier to do push-ups for making a mistake. I have no clue how many push-ups I've done in my Army career for doing stupid stuff. But when I got smoked for doing something stupid, I learned from it. Apparently, Zisha wasn't catching on because he kept making the same mistakes over and over, and he continued to pay the price for these blunders.

After being there for about ten days, I saw Zisha getting smoked once again. When he was cut loose, I pulled him down to my CHU and sat him down at the picnic table just outside my door. I thought it was time to let him know that what he was going through was normal.

"First of all, I want you to relax and listen to what I have to say," I said. "You're the new guy. When I was the new guy, I got smoked for hours because I called my squad leader 'the short guy' because I didn't remember his name. I never forgot his name after that. The new guy always gets fucked with."

Zisha just stared at me.

"Look, I just want you to know that eventually, this is going to get better. Your newness will wear off, and you'll stop getting smoked so much."

Zisha just stared at me.

"All righty then. You just have to start doing your job and stop making so many mistakes. And don't take all this stuff personal. It's just the way of the Army. It will get better. I promise you it will."

Zisha just stared at me.

"OK. Well, learn your job and stop making mistakes, and you'll be fine. Do you understand?"

Zisha stared at me and nodded his head. At least I knew he could hear me.

About that time, Fox walked up and reiterated some of the things I'd told Zisha. Zisha just stared at Fox. It was almost uncomfortable to have him sit there and just stare at me. It wasn't a menacing stare. It was like he was listening, soaking it in, and not responding. It was just weird. So I turned to Fox and started talking about something. I let Zisha sit there, hoping he'd feel some kind of refuge, but I had said what I wanted to say to him. Eventually, he got up without saying a word and walked off.

"That was fucking weird," I said to Fox.

"I know," Fox told me. "He just sat there staring at us. I wonder if he heard us."

"I'm sure he did," I replied. "Maybe he just feels intimidated and didn't think he could respond. Whatever. He'll be OK."

Later that day, I was walking to the eating area to get dinner. There was a picnic table around the corner from the kitchen tent, and Zisha was eating by himself at that table. When I got closer to the eating area, I saw Brooks eating dinner. I knew Brooks was in the same squad as Zisha, and I thought to myself, *these kids are doing nothing to help Zisha out.*

"Brooks."

"Yes, Sergeant?"

"Is Zisha in your squad?"

"Yes, Sergeant."

"Then get your ass up and go around that corner and eat dinner with him!" I yelled. "And anyone else in his squad, better get your ass over there and eat with him too. It's no wonder he keeps fucking up. No one here is helping him out."

A few of the guys got up and walked over to the table Zisha was eating at. I couldn't really tell if they did it to make him feel part of the platoon or if they just did it because I had told them to do it. At any rate, at least he didn't have to eat that meal by himself.

One night I was lying in my bed and someone knocked on my door. It was Carden, and when he stuck his head in, he asked, "Is Zisha in here?"

"Why the fuck would Zisha be in here?" I asked.

"I don't know," Carden said back. "But we can't find him."

My first thought was that Zisha had somehow been abducted by the Taliban, which personally was my worst fear while serving in a combat zone. I told Carden I hadn't seen him, and he left.

Early the next morning, I relieved Carden on SOG and asked him if he ever found Zisha.

"Yeah," he said. "He was sleeping in one of the shitters."

"What?" I gasped. "Why was he sleeping in the shitter?"

"I don't know," Carden said with concern in his voice. "But he was in that first one too, the one where everyone goes to piss in and ends up pissing all over the place. That's just fucking weird, man."

I couldn't imagine sleeping in one of those porta-johns. Not only did they smell rotten, but they were hot and definitely not sanitary. Not to mention, it's impossible to lie down.

I worked through my SOG shift, and as the sun was coming up, Zisha came to the TOC to get a new battery to go up for his guard shift.

"Were you sleeping in a shitter last night?" I asked him.

"Yes, Sergeant," he squeaked.

"Why in the hell were you sleeping in a shitter?" I asked him.

"Because I didn't feel like I deserved a CHU," Zisha said in a whisper.

"Hey! That's bullshit!" I said. "You're a goddamn American soldier, and you deserve a fucking CHU. Don't you ever sleep in a shitter again, OK?"

"Roger, Sergeant," he responded and walked off to the tower to pull guard duty.

I never really inquired as to why he felt like he didn't deserve his CHU or what had happened for him to go sleep in a porta-john. I assumed he had been smoked and was imposing some kind of self-punishment. I'm no psychiatrist, but I maybe should have taken that as some sort of sign. But people do weird things on deployments. That was definitely weird.

A few days later, I was sitting outside my CHU, smoking a cigarette and thinking about Zisha. I guess I have a soft spot for weaklings. Obviously, I do since I had Christiansen in my squad, not to mention a few other kids I've somewhat mentored in the past. I got a wild hair and decided I'd try to pull Zisha into Weapons Squad.

Our RTO, Specialist Bedient, was about to go on R & R, and when he got back, he was going to be reassigned to the headquarters platoon. Apparently, he had some kind of allergy and wasn't able to go on patrols. My scheme involved training Zisha to be Bedient's replacement.

At about 1400, I pulled Zisha down to my CHU and told him to get his medium rucksack and come back. When he came back, I opened his pack and put a radio, several batteries, a handful of water bottles, and about one hundred rounds of 7.62 mm ammunition. It was roughly about fifty pounds in weight. I had Zisha get in full kit, and as he stood in front of me, I explained what I was doing.

"Zisha, this is *not* a smoking. This is an assessment. Do you understand?"

"Yes, Sergeant."

"OK, then here's what I want you to do. I want you to walk the inner perimeter of the COP until you've gone roughly a thousand meters." I handed him my GPS watch so he could judge his distance. "When you've gone a click, come to me. I'll be out there watching you. Drink water and don't fall out. If you can do this, I'll see about getting you trained on the radio."

Zisha looked at me a little funny. I think he even smiled. Then I helped him load the pack on his back, and I stood in the hot sun during the hottest part of that Afghan day and watched him walk twice around the interior of COP Palace. When he got to me, he showed me the watch, which indicated he had walked just a little more than a kilometer.

We were standing next to the drive-up ramp on the southeast corner of the COP, and I moved to where the Hesco barrier was about the same height as some of the grape walls we jumped over in sector.

"I want you to climb on top of this Hesco and then climb down," I instructed him.

With all his gear on and weapon in hand, he struggled to get over the barrier. When he finally did, he fell off when he was coming down. After I made sure he was OK, I demonstrated how we often got up and over the walls and a technique I used for coming down. He tried again, and this time he was successful.

Honestly, he had passed my tests. I can't say that he had passed with flying colors, but he showed me that with a little effort on his part and a whole lot of work, he might be able to go on a patrol with the platoon. It was a long shot, but I thought there was a chance.

Bedient was on radio guard at the time, so I had Zisha download all his gear and go into the TOC. I told Bedient I wanted him to start training Zisha on how to fill the radios or load them with the proper frequencies. Zisha sat down with Bedient for about three hours. I occasionally went in to check on them to see if Zisha was making any progress, and Bedient assured me that Zisha was learning it.

Zisha was on the guard roster for the next shift. He was supposed to be in Tower 1, but I swapped him with the next radio guard so Zisha could get time talking on the radio. I had Bedient stay with Zisha for a while so Zisha could ask questions and so Bedient could keep an eye on him to make sure he didn't make too many mistakes.

My plan was genius. And so far, it was working.

About an hour into this, Lieutenant Labowski called me to the radio shack.

"Why is Zisha on the radio?" he asked.

"Because I'm going to make him my new RTO when Bedient leaves," I said proudly.

"No. No. That's not gonna work," Lieutenant Labowski said to me.

"Sir, we need an RTO that will go on patrols with us," I lobbied. "Bedient hasn't been able to go out, and we can train Zisha on the radio. He's already learned how to fill them, and he'll pick the rest up."

"Sergeant Wes," Lieutenant Labowski said in his reasoning tone, "I see what you're doing here, and I respect that. But this isn't going to happen. Zisha is way too weak to carry all that equipment on a patrol. And listen to him. I've been watching him for just a few minutes, and he's forgotten call signs and missed incoming transmissions. How is he going to react under fire?"

I poked my head into the TOC and watched Zisha stutter through a radio check.

"Sir," I said, "I know he sucks, but we can train him. It'll work. I think he can do it."

"Look, this isn't going to happen," Lieutenant Labowski said. "That's one of the most important and stressful jobs in platoon. We need someone reliable to be RTO, and frankly, Zisha hasn't proven himself. I appreciate what you're doing, but it's not going to happen."

"Yes, sir," I said. I was beaten, and I didn't have a leg to stand on. Everything the LT said was true. We couldn't risk taking Zisha on a patrol as an RTO. He was physically weak, and he was incompetent on the radio. Additionally, I was about to go on my midtour leave, and even if I was able to pull Zisha into my squad, I couldn't guarantee him the Weapons Squad *blanket of security* that my guys enjoyed. I couldn't even guarantee it for my squad while I was gone.

I asked Zisha to step outside the TOC for a minute to talk to him. When he came out, I looked him in his eyes and let him know I'd failed.

"Zisha, I tried to make you an RTO and move you into my squad, but that's not going to happen right now," I said. "But look, don't give up hope. I'm going on R & R, and when I get back, we can try this again. I need you to go to the gym and beef up. I also want you to keep learning everything you can about the radio."

"Yes, Sergeant," he said, and I sent him back in to finish his radio guard shift.

I've already talked about nicknames in the Army. Eventually, everyone gets one; and in the infantry, your nickname may not always be desirable. Mine was *Dusty Balls*. Christiansen was called *Dump* for a long time. We had a kid we called *Titties*. The LT was often referred to as *the Jew*, although there were only a few of us that would call him that to his face.

So there were a lot of nicknames at Palace, but when I heard Carden call Zisha *Dragon Lady*, I had to chuckle. I looked at Carden and rolled my eyes.

"That's fucked up," I said, but I still thought it was funny. Zisha smiled at the reference when it first started, and I didn't see anything too out of line with it. At least no one was calling him derogatory names like gook or chink, which I feel would have been over the line. I remember hearing a few other nicknames for Zisha, including *Soy Sauce* and *Fortune Cookie*. These could easily be construed as racial slurs, but at the time, it seemed harmless.

Zisha was basically a good kid from what I could gather. He was very quiet and seemed rather intelligent. Since he wasn't in my squad, I didn't have much interaction with him, but I hated to see him get smoked as much as he did, whether he deserved it or not.

I need to clarify that when I say I saw him get smoked *a lot*. I mean it was more than anyone else on the COP. I don't think it was anyone zeroing in on him or singling him out, but he was the new guy, and he did make more mistakes than the other joes in the platoon. Oddly enough, Berhe showed up about a week after Zisha and got smoked much less than Zisha did. But Berhe was much better at doing his job, and when he did get smoked, he learned from it. Zisha obviously didn't.

On 12 September, I was in the TOC making arrangements for my ride to Sperwan Ghar, which was my first stop on my way home for midtour leave. When I walked out of the radio room, I nearly bumped into Zisha.

"I'm sorry, Sergeant," he said to me, and I told him it was OK, but I noticed he still looked as scared as he did the first day he showed up at COP Palace. New privates seem to all have that "deer in the headlights" look when they get somewhere new because they don't know what's going to happen next. But Zisha had been there for three weeks.

I was walking toward my CHU to pick up my bags, and I walked past Carden. In passing, I told him to take it easy on Zisha because he still looked scared. Carden merely said, "OK."

I kept walking.

NINETEEN

WHEN THE SHIT HIT THE FAN

If I were asked to give what I consider the single most useful bit of advice for all humanity it would be this: Expect trouble as an inevitable part of life and when it comes, hold your head high, look it squarely in eye and say, "I will be bigger than you. You cannot defeat me."

—Ann Landers

I left Palace on September 12 for leave. When the clip was ready to take me to my first stop, Sperwan Ghar, I grabbed my bag and headed for the Stryker. My luggage consisted of my medium rucksack filled with a book, my journal, five cans of Red Seal Long Cut Wintergreen, a pack of cigarettes, my laptop, a hygiene kit, two pairs of socks, a PT uniform, tennis shoes, and shower shoes. I was traveling as light as I could. I didn't want to check any baggage because that would have meant a longer wait at the airport when I got home, and I didn't want to waste any of my precious leave.

As I climbed the ramp of the Stryker, I asked the private in the VC position if I was on one of the new V-hulled Strykers we'd just gotten from KAF. The V-hulled Strykers supposedly withstand an IED blast better than a flat-hulled vehicle. He said it was, so I felt a little more comfortable. I wasn't leaving anything to chance. This was my time to get away from this place for almost a month, and I didn't want to be one of the stories of the guy getting blown up while he was on his way out the door for midtour leave. The trip from Palace to Sperwan Ghar should be the most dangerous leg of my journey home, unless the boredom caused me to kill myself. I didn't see that happening.

I'd traveled enough between Palace and Sperwan Ghar to know where we were without looking outside a hatch. The Stryker left Palace going north on Route Q. When it stopped, I knew we were about to make the right-hand turn onto Route H.

After that turn, I felt the uneven asphalt as the vehicle ran over the spot in the road that Van Bockel's truck was hit by an IED, and we kept rolling. I held my breath as we crossed over this broken piece of road, knowing full well that if there was an IED there once, there could easily be one there again. I slowly exhaled as we cleared the spot and made the curves heading toward ACP 16 and another right turn toward Sperwan Ghar.

When the Stryker slowed and turned into the company's FOB, I breathed a sigh. I had made it to my first leg and was ready to leave there by the time we pulled in. The truck came to a stop outside the company TOC and the ramp lowered. I shook hands with the guys on the truck and thanked them for the ride. I went inside the company TOC and boisterously yelled out, "When's my flight?" I don't think anyone even looked up. I stood in the doorway with my helmet in hand just staring at these TOC roaches, clacking away at computers. Finally, one turned to me and said, "We're working on getting you out of here, but we don't know when the flight will be. We'll find out later on this evening."

A platoon sergeant from another platoon walked in. I shook his hand, and he asked why I was there. I told him I was going on leave, and he told me to stay in his room. I gathered my stuff and followed him to his room, which was more of a castle. He had a couch, TV, coffeemaker, refrigerator, and a DVD player. The room was huge, and he shared it with his platoon leader. My buddy pointed out a bed I could sleep in, and we talked for a little while.

Later that day, a runner came to the room and said the next flight out to KAF was the following day at 1300. I was staying the night, but I had expected that. At least I was safe and with good company.

I didn't sleep much that night. It was hard to get the excitement of going home out of my head. I watched some movies on my buddy's DVD player and eventually dozed off reading a book. I woke up the next morning and repacked my bag. I killed time until just before 1300, when I gathered my gear and went outside with the rest of the guys going on leave. Eventually, the sound of the rotor blades became audible, and the first Blackhawk landed, unloading all the guys coming back from leave. As they filed off, we filed past them toward the birds, and I ran into Alley. We shook hands, hugged a hello, and I kept going.

The first bird filled up before I got a seat, so I went back behind the barrier and waited until the second Blackhawk landed. I got on, buckled in, and we were off. As the helicopter flew over Panjwei'i, I marveled at the beauty of this place I had grown to hate so much. The grape fields, from this height, were plush green orchards, and the architecture of the walls surrounding each field was a work of art. I wished I hadn't packed my camera so deep into my bag so I could get a photo of what the land looked like from a safe location. I thought that one day I might appreciate having had the opportunity to experience this area.

Flying over the desert was a site too. The miles and miles of vast nothingness was mind boggling. It seemed like the red sand from the desert went on forever.

And though I was glad I was not down there on the ground, I couldn't help thinking, *This is a beautiful country. I wouldn't go here on a honeymoon, but it is a beautiful country.*

The flight from Sperwan Ghar to KAF had one stop in between where we picked up another group of guys going on leave. When we landed at KAF, we all piled off the Blackhawks and went into a mud building and waited for a ride to Camp Roberts, where we would be staying until we caught a C-17 flight to Ali Al Saleem, Kuwait. I was hoping that flight would be sooner rather than later. I was in for a surprise.

Our ride picked us up and took us to Camp Roberts, and after signing in there, the liaison officer (LNO) told us the next flight out was on the seventeenth . . . four days from now. I was heartbroken. What was I going to do at KAF for four days to keep myself from going insane?

I slept as much as I could. It was the same tactic I'd used coming into country when we stayed at Manas Air Base several months earlier. There were two accountability formations a day, so I'd make those formations, go eat, tried not to spend money at the boardwalk, and slept as much as I could. Time passed, and finally, the morning of the seventeenth arrived. I repacked my bag and caught the truck to the outbound terminal.

The flight from KAF to Ali was about four hours long, and I was too wired to sleep. When we got there, we loaded shuttle busses that took us from the flight line to the out-processing center, where we completed our leave packets and were assigned flights back to the States. If your final destination was west of the Mississippi River, you were going to Dallas. Anywhere east of the Mississippi River, the flight was going to Atlanta. My group, the Dallas group, was given a time for the next formation, where we were told to be with all our bags and ready to go. I was in Kuwait for about fifteen hours before I loaded a commercial airline and watched the lights of Kuwait City turn into the blackness of the Persian Gulf and then on to Leipzig, Germany—the final stop before making it back to American soil.

After the two-hour stopover in Germany, we reloaded the plane and headed for the USA. Apparently, the Atlanta flight was full, so we were making a stop in Georgia to drop off some troops. When we landed, I was so happy to see the southern pine trees and the hustle of the Atlanta traffic. We got off the plane for another two-hour layover before reloading for Dallas. I stopped in Dallas and spent a couple hours with my mom, who'd driven to the airport to see me. My wife was with her, and I was surprised at how happy I was to see her. Three years had passed since we'd had many nice things to say to each other, but I was actually happy she had come out. Hindsight being twenty-twenty, I should have ended my journey there. But thinking back, there are a lot of things that I should have done differently. I made it to my final destination, which I'm going to leave a mystery. Some things are better left unsaid. It was September 19—a week since I'd left COP Palace.

I think when you're so hyped up and ready to get away from a bad situation, when you get to where you're going, you realize your expectations were unrealistically high and there's a lot of disappointment involved when reality it doesn't live up to what you expected. My leave was terrible. I ran into one pitfall after another. I got to the point where I was counting days until I went back to Afghanistan.

The only actual highlights of these two weeks were visiting my friends, Jake and Karen Jegelewicz. I also got to see Jake's son, my longtime friend, Jeff Jegelewicz, and his wife and kids. Both families took me in, and I had a great visit. Other than that, my leave sucked.

The night before I left to return to Afghanistan, I was watching a DVD when my phone rang. I didn't recognize the number. In fact, it looked like a foreign number leading me to believe someone was calling me from COP Palace. I answered it.

"This is Dugas, and I don't have much time," said the voice before the reception started to break up. "I just wanted you to know . . . shit . . . turd . . . drinking . . . hand grenade . . . turds . . ."

"I didn't hear that," I responded. "Say that again. I didn't understand you."

"Shit storm . . . drinking . . . turd . . . gren . . ." and the phone went dead.

I held the phone for a moment trying to piece together what I had heard. What a strange phone call. We all had cell phones at Palace, but the reception there was so bad it was nearly impossible to place a phone call longer than two minutes. I wished I had heard what he had said, and I was really confused.

I contacted Dugas's wife and asked her if she knew what was going on.

"He's been really stressed out lately," she said. "And after that kid killed himself, he's been sort of a wreck."

"What?" I shot back. "Someone killed himself? Who?"

"I don't know," she said. "It happened about three days ago, and I don't know who it was."

I got off the phone with her, and now my mind was going crazy. I was certain no one from Weapons Squad would have killed himself, so who could it have been? My mind started going from one face to another of the men still at COP Palace. My guess was that it was Brooks because he had been going through a family crisis and wasn't able to get leave any sooner. But I couldn't be satisfied with just a guess.

I called someone from the Family Readiness Group (FRG) at Fort Wainwright, and I was assured that everything was OK and no one had committed suicide. I wasn't satisfied. I'd known through experiences in the past that the FRG couldn't be trusted, but I didn't know what else to do. I called the Fairbanks newspaper and talked to the reporter that covered military stories.

"Hi. My name is Staff Sergeant Westenrieder, and I'm on leave from Afghanistan," I identified myself. "I just heard that someone from my platoon killed himself over there. I was wondering if you could give me any information on this."

"Well, we got a release the other day," explained the reporter. "It doesn't say he committed suicide, but we've been doing this long enough to read between the lines."

"Who was it?"

I braced myself for the bad news. I wasn't sure how I'd handle it if it was someone I cared about.

"It was Pvt. Mikey Zisha of New York," the reporter answered.

I was a little stunned. Why would he kill himself? He had only been there a few weeks when I left.

"Are you still there?" the reporter's voice came over the phone.

"Yes. I'm still here," I replied. "I'm just trying to wrap my head around that one. I can't imagine why he would have killed himself. But thank you for your help."

I hung up the phone and started to piece things together. Dugas had called, and even though his conversation had been distorted, I was able to hear the words *shit storm*, *drinking*, and *hand grenade*. Now that I knew Zisha had killed himself, I used my imagination and determined that during the investigation of the suicide, which would not be uncommon, the fact that I had been drinking and had thrown the hand grenade over the south wall of Palace had come out.

Should I worry?

I initially decided I was going to deny everything. No one saw me throw the grenade, and that wasn't uncommon anyway. There were several instances where grenades had been tossed over the walls at Palace. But the drinking thing could get me into serious trouble. The only one who saw me drink, for sure, was Dugas and he had been drinking with me. Surely he knew the old Army adage, "deny, deny, deny!"

But I still worried.

The next day, I made it to Dallas and was waiting at my terminal to fly out. I got a phone call from Schwartz's mother.

"Casey, have you heard?" she asked.

"About that kid killing himself? Yeah. I got a call from Dugas last night. I couldn't hear anything he said, but I found out from the newspaper in Fairbanks about that kid killing himself."

"Yeah. Will just called me. He's freaking out. Most of the NCOs from Third Platoon have been relieved and moved out of Palace. Dugas and Lieutenant Labowski are gone too!"

My head started to spin.

"Holy shit! What the hell is going on over there?"

"I don't know, Casey. But I wanted to call you and tell you what Will told me."

"Well, thanks for the call. If you talk to Will, let him know everything is going to be OK. I'm in Dallas flying out today. I'll be back there in about a week, and I'm sure it'll all be OK. Thanks for calling."

I got off the phone with her and tried to sort out what I knew. They obviously knew I had been drinking at COP Palace. But who were *they*? Was it the company commander? The battalion commander? Surely I could talk my way out of this. But why had everyone been relieved? And who was left? I had so many questions with almost no answers.

The flight back to Afghanistan took me back through Germany and Kuwait. I spent several hours in Kuwait before loading another Air Force C-17 to Kandahar Airfield. I couldn't sleep. I had no idea what I was going back to. I had no idea if I would still have a job. I was stressed beyond my limits, and I couldn't stop thinking about it. Not even for a minute.

When I finally got to Kandahar Airfield, I found out it would be several days before I would be flown back into Panjwei'i. At this point, I hadn't slept in almost three days, and I decided I needed to try to put my mind at ease.

I went to the JAG office at KAF and waited my turn. After a short time, an attorney pulled me into his office.

"Can I get an Article 15 or in any trouble if someone accused me of drinking, and there's no proof?" I asked.

"That I can't answer for you," he replied. "In a situation like that, you'll need to go to TDS (Trial Defense Services) and ask that question."

After getting directions to TDS, I walked out of the JAG office and almost decided not to mess with it. But my mind was running a million miles per hour, and I couldn't pass it up. I walked up the outside stairs to get to the TDS office, and when I walked in, I told the guy sitting at a desk that I needed to speak to an attorney. So I sat in the waiting area until an attorney came in and invited me into his office.

Again, I asked my question.

"Can I get an Article 15 or in any trouble if someone accused me of drinking and there's no proof?"

"I need to know more," he explained. "What all happened."

I gave him the story about the phone call I received from Dugas, and when I mentioned the hand grenade, he stopped me.

"You threw a hand grenade over the wall?" he asked.

"Yes, sir, I did. But that's no big deal," I said.

"No big deal?" he shot back at me. "You threw a live grenade over the wall. I wouldn't stress about the drinking. You threw a grenade over the wall. You're fucked!"

I couldn't believe what I was hearing. This whole time I was worried about the drinking, and he was telling me that part was no big deal, but instead I was screwed because of the grenade I threw. None of this was making sense to me. I wanted to tell him he was just a POG, and he didn't understand, but I wasn't about to try to piss this guy off.

"Here's what you're going to do," the attorney said to me. "When you start getting questioned about this, you need to say, 'I have nothing to say at this time, and I would like an attorney.' Do you understand?"

"Yes, sir," I said. "I understand."

"No," he said. "I want you to tell me what you're going to say."

"Really, sir?" I asked. "OK. When I have to answer questions about this, I'm going to say, 'I have nothing to say at this time.'"

"And?"

"And I'm going to say, 'I want an attorney.'"

"Say it again."

"I have nothing to say at this time, and I want an attorney."

"Say it again."

I thought he was kidding. But I followed his instructions and repeated his words back to him again.

"Now when you leave this office, you don't talk to anyone about anything that has to do with any of this. Do you understand me?

"Yes, sir."

I got up, shook his hand, and walked out of his office and headed back to Camp Roberts. That night, I still couldn't sleep. The words *You're fucked!* from the attorney kept running through my head. But I was still more worried about the drinking. The hand grenade was no big deal as far as I was concerned.

The next day, I walked back to the PX and stopped off to get a haircut. I was supposed to fly out the next day and figured I should look decent. As I was walking back to Camp Roberts, a vehicle pulled over in front of me. It was the LNO.

"I can't believe I found you," he said. "I need to take you somewhere. They've been looking for you."

"Who's been looking for me?" I asked.

"CID," he said. "They want to ask you some questions. I don't really know what it's about."

"I'm pretty sure I do," I said back as I climbed into the backseat of the car.

The LNO dropped me off at an obscure little office, and I went inside. I gave my name to someone behind a desk and sat in a chair, waiting to be called. I had no idea what to expect. I had never had to deal with the Criminal Investigation Division before. I'd always heard they were dirty bastards, but I figured I could handle it. After all, what could they want from me? I waited for nearly an hour before I was called in to an office.

A warrant officer came in and sat down by me. He had a stack of papers he set on the table, and then he turned to me.

"Hello, Sergeant Westenrieder. My name is CW2 John Thomas," he said. Then he tore the warrant officer rank off the front of his shirt and tossed it on the table. "I know you're a staff sergeant, and I'm a CW2, but now we're the same rank."

I wanted to laugh. This was some stupid ploy this guy probably learned in CID school to try to make the person getting interrogated feel more comfortable. He must have thought I was an idiot.

"Sir, you can take your rank off all you want, but I'm still a staff sergeant, and you're still a warrant officer. That won't change."

He shifted in his seat. I stared at him, trying not to look nervous.

"Do you know why you're here?" he asked.

"Yes, sir," I responded. "I'm here because that kid killed himself."

"Well, he may not have killed himself," the agent said, staring at me.

That statement hit me in an awkward way. What was he implying? Was he suggesting that Zisha had been murdered? I felt a chill run down my spine, but I tried to remain calm.

"Right now we have relieved eight soldiers from their duties at COP Palace," the agent continued. "So far, these are the names: Lieutenant Labowski, Staff Sergeant Dugas, Staff Sergeant Van Bockel, Sergeant Hurst, Sergeant Holcomb, Sergeant Carden, Specialist Offutt, and Specialist Curtis."

I just sat there staring. I didn't know what to say. I was still trying to process the inference that Zisha may have been murdered. I think the agent asked me a few more questions about some of the guys he'd mentioned, but I didn't have anything to say about them. So he turned on me.

"There was drinking going on at Palace," he stated. "Did you drink at COP Palace?"

"Yes, sir, I did."

"How many times did you drink?"

"I'm not sure. Maybe two or three times."

"Who did you drink with?"

"I'm not going to tell you that."

"You have to tell me."

"No, sir, I won't."

"You can tell me, sergeant. I already know."

"Well, sir, if you already know I don't have to tell you."

I think he got pissed and changed his line of questioning.

"OK. Let's talk about the hand grenade that was thrown over the south wall."

Suddenly, the words from the attorney screamed in my head. *You're fucked!* I also considered that I had no idea what Dugas had said about the incident, and since he was the one who told me to throw it, I didn't want to get him into any more trouble than he might already be in. I took the lawyer option.

"I would like an attorney," I told the agent.

He wasn't happy to hear me say those words, and I could tell he was angry. He fished through some papers, and the whole time he was telling me how Palace was some kind of *den of inequity*, and he had never seen such a *circus* in all his years in the Army. All I could do was sit quietly and keep my mouth shut.

I signed some papers, and when he was done with me, he asked me if I knew where TDS was. I told him I did.

"Well, you need to go up there and get an attorney," he said. "And when you get one, you need to tell them you want immunity."

This was another shocking statement that took me by surprise. This clown didn't want me. He just wanted to know what I knew or he wanted me to roll over on my buddies. Immunity? No wonder he was so pissed when I asked for an attorney.

I left the CID office and went straight to the TDS office. When I got into the attorney's office, I told him I'd been interrogated by CID.

"You got picked up by CID?" he asked. "Why is CID involved in this?"

"It has something to do with a kid in my platoon killing himself," I explained.

The attorney's eyes narrowed.

"Pvt. Mikey Zisha?" he asked.

"Yes, sir," I answered. "I guess you've heard about it."

"I want to show you something," the attorney said as he pulled up a website on his computer. It was the front page of the *New York Times*. One of the stories on the front page was about Mikey Zisha.

"This is huge," he said to me. "This is on the front page of the *New York Times*. Yes, I've heard about it. Everyone's heard about it. I won't be surprised if the president hasn't already been briefed about it."

My head started to swim again. I had no idea of the magnitude of this thing. Even at that point, I didn't realize how big this thing had gotten.

He asked me to tell me my part of the story. I explained about the bottle of vodka I'd received in the mail. I told him how Dugas and I had drank a few drinks that night, and he'd told me to throw the grenade. He sat listening to me and nodding his head. When I was done with the story, he sat up.

"OK," he said. "That makes more sense now. I don't want you to talk to anyone about this at all. I'm your attorney, and if anyone tries to question you, you tell them you have an attorney, and you don't have to make any statements. Do you understand?"

"Yes, sir," I answered. "But I should tell you I started to answer some of the CID agent's questions."

His eyes got really big, and his face got red.

"What the fuck?" he yelled at me. "Didn't you sit there in that same chair just yesterday and hear me tell you what to tell anyone that questioned you? Remember repeating back to me, 'I have nothing to say at this time, and I would like an attorney,' or did I just dream that?"

"No, sir, you didn't dream it. I guess I fucked up."

"Yes! You fucked up!" he said, almost in a rage. "I can't believe you talked to them. I told you what to say, and you just blew me off. Look, Sergeant, if I'm going to represent you, you have to listen to what I tell you. If you can't do that, I can't represent you. Do you understand me?"

"Yes, sir."

"OK," he said. "Now I'm going to make this as simple as possible. You need to *shut the fuck up!* Do not talk to anyone else about any of this. Do you understand me when I'm telling you to shut the fuck up? Is that simple enough?"

"Yes, sir."

I left the lawyer's office and went back to Camp Roberts, sat on my bunk, and tried to soak it all in. Dugas hadn't lied when he called this situation a shit storm, and I was right in the middle of it. I pulled out my journal and went through every page. I had some incriminating stories about some of the other guys in Third Platoon, and my first thought was that once they found out I had a journal, they would try to subpoena it. I started tearing out pages. Then I walked to the post office and sent the journal home. I burned the pages with the incriminating stories and went back to my bunk at Camp Roberts.

I didn't sleep that night. The next day, I flew back to Sperwan Ghar, and things weren't going to get any better anytime soon. Throughout my entire military career, I'd never been in trouble. Sure I'd been smoked for doing stupid things, but I had never even received a negative counseling statement. I guess when it rains, it pours, and this shit storm was just beginning.

Author's Note: After I left for midtour leave, I stopped writing in my journal. I made note of many of the important dates, but since I no longer kept a journal, a lot of what follows this chapter is from memory and notes I kept on the side.

TWENTY

FROM HEROES TO ZEROES

A lie gets halfway around the world before the truth has a
chance to get its pants on.

—Winston Churchill

On 10 October, I climbed onto a CH-47 Chinook helicopter to make my way back to my unit. I heard that since Zisha's suicide and all the issues surrounding it, Third Platoon was moved to Sperwan Ghar, and Second Platoon had taken over duties at Palace. Of course it was still just a rumor, and I'd find out soon enough.

The chopper was crammed with personnel and equipment, and when it finally landed at Sperwan Ghar, I struggled to get my gear and myself off the bird. At the bottom of the ramp was Captain Allred.

"Hey, sir!" I yelled over the thumping of the propellers. "Is Third Platoon here?"

He pointed in the direction of the command post building and said, "They got here yesterday." Then he turned around and walked away from me. It was a little unnerving since he was usually very talkative. I knew something wasn't right.

I walked into the building and set my gear on a table. I found the company armor and told him I needed to get my weapon, which was checked in before I went on leave.

"I need to check and see if we're supposed to issue your weapon back to you," he said.

Now I knew I was in this pretty deep. I started noticing people who were friendly to me before walk by me and not say anything, or worse, ignore me when I talked to them. I wasn't even sure if I was going to be reissued my weapon.

The platoon sergeant I had stayed with when I left walked by and said he needed to speak to me, but he wanted to go outside where no one would see us. This was all too much like some eerie spy movie.

"Don't talk about any of this on the phone or the Internet," he told me. "Everything you guys say or do is being monitored."

"Are you kidding me?" I asked. "What's going on? What happened out there?"

"There are all kinds of rumors," he said. "Stuff like you guys were making Zisha hold a grenade in the guard tower with the pin pulled so he'd stay awake. And that you guys beat the shit out of him all the time. Stuff like that. And they're saying you guys were smoking pot out there."

I couldn't believe what I was hearing. I'm pretty sure no one would have made anyone, including Zisha, hold a live grenade on guard duty with the pin pulled. That's just stupid. I never saw anyone put a finger on Zisha. And I never even heard of anyone smoking pot. But then I remembered the patrol I'd gone on where I found the small bag of marijuana seeds. I should have kept my mouth shut, but I didn't want my friend to think I was involved in any kind of illegal drug use.

"Look," I told my friend. "I've never heard of any of that. But there was an instance where I found some pot seeds in a baggie when we were on patrol once. I put them in my assault bag to try to figure out who had done it, but I forgot about them. Shit! I hope I got rid of them before they went through my stuff!"

"Well, I hope so too," he said. "That's all you need right now."

The conversation ended with a "good luck" and a handshake. Now I had something else to worry about.

I went back into the building, and Third Platoon's new platoon sergeant walked up to me and said he needed my NVGs and any other squad equipment I had. I was obviously getting relieved of duty until this thing played out. I had left all this equipment with Schwartz. He had someone get Schwartz and bring all of my gear and gave me a hand receipt as evidence that I had turned the equipment over to him. When he walked off, I tried to talk to Schwartz, but the conversation was very limited.

"What the fuck is going on?" I asked.

"It's crazy," he said. "We're not even supposed to talk to you."

"Well, shit," I said. "I don't want to get you in trouble. I guess I'll be seeing you around. I have no idea what they're going to do to me."

"The rest of the guys are at Zangabad," he informed me. "I don't know what they're doing there. You'll probably be there too."

"Great," I said. "I'll be right next to the fucking flagpole. I guess they want to keep an eye on us."

We shook hands and parted ways as my old roommate, Sergeant Moreton, walked up and told me he was leading the convoy back to Palace, where I could pick up my stuff.

"My stuff is still at Palace?" I asked. "Why didn't they move it here?"

"I don't know," Moreton said. "We were told to leave it where it was and not touch it."

I didn't understand the logic in that, but I already had too much on my mind. Eventually, the trucks were ready, and I climbed on to Moreton's truck and headed toward Palace. The whole way there, I had a million things running through my head.

I even hoped we'd hit an IED, and all this would be over. I could feel the bottom falling out from under my feet, and I had no idea where this fall would end. We made it to Palace without getting hit by an IED, and I headed to my old CHU to gather my stuff.

The first thing I did was pick up my assault bag and open the outside pocket to see if those marijuana seeds were still there. I almost panicked when I found the small bag of pot seeds. I stuffed them into my pocket as my mind was racing with ways to get rid of these. All I needed at this point was to get accused of possessing marijuana.

There were people helping me load my stuff onto one of the Strykers. I couldn't believe how much stuff I had accumulated over the time I spent at Palace. I didn't even know where it had all come from. While the guys were putting stuff on the trucks, I grabbed a trash bag and stuffed it full of stuff I knew I wouldn't need, to include the bag of pot seeds, and carried it to the burn pit. I felt a bit of relief as the bag of garbage caught fire. I had dodged one more bullet in Panjwei'i.

The Stryker was starting feel more like a prison bus. When it pulled into Zangabad, I had no idea what I was supposed to do, so I found the acting first sergeant to try to get some guidance.

"The rest of the guys are staying in this tent here," he said, pointing to a large tent connected to the MWR tent. "I'm not sure if there's room in there for you."

My mind went back to what my attorney had said, "Shut the fuck up," and I made a quick decision.

"My lawyer said I'm not supposed to have any contact with those guys," I said, not really lying, but trying to keep my distance from them. "If it's possible, I'd like somewhere else to avoid any problems."

He went to his office and came back with my tent assignment. Moreton and a few others helped me drag all my stuff to Tent 14. This tent housed about six other people from one of the staff offices at the battalion level. Some of them were civilian contractors. The others were higher-ranking NCOs and one officer. I had a bunk and a small locker. The bunk next to mine was empty, so I piled all my stuff onto the empty bunk and started to try to settle in. There's an old quote from actress Lillian Russell that goes something like "We all have a fear of the unknown. What one does with that fear will make all the difference in the world." Well, there was plenty of unknown for me at this point, and I have to admit it was scary. But what would I do with it? I didn't even know what I was supposed to do at all.

I sat the remainder of the day, staring at the stuff on the bunk next to me. Every time the door opened, I jumped, expecting to be summoned to the battalion commander's office. But no one came for me. I went to the chow hall for dinner, and on the way back, I stepped into one of the porta-johns to take a piss. When I was leaving, I saw Carden and Van Bockel. They tried to talk to me, and I put up my hand.

"Don't take this personally," I said to them. "I'm not supposed to talk to you. I don't know what happened after I left, and I don't want to know, but I can't talk to you guys."

I turned around and walked back to my tent. As I sat that evening, staring at my pile of stuff, I thought back on how I'd acted with Carden and Van Bockel and realized I was no better than the assholes that ignored me at Sperwan Ghar and the others here at Zangabad who avoided making eye contact with me. I realized I was becoming an asshole. I was no better than them. In fact, I was in the same boat as them, so why should I treat them like they didn't exist? I decided I'd make amends for that conversation in the near future.

A few days later, I got word that Captain Allred and our company first sergeant had been relieved and replaced. This was getting bigger, and I wondered how far up this would go.

Then the waiting began. I sat in my tent as much as possible to try and avoid as many people as I could. I tried to stay inside during daylight hours because I figured I'd be less noticeable at night. I learned that Lieutenant Labowski was actually in the tent right behind mine, and Dugas had been sent to Masum Ghar. Van Bockel, Carden, Hurst, Holcomb, Curtis, and Offutt were in a tent together. I felt isolated, and I had no clue what would happen next or what I was supposed to be doing. The *unknown* started to wear me down.

I sat in a chair, staring at the door of the tent, waiting for something to happen. Nothing happened. One of the civilian contractors approached me one day when he realized I didn't do anything.

"I'd sure like to have your job," he said. "How do I go about that?"

"Easy," I told him. "Get into trouble."

"Oh," he responded. "I guess I don't want your job after all."

And that was one of the few times he and I spoke. Word was getting around about what we had allegedly done to Zisha, and I was starting to feel more and more like a leper. On the third day, I left the tent to go eat breakfast. I returned and saw the command sergeant major standing on the steps of the tent with two other NCOs.

"Sergeant," he said, looking at me. "We're going to conduct a health and welfare search of your belongings. Is there anything you want to say to me before we begin?"

I wasn't completely shocked yet. I told him I was fine with them searching my stuff. He handed me a memo and told me to read it before they began the search. I held the memo in my hand and *that's* when I was shocked. The memo described a sworn statement from my *friend* at Sperwan Ghar who said that I participated in the use of marijuana and that I had marijuana in my possession.

"Sergeant Major," I said as I handed back the memo. "I need you to search every nook and cranny of my shit. I need you to make sure you don't find anything in there that I'm not supposed to have."

And the search began. I stood with my arms folded next to my locker as the three NCOs rifled through all my stuff looking for any evidence of anything illegal. Some of the residents of the tent walked in and out during the search, and I could feel my dirt-bag status growing. After almost an hour of searching, the three found nothing and left my belongings scattered all over the floor of the tent.

I was livid. I couldn't believe I had just had my belongings searched because a *friend* I had confided in had taken what I said, twisted it, and reported it to CID in a sworn statement. What did he have to gain by doing that? Why would he betray me like that? Shock doesn't exactly even begin to describe how I felt. It was time to break my silence with the others.

I spent about two hours going through all my stuff. I put away stuff that I wanted to keep, bagged up garbage I didn't need, and made a pile of stuff I could donate to the chaplain's Free-X. I pushed my keep pile under my bunk, trashed all the garbage, then took all the donations to the chaplain's office. On my way back to the tent, I made a pit stop to visit the guys I wasn't supposed to visit.

"Oh," someone said as I walked into their domain. "You've decided to come visit us."

I felt like an asshole. They had every right to treat me like that, and I couldn't even argue with them.

"I was only doing what my attorney told me to do," I tried to explain. I think they understood, but it took a while for them to warm up to me. I told them my story starting with the phone call from Dugas up until the health and welfare search and the sworn statement. In turn, I learned a lot of what had actually happened from the time I left until the time I got the call from Dugas. It was obvious that a lot of the stories I had heard, like making Zisha sit in a guard tower with a pin pulled on a hand grenade, were completely fabricated. I learned of a few incidents where Zisha had been actually physically assaulted, but no one ever beat him up on a regular basis as the stories had grown to be. And to the guys that did touch Zisha, I told them they would deserve anything they had coming to them because they knew better. They agreed.

I felt much better that I had started mending the gap between myself and these other soldiers. I talked to Lieutenant Labowski a few times, but he was very firm that he didn't want to talk to any of us about anything that happened at Palace or any of the accusations. I didn't blame him, but it was frustrating for me. One night, I was lying in my bunk trying to go to sleep when the door opened. I didn't even look to see who it was. A light shown in my face, and I heard someone say, "Hey, motherfucker. Get your ass out of bed." I recognized the voice immediately. It was Dugas.

I jumped up, and we shook hands.

"We need to talk," I said.

"I know, but we can't do it in here," he said. "Let's go outside."

We went to the side of the tent close enough to the air-conditioning unit that we could still hear each other, but the sound of the running air conditioner would drown out our conversation from anyone that might be listening. Yes, Dugas was still paranoid, but he made more sense to me now.

We talked for a few minutes about where he was and what he was doing. He was at Masum Ghar, pulling gate guard duty, which was a form of humiliation for someone who had just weeks earlier been a platoon sergeant for an infantry platoon.

He told me he was on his way back to Masum Ghar from KAF, where he had gone for a dental appointment. I told him about getting to Sperwan Ghar, picking up my stuff, and the health and welfare inspection.

"Why would he do something like that?" Dugas asked, referring to the sworn statement of our mutual *friend*.

"I don't know," I said. "But I got a lawyer right after all this came down. I didn't want to say anything about that hand grenade or us drinking together because I didn't know what you had already told them."

"That's cool," he said. "I wish I had gotten a lawyer when all this came down. I just didn't know it was going to blow up like it did."

"I know," I said. "You do realize that you're the one who told me to throw that grenade, right?"

"Yeah," Dugas said. "That's the story I told them too."

I breathed a sigh of relief. Dugas had to leave to get back to his ride to Masum Ghar, so we shook hands, and I told him to hang in there. He told me the same and then disappeared into the darkness.

Time crept by at Zangabad. The fear of the unknown grew more every day that no one could tell us what was going on. I spent my days watching the door of the tent, waiting for it to open. When it got dark, I'd creep over to spend time with the rest of the guys. We'd build a fire in a burn pit behind their tent and watch the broken pallets burn to ashes before I'd find my way back to my tent and try to sleep. When the sun came up the next day, it all started again. It was like a sick version of *Groundhog Day*.

Eventually, Third Platoon moved back to Zangabad. COP Palace got closed down and Second Platoon moved to Zangabad. Then First Platoon's COP was closed down, and they also moved to Zangabad. Charlie Company was all in one place, and they all had orders *not* to talk to any of us.

We were treated like outcasts. People we knew or people that once looked up to us walked by us with their heads down. People would see us walking to the chow hall and cross the dirt road to avoid us. The ones who did talk to us would do it in the shadows, and we would go back to our group and report the new propaganda that was being spread around the company.

I saw a friend of mine outside the MWR tent. He was in Headquarters Platoon, and I knew he liked coffee, and I had a coffeemaker in my tent, so I invited him over for a cup of joe. He threw his hands up in a gesture like he was pushing me away.

"I don't want anything to do with you guys," he said. "I don't need that kind of trouble."

"What are you talking about?" I asked. "It's a cup of coffee. We're not conspiring to do anything. We don't even have to talk about any of this crap. It's just a cup of coffee! No more."

"No, man," he said and pointed a finger at me. "They're gunning for you. You're going to prison."

"What the fuck are you talking about?" I yelled at him. "You don't know a fucking thing! In fact, fuck you! No coffee for you!"

I stormed off. Things were getting out of hand. The rumors were growing, and now people were talking about prison. I didn't know what to think, and no one in any sort of leadership position would talk to us and tell us what was going on. We were being ignored. None of us had jobs, and we reported to no one.

After about six weeks of living in Tent 14, the space became more limited. A group of civilian contractors showed up to Zangabad, and they started moving cots into the tent. I didn't feel comfortable, so I went to the "outcast" tent and asked if I could move in. After shuffling some gear around, I had room and a cot. A few of the guys helped me move my gear from Tent 14 to my new home, and I settled in the best I could.

It wasn't easy to settle into this new environment. There were six other infantrymen in this tent with no jobs, no supervision, and essentially no one to say "don't do that" about anything. Haircuts and shaving became something of a nuisance. Since most of the guys in the tent were already heavily medicated, sleeping was the main pastime. The Internet tent was merely steps away, so it was easy for us to walk into the computer room and get on a computer. Then strange things started showing up in the mail. Blow guns, throwing knives, a spear, a deer target, and a compound bow. But what took the cake was one day when Carden walked into the tent and made an announcement.

"I just ordered a tattoo gun!" he blurted out.

"Dude," I said. "I can't see anything good coming from this."

"No," he said. "It's gonna be awesome!"

He went to the back area of the tent and started making room for what he called the tattoo parlor. All I could do was shake my head. This entire time I was trying to remain low key and off the radar, then I moved in with the wild bunch. Between Carden ordering a tattoo gun and Holcomb growing dreadlocks, I wondered where it would end.

A couple weeks later, Carden burst into the tent holding a package over his head. He wasn't kidding. He had ordered a tattoo gun. The box was torn open, and Holcomb watched the DVD explaining how to tattoo. Before the instructional video was even over, Carden was yelling at Holcomb to get started. I couldn't believe that I wasn't dreaming this.

Within a couple hours, Carden had a tattoo of a skeleton on his leg. I stared at it in awe. They had really done it. They were giving each other tattoos. I was shocked. And all I could say was "I'm next!"

I wasn't the next in line, but I did get my share of what we later called our prison tattoos. The first one I got from Curtis, and it was so bad it's funny. The others I got from Holcomb. One was pretty good, but the other one I later spent hundreds of dollars having a professional cover up.

Living with these guys and being this close to the Internet helped the days go by a little easier, and the camaraderie was priceless. But time went by slowly, and there was still no word about what would happen until 21 December, when the first sergeant saw me and told me to get everyone together and get them ready to go to Masum Ghar.

"Make sure they all shave," he told me. "And don't ask why you're going because I don't know. All I know is you all need to get ready to leave in an hour."

I went back to the tent and woke everyone up. We all shaved and got cleaned up the best we could. Within an hour, the sergeant major rounded us up and told us to all get haircuts when we got to Masum Ghar because we would be seeing the brigade commander there. We were all about to have our charges read to us.

From the time I got back to Afghanistan until that day, I had expected to get an Article 15 for my piece in all that had happened. An Article 15 in the military is a form of nonjudicial punishment usually handed down for minor infractions. I had violated an order which stated we could not consume alcohol, and as far as I was concerned, that was a minor infraction. So I prepared myself to be read charges and levied a Field Grade Article 15, which was the stiffest level of such form of punishment.

We sat in a small room in the brigade legal building and waited our turn to have our charges read to us. My name was called. I stood up and knocked on the door. After being told to enter, I walked to the table where the brigade commander sat, saluted him, and reported.

I don't remember much of what happened in the short time that I was in there. The last thing I remember hearing were the words "general court-martial," and after that, everything was a blur. I couldn't believe that I was getting a court-martial for drinking alcohol and throwing a hand grenade. What I hadn't heard during the reading was that I was also being charged with two additional charges that I wasn't even aware of.

My four charges were: Violation of General Order Number 1 (the drinking), Destruction of Government Property Under $500 (throwing the hand grenade), Aggravated Assault and Reckless Endangerment of two soldiers who were in the guard tower when I threw the grenade. And as bad as I thought my outcome was, I was one of the lucky ones. I was levied the fewest charges of the group. The others were charged with a myriad of sanctions ranging from Dereliction of Duty to Involuntary Manslaughter or Negligent Homicide. Some were charged with Assault, and most were charged with Maltreatment. When we had all been read, we sat in the chow hall at Masum Ghar and compared charges.

The sergeant major came into the chow hall and told us that we were going back to Zangabad, and when we got there, we needed to pack up all of our stuff because we were being moved to KAF. After months of sitting around, doing nothing, things seemed to be moving fast—almost too fast.

We got back to Zangabad and started packing. We threw away as much as we could and packed up the rest. While we were packing, the new Charlie Company commander walked into the tent. He gathered us together and gave us a briefing of sorts.

"When you guys get to Kandahar Airfield, you need to do the best you can to stay out of trouble," he said. "People will be watching you. You're going to be put in CHUs, so there will be two men to each CHU. And when you get there, you are going to have to give up the firing pins in your weapons."

First of all, I wondered how he figured there would be two men to each CHU since there were nine of us. Secondly, I was confused as to why we would be rendering our weapons useless by taking out the firing pin.

"Sir, why are they going to take our firing pins?" I asked respectfully.

"Don't fucking worry about it," was his response.

I didn't know how to respond. It took all I could to keep from calling him an asshole. Don't worry about it? Like it or not, KAF is still in the middle of a combat zone, and we were going to have nonfunctioning weapons. You bet your ass I was *fucking* worried about it. I really hoped that this captain was speaking out of his ass, but I didn't see any reason why he needed to talk to me the way he did.

We loaded our gear onto a cargo truck and climbed onto Strykers. The convoy made a stop at Masum Ghar to pick up Dugas, and after a short stay, we headed to Kandahar Airfield.

TWENTY-ONE

The Palace Eight . . . or Nine

A man has to build a thousand bridges before he is known as
a bridge-builder, but if he sucks one dick he's forever known
as a cocksucker.
—Quote my dad always told me. Author unknown.

It was about 0200 when we arrived at Kandahar Airfield. I hadn't slept any while riding in the truck because, again, I didn't know what to expect when I got there, and I was riding in a separate Stryker from the rest of our group. I didn't have anyone to chat with to make me feel more comfortable about our situation.

When I got off the truck, I didn't recognize any of the buildings around us. That's not surprising because it wasn't like I had spent much time at KAF. That was about to change, but I was still a little disoriented. We were led into a conference room and sat around a large table, waiting for instruction. It wasn't long at all before a first sergeant and a sergeant major were briefing us on the rules of their unit. A man with a stack of keys went around the table and issued keys to CHUs that we would be staying in.

At the end of the briefing, a handful of sandwich bags were passed around the table, and we were each instructed to remove the bolt carrier from our weapon, take the firing pin out of the bolt carrier, then to reassemble the weapon. The firing pin went inside the sandwich bag, and we wrote our weapon's serial number on the outside of the baggie with a black marker. Of course we had been warned this was coming, but it never really hit any of us until we had to actually do it. Then we had to come to terms that we would be carrying around a useless weapon. I'm pretty sure Lieutenant Labowski took it the hardest out of all us at the time. I didn't know that he was aware that was going to happen. Regardless, we gave up our firing pins with little drama.

We moved over to the barracks, which were a series of CHUs placed together, two high, with a shower and a latrine on each level. We were given four rooms to occupy, which meant three rooms would have two people and the other would have three. I ended up in the same room with Lieutenant Labowski and Dugas. The others would eventually shuffle around to different rooms, but that was our home until the end of our deployment.

It took a while to get settled in. Most of our stuff was put in a storage unit, and we had pretty much our bare necessities. Dugas was paranoid about the place being bugged, and he spent time inspecting all the outlets and light fixtures. I just wanted to try to sleep, and eventually, everything calmed down.

I didn't sleep that night, and I know Dugas didn't either.

The following day, we loaded onto a shuttle bus provided to us by the battalion and drove to TDS. Amazingly, I was the only one of the group who got an attorney. And something unknown to me before this: If an attorney represents one person in a trial of this magnitude, this attorney cannot represent anyone else involved in the matter. There were nine of us and only two attorneys at KAF.

My attorney gathered us all together and gave us the "keep your fucking mouth shut" speech. When he found out the firing pins had been taken out of our M4s, he said that we would still be required to carry our weapons. His advice was for us to remain under the radar as much as possible.

When he was done talking to the group, he pulled me into his office and started going over my charges. I was nervous to begin with, but when he said the Aggravated Assault charge carried a maximum sentence of fifteen years, I nearly jumped out of my skin.

"Fifteen years?" I exclaimed

"Yes, but that doesn't mean that's what you'll get," he said, trying to keep me calm. I thought I was going to have a heart attack. He explained he was going to try to negotiate a deal to reduce my charges, and while he was explaining the ins and outs of what he was planning, my mind kept going back to "fifteen years."

How could this happen? I know I wasn't the only guy that ever took a drink on a deployment. But how often were other offenders of this *crime* referred to a general court-martial? We threw countless grenades over the walls at COP Palace. It was a combat zone, so why was this suddenly a general court-martial offense?

How could this be happening to the others? I'm pretty sure Zisha was not the first soldier to kill himself during a deployment, so why were these eight men being charged with his death? I had never heard of anything going this far over a suicide. I became convinced that had Zisha not killed himself, my issue wouldn't even be an issue. My attorney agreed. I had become a victim of circumstance. Come to think of it, we all had.

After our charges were read by the colonel, our cases officially became criminal, newsworthy cases. Everyone's name was released to the media. My name was the only one that wasn't printed in every major newspaper in America and likely other newspapers around the world. The Army's *Stars and Stripes* ran a story about the charges filed against the eight soldiers from COP Palace and graciously left my name out of it.

Dugas started staying up late, scouring the Internet for stories written about us . . . or them. I was lucky that I was never named in any of the stories printed. Especially since most of what was written was complete garbage and completely untrue. None of us could believe that most of what was written was so far-fetched to the point of near insanity. One report in a newspaper even said that Mikey Zisha was murdered by his superiors, explaining that the men charged for his death had actually pulled the trigger.

I tried to get Dugas and the others to stop looking up these stories on the Internet, but it was no use. Something inside Dugas wouldn't let him stop. I didn't want to even hear about what he was reading, but that never stopped him from telling me.

Some of the things reported in the media included the alleged incident of making Zisha hold a hand grenade in the tower with the pin pulled to keep him from falling asleep. There were also reports stating Zisha was made to low crawl more than one hundred meters over large rocks, he was continuously assaulted, was dragged about seventy meters over the rocks, and was belittled in countless ways. Reports claimed Zisha was required to tie full sandbags to his wrists and walk around with them all day. One incident included Zisha wearing a green construction hat while he was put in charge of a detail but was only allowed to communicate to the rest of the platoon by speaking Chinese while Christiansen was his translator. Some of those stories, as it turned out, had some truth to them, but they were greatly exaggerated.

Because Zisha was Chinese, A Chinese activist group from New York mounted protests, saying that Zisha was mistreated because of his race. Also, there were claims the he was only Chinese-American soldier in our unit.

I found the racial end of the argument offensive. Zisha was not the only Chinese soldier in our unit. In fact, the first RTO when I got to this platoon was Chinese and never felt like he was ridiculed for being Asian. Not to mention all the Black and Mexican soldiers. I am German. Lieutenant Labowski was Jewish. We worked daily with Muslim interpreters. Race or religion held no bearing on the treatment Zisha received. Zisha was a good kid on a personal level, but there was no evidence to support the fact that he was a good soldier, and that had absolutely nothing to do with his heritage. I had tried to work with him, and I knew firsthand that he was physically weak. I did believe that he had potential, but he never should have been put at COP Palace, and that, again, has nothing to do with his ethnic background.

In addition to the stress of the impending courts-martial, we were in a new strange place. We weren't accustomed to the sounds of KAF. There were rocket attack warnings, an A-10 gun range, another common noise which we later attributed to an AC-130 firing range, and all the loud sounds which accompanied a large FOB. We weren't used to any of it, and for Dugas and me, it was the beginning of a long bout with insomnia.

"Did you sleep last night?" Dugas would periodically ask.

"No," I'd reply.

"I know," he'd say. "I could hear your eyes blinking."

And it wasn't that we wanted to stay awake. We would eventually try every form of sleeping aid the clinics would give us. Dugas started counting the rivets in the walls of the CHU. When he was done counting them, he started naming them, and that's when I started to worry about him. He was becoming angrier as time went by. I had been going to a psychiatrist at KAF at the request, or the order, of my attorney. Most of the others had also been seeking counseling or psychiatric help, but Dugas held out.

"You need to go talk to someone," I told him one day after he told me I should go kill myself. I think he was kidding when he said it, but he still sounded angry.

"Go fuck yourself," he said.

"I'm going to go talk to the chaplain and tell him you're having anger issues," I said.

"If you do that, I'll rip off your head and show it to you," he said back to me.

Later that day, I looked for the chaplain; and when I found him, I told him that I was worried about Dugas, and I thought he needed to be command referred to get some counseling. The chaplain said he would talk to Dugas, and I started to wonder what my head was going to look like when Dugas ripped it off and showed it to me.

When the chaplain came into our CHU to talk to Dugas, he made it sound like he was just stopping by for a visit. I was thankful he didn't throw me under the bus, and when he asked Dugas how he was doing, it got ugly.

"How the fuck do you think I'm doing, *sir*?" Dugas spat at the chaplain.

"Well, I'm sure you're under some pressure," the chaplain replied.

Dugas hit the ceiling. I don't remember everything he said to the chaplain because he said it so fast, but I'm sure there were some racial obscenities thrown out, a whole lot of F bombs, and you could cut the tension in the room with a knife. I didn't know whether I should laugh or gasp. The chaplain let him finish his tirade and expressed his concern about the anger he felt from Dugas. Dugas told him to go fuck himself.

The chaplain left me alone with Dugas.

"Did you set that shit up?"

My eyes were as wide as saucers. I didn't want to admit it because I was afraid Dugas was going to kill me, but I had to be honest with him.

"I did, but I didn't think you were going to bite his head off," I said.

"Well, fuck!" he yelled. "I just cussed out the chaplain! I'm going to Hell. I need to go apologize to him."

Later, Dugas did apologize to the chaplain, who accepted it wholeheartedly, and he started to see a counselor. After a few sessions and some medication, Dugas actually even thanked me for telling the chaplain in the first place.

Since we had access to the Internet, we were able to check our e-mail and Facebook pages. It didn't take long before someone came across a Facebook page called Justice for Mikey Zisha. On the page were death threats to people involved and a treasure chest of misinformation about what really happened. In an attempt to even things out, someone's wife started a Facebook page on our behalf. She called it Support the Palace 8. I think someone forgot to tell her there were nine of us there, so at first, I *liked* the page; but later, I felt left out, so I *unliked* the page. That brought questions from the wife, and I told her why. Since then, it's been a bit of a joke that I'm the odd man out.

Eventually, the Palace Eight were all assigned military attorneys. Four of the guys decided to exercise the option of obtaining civilian legal counsel as well. I decided to stay with my free military lawyer because after hearing the astronomical fees the others were paying, there was no way I would be able to afford a civilian lawyer. I don't know who paid the most in legal fees. I know Dugas paid more than forty thousand dollars for his lawyer, and Van Bockel paid about fifty-five thousand dollars. Hurst paid around forty-five thousand dollars. Lieutenant Labowski also had high-priced civilian attorneys but never admitted the amount paid. It had to be huge. I never felt like my charges were worthy of paying that much money for a civilian attorney, and it helped that my military attorney was confident in his abilities. He was also very aggressive in dealing with the prosecutors.

Now that the Palace Eight/Nine all had legal counsel, the next step in the court-martial procedure was the Article 32 hearings, which determined if there was enough evidence for the cases to go to trial. We all had high hopes because we didn't believe there was any chance they could prove that anyone involved in this fiasco had been the cause of Zisha killing himself. But what we later learned is that the Article 32 hearing is nothing more than a formality. The presiding officer in the Article 32 hearing could recommend a case be completely thrown out, but that's all it was—a recommendation. When the recommendation reached the commander, he could listen to the recommendation, or he could throw out the recommendation. It was obvious that these cases were not going away. They were too high profile.

At the end of January, Offutt was the first one to go to the Article 32 hearing. We waited around the CHUs pretty much all day, waiting to hear the outcome. The recommendation was that he would go to trial, but the manslaughter charge was dropped, leaving negligent homicide the most serious charge he was facing. Basically, he could do up to three years in prison if he was found guilty of this charge. The manslaughter charge carried a maximum sentence of ten years.

As the Article 32 hearings came and went, everyone involved had charges that were dropped or the level of the court-martial dropped from a general court-martial to a special court-martial, which was one step below a general court-martial. During this process, I was working with my attorney to strike a deal and the mistakes the prosecution was making during the Article 32 hearings bode well for me. My lawyer called me into his office one day and had me answer a list of questions he had received from the prosecution. I answered the questions the best I could without making my friends look too guilty. There were a lot of questions I knew absolutely nothing about. I had to keep reminding people that I was not around when most of the alleged abuse had taken place, and with that in mind, I was pretty sure I wouldn't get a deal, but I played along the best I could.

The day of my Article 32 hearing, I went to the courthouse and met my attorney who told me that the prosecution had offered a deal. I couldn't believe it.

"What is the deal?" I asked. "And if he's offering a deal, why are we here?"

"We still have to do the Article 32 in case this deal falls through or you don't accept it," he said. "I don't know what the deal is yet, but we'll find out when this is over."

I didn't really like the sound of that, but I had no choice. My hearing started, and I can't remember much of what was said or done because I focused on a seal affixed to the front of the presiding officer's bench. I think it was the JAG seal. I know they called Wyscaver as a witness against me, and he told the truth as he knew it, but it wasn't damning. The worst part of the hearing was listening to the prosecutor stand up in front of the presiding officer and smash my character with an exaggerated story of what happened. When he described my story, he made it sound like I was completely hammered drunk walking around COP Palace, throwing hand grenades over the walls. He said I was disturbing the local population around Palace, and they didn't deserve to be treated the way I was treating them. I was fuming by the time he sat down. One of the common themes emerging from this whole thing was how much people knew about what happened at COP Palace even though they were *never* at COP Palace. It was frustrating to say the least.

The hearing only lasted an hour and a half, and when it was over, I followed my lawyer back to his office and waited for the prosecutor to show up and give his deal. It seemed like an eternity before he showed up with the paperwork. He talked with my lawyer, and when they were done talking, he stood in the office and looked at me.

"You were pretty pissed at me at your hearing weren't you?" he asked.

"Yes, sir, I was very pissed," I told him.

"You do understand I'm just doing my job," he responded.

"Whatever, sir," I said. "I understand you were doing your job. I just think you should be more honest when doing your job."

I sat alone with my lawyer as he reviewed the paperwork describing the deal I would make. In return for staying out of trouble and agreeing to testify, the government dropped the charges of Aggravated Assault and Reckless Endangerment. I also had to plead guilty to violating General Order Number 1 and Destruction of Government Property. My Article 32 hearing result dropped my case to a special court-martial. With the deal, it was dropped down to a summary court-martial, which is the lowest form of court-martial.

I couldn't sign it fast it enough.

It took several days before the brigade commander would sign off on the deal, but he did, and I was back in my lawyer's office the next day.

"Are you OK with being there with the rest of the guys?" he asked.

"Of course I am," I said. "Why wouldn't I be?"

"Because you signed a deal to testify against them," he explained. "Are you sure you feel safe?"

Did I feel safe? What kind of question was that? I wanted to laugh at my lawyer. Every one of the Palace Eight understood what I was doing. I went to great lengths to let them know that I knew nothing about any one of them that would damage their cases. I showed them copies of the questions the prosecutors asked me and the answers I gave for each one. Of course I felt safe around the rest of these guys. I thought that was absurd.

I left his office and walked back to the CHU. I'm sure every five feet I was thanking God for pulling me out of what could have been a long prison term. With a summary court-martial, the most punishment I could incur would be a loss of two-thirds of a month's pay and a demotion of one pay grade. Not to mention anything I was found guilty of in a summary court-martial would be considered a misdemeanor. Basically, I was in for a slap on the wrist.

I got back to the CHU and let everyone know my news. I think some of the guys were a little sour about me taking a deal. I didn't blame them, and I felt like they were a little worried I'd throw them under the bus, so I assured all of them that it would never happen. But I never felt threatened by any of them.

Dugas and I went to the gym and worked out, and when we got back, I was met by an NCO from battalion.

"You need to pack up all your stuff," he said.

"Why?"

"You're moving," he replied.

"Why am I moving? Where am I going?"

"I've got you a room in another CHU," he said. "I don't know why, I'm just doing what I'm told."

I was livid. I was finally in a daily pattern and was comfortable with my surroundings again. Now I was going to have to pack up and move. I couldn't even imagine what it would look like to the rest of the guys. I didn't have any proof, but I was pretty certain that my attorney had a hand in this. I'd later find out I was right.

I packed my stuff and loaded it onto a truck. The truck carried me about a half mile away from where I had been, and the guy helped me carry my stuff upstairs into the CHU I was now assigned to. I didn't have a roommate, and this place was close to the POG coffee shop and the post office, but it was far from my friends. After everything was unloaded, I walked back to my old *home* and talked to Dugas, so he'd know where I was. We agreed to keep our daily schedule. It just involved me walking an extra mile to do it. I was lonely there, so the walk was worth it.

After a week of living on my own and walking back and forth between the CHUs, I was summoned to the LNO office. The LNO told me he'd talked to my first sergeant, and they were putting me on the first battalion lift back to the States. I couldn't believe my ears! It was already the end of March, so I could possibly be back in America by early April. He told me to go back and see him the next day, and he'd give me times and dates for my itinerary.

I rushed back to my CHU and started packing. I had everything ready to go. I couldn't get out of Afghanistan fast enough. The past year had by far been the absolute worst year of my life, and I had completely lost faith in the mission we were doing there, the United States Army, and anything else that had to do with us being there. I was ready to go home.

The next day, I went back to the LNO office.

"Plans have changed," he told me. "Now you're going to Masum Ghar to help them break down the brigade headquarters."

"Excuse me?" I asked with much sarcasm. "This is bullshit. I want to call my first sergeant."

He handed me the phone and dialed the number.

"First Sergeant, what is this shit about me going to Masum Ghar to break down brigade?" I asked.

"Look, I know you're pissed, and I'm doing everything I can for you," he explained. "I had you on the first lift, but someone caught your name on it and threw a fit. It was over my head, and there's nothing I could do about it. I'm sorry."

It felt like a trap door I had been standing on was opened up, and I was dropped into a pool of shit. I looked at the LNO.

"So when am I going to Masum Ghar?" I asked.

"I'm trying to find you a flight right now," he said. "It'll probably be three of four days."

Then I had an epiphany.

"I'm not getting on that bird until I get my firing pin back," I said, catching him off guard.

"Well, I can't make that decision," he said. "I'll talk to the sergeant major."

"That's fine, but I will not get on that chopper unless I have a functional weapon," I repeated. "I'll go straight to my lawyer with that. In fact, I think I'll go talk to him now."

I stormed out of the LNO office, but I didn't go talk to my lawyer. I just wanted them to stew on what I'd said. The next day, I went back to the LNO office, and plans had changed again.

"You're going to be on lift twelve," the LNO reported.

"When does that leave? Am I still going to Masum Ghar?" I asked.

"I'm not sure when it leaves," he answered. "And no, you're not going to Masum Ghar."

I should have left it alone at that, but I couldn't help it.

"Son of a bitch," I said loudly. "You're going to tell me sergeant major would rather send me home than give me a firing pin for my weapon? This is unbelievable!"

I laughed my way over to the office that was set up to manifest the flights out of KAF. I ran into a lieutenant that I had known before the deployment. He helped me get on a manifest and gave me times and dates. I was set, but when I got back to my CHU, I feared the knock on my door that would come and tell me things had changed again. Luckily, that knock never came.

Another week passed before I moved to Hotel California, which is a temporary barracks near the boardwalk. There I stacked my bags and took a bunk and waited. Several days went by, and I was lonely again. The large tent was packed with people, but everyone knew who I was. I felt like an outsider. I heard whispers and caught a lot of stares. Maybe I was just being paranoid, but oddly enough, very few people even talked to me, and I was often left out of the briefings about the delays in our flight status. So all I could do was continue to wait and do my best to keep myself informed about what was going on.

On 14 April 2011, I boarded a C-17 Globemaster headed for Manas Air Base, Kyrgyzstan.

I was going home.

TWENTY-TWO

WHEN WILL THIS END?

Always do sober what you said you'd do drunk. That will
teach you to keep your mouth shut.

—Ernest Hemingway

To this day, I don't know how I was manifested on that flight out of Afghanistan. Other than myself, there were only two other people from my battalion, and they were officers. Despite the fact that there were only three soldiers from 3-21 Infantry flying that day, we were responsible for the bags of two other soldiers from our battalion. So when it came time for pushing bags through customs at Manas Airbase, who do you think was responsible for inspecting the bags of these other two soldiers? It's safe to say it wasn't going to be one of the officers.

I had gone to the inspection formation in my PT uniform. Since the shorts don't have pockets, I had my wallet and a few other things in a plastic bag. When I was asked to inspect the unaccompanied luggage, I set my plastic bag on top of a concrete barrier and started dumping bags. When I was done, my wallet was gone. Luckily, there was only a small amount of cash missing, and the customs officials had my military ID. The credit cards were easy enough to cancel, but my driver's license was gone. Typically, that's not such an issue, but I'd need a driver's license to get my car out of storage when I got back to Alaska. My luck wasn't getting any better.

I made arrangements with a girl Carden knew to pick me up from Fort Wainwright upon my return to Alaska. I had already, through Internet and e-mail, rented a cabin outside of Fairbanks. Carden's friend picked me up and had thought ahead. She'd brought a bottle of vodka and six-pack of soda. On the way to my new cabin, I started catching up on the drinking I'd missed out on, and it didn't take long. Luckily, she was also able to take me to the DMV, so I could replace my stolen driver's license, which I did in full uniform while trying not to breathe on any of the people behind the desk. The funny thing is I think it was the best driver's license picture I've ever taken if for no other reason because I know I was hammered drunk when I had it made.

My first day back at work, I didn't know where I stood. I was no longer in Charlie Company, and I wasn't sure who was in charge of me. I had been reassigned to Headquarters and Headquarters Company (HHC), which, with the exception of the company scouts team, is a company of POGs. I asked the first sergeant who he wanted me to form up with at the morning formation, and he wasn't even sure where I should stand. Eventually, I made it to the S-3 shop, which is the battalion's operations staff. After PT that day, I showered and went to work. I was in the office for about twenty minutes when the operations sergeant major, the NCO in charge of this office, saw me standing next to a desk.

"Westenrieder, what the fuck are you doing in here?" he bellowed in front of the whole room.

"I work here, Sergeant Major," I replied as I assumed the position of parade rest.

"Who the fuck told you that?" he screamed, and before I could answer, he continued with "Get your ass in my office."

I stepped into his office, expecting an ass chewing, so I shut the door behind me. He stood glaring at me behind his desk while I explained.

"Sergeant Major, I was told by the first sergeant to work in your office while the roster is being worked out," I said, trying to clarify why I was there. "I don't know what you want me to do, but I'm here."

"Well, nobody fucking told me anything about this," he said. "I don't know why they think they can just dump people in here."

I stood silent. I had nothing to say, and his harsh demeanor softened a little bit.

"Sit down and relax," he said in a much calmer voice, and I was a little surprised as I took my chair.

"What's going on with all this?" he asked. "And what's going on with you?"

"Well, Sergeant Major, I can't talk about this with anyone," I explained. "I can tell you that I signed a plea agreement, and I'll be going to a summary court-martial. Other than that, I can't legally talk about it."

"Do you think you'll stay in the Army after all this?"

"From what I understand, I'll be looking at a chapter (separation) when the dust settles from all of this," I said

"That's what I think too," he said. "And that's what pisses me off about them sending you over here. I can't really train you to do a job in this office only to have you chaptered out of the army in six months or however long this is gonna take."

"I totally understand, Sergeant Major," I said.

"This whole thing pisses me off. None of this ever should have gone this far," he said, and I'm sure my eyes started to widen. "It's not good that the kid killed himself, but they've taken all this too far. Do you have any idea how much it's going to cost to court-martial nine guys? This whole thing is ridiculous. I hate this fucking battalion. I'm only hanging on here for about another year, then I'm going to fucking retire."

As he was saying all of this, I started to feel a little warm. I'm not sure if it was warmth from knowing a battalion sergeant major was actually showing support or if it was anger that he was finally showing support when the door was shut, and I was the only one who could hear it.

I left his office a little confused. I told another staff sergeant in the office I had an appointment and made sure he had my number, so he could call if anyone needed me. I didn't have an appointment. I went home.

The second day back to work, I fell in again with the S-3 shop. I really had nowhere else to go and no other guidance. I thought when I got back to Fort Wainwright that the feeling of isolation would start to go away, but the shadow of the past seven months was still following me around like a lingering fart. No one wanted to talk to me, and the sergeant major was the only person to even bring up what had happened, so when I told the section sergeant I was going to do PT on my own, he didn't even bat an eye as he waved me off.

I showed up in the S-3 office again and was just walking into the door of the office when the battalion's command sergeant major saw me and pulled me across the hall.

"What are you doing, Westenrieder?" he asked rather bluntly, and I assumed he wanted to know why I was working in the S-3 shop.

"Sergeant Major, I was told to fall in with the S-3 shop for formations, and I would fall under that office until I was assigned a duty position."

"That's not what I meant," he said. "I want to know what's going to happen to you when this is over."

I gave him the same answer I'd given the operations sergeant major, saying I expected to be separated from the Army at the conclusion of all the trials. He nodded his head in agreement.

"I'd say that sounds about right," he said. "You need to keep your nose clean around here and not talk about this with any of my soldiers. Do you understand me, Staff Sergeant?"

"Roger that, Sergeant Major," I responded as I snapped to attention, did an about face, and a forward march straight out of his office. I was back at work for two days and already had an ass chewing by the two top battalion NCOs.

Who would be next, I wondered. *The colonel?*

I answered my own question by walking across the hall to the S-3 office and found the same sergeant I'd talked to the day prior.

"I've got another appointment," I said. "In fact, you have my number. I'm going to avoid this place, so if anyone needs me from here on out, call me. I'm not about to come to work every day and get my ass chewed just for being here."

I walked out the door and went straight to my car and drove home. After that day, I showed up in the morning for accountability. I did PT, and then I went home, and no one ever asked a question.

A few weeks went by and I got word that there were prosecuting attorneys in Alaska interviewing the possible witnesses for the upcoming trials. I got a phone call from my lawyer, telling me I had to meet with the prosecutors. He gave me a date, time, and said I had to meet them at the brigade conference room. I showed up on time and waited outside the empty conference room for nearly a half hour before a short major came down the hall, identified himself as one of the prosecutors, and said the meeting place had changed. At least I knew I wasn't wrong, and I followed him to a small office where the other attorney was waiting.

The major seemed pretty nice. The other attorney, a captain, was really cocky. I sat with them for an hour and a half and answered their questions about everything I knew. I talked about Carden, Hurst, Lieutenant Labowski, Curtis, and Van Bockel. Oddly enough, questions about Dugas were limited, and I didn't know anything about Offutt or Holcomb. After ninety minutes of questioning, I felt drained only to find out they wanted to talk to me again in two days. So I met them again two days later, and they drilled me for another two hours.

A lot of the questions they asked were simply fact-finding questions, but many times they would take what I had said, twist it around, and try to make it sound like I meant something else. I spent a lot of time telling them, "No, that's not what I meant when I said that." After those two hours, I was completely drained, and I knew this was only going to get worse as the trials started.

I left this meeting and went to the company headquarters, where I turned in a leave form. I went to Texas for the month of June, where I tried for thirty days to forget I was in the Army.

At the beginning of July, I got back to Alaska, and things started to get weird. I was under the impression that the courts-martial would be handled in Alaska. We were stationed in Alaska, Zisha was in our unit in Alaska, and all the witnesses that would be called were in Alaska. Rumors started circulating that the trials would be held at Fort Bragg in North Carolina. When I heard that, I laughed. There is no way they are going to fly everyone back and forth to Fort Bragg for all these trials. My attorney called me not long after I got back and put the rumor to bed It was fact, not rumor.

"This is unbelievable, sir," I told him. "Are they really going to spend the money to fly me back and forth to Alaska for every one of these courts-martial?"

"Not exactly," he said. "You're going to go down there on July 18 and stay for a while."

"How long is a while?" I asked.

"However long they tell you to go," he answered.

This was just getting deeper, and I was getting more and more annoyed. I had just signed a lease on a cabin in the woods, I was settling into an everyday routine, and now I was going to be pulled out of it. I was getting angry about something that had happened repeatedly over the past year, and as usual, there was nothing I could do about it. I tried to think of excuses to get out of having to go to Fort Bragg, but nothing I could come up with would get me out of it.

Later that week, I got a call from the HHC training room requesting that I go to the S-3 office and fill out the forms needed to get paid for a temporary duty assignment (TDY). A few days later, I got an itinerary for Fayetteville, North Carolina, leaving July 18. Forces far beyond my control were in motion. It felt like I was caught in a tidal wave of circumstances that were pulling me further and further into deep, dark waters. I was told I would be back at the beginning of September, so I packed light, and on July 18, I boarded a plane with a group of other witnesses bound for Fayetteville, North Carolina . . . the place I had reenlisted to leave just two years earlier.

I wish I could put into words the disgust I have of what happened next. The late comedian George Carlin made fun of the term *military intelligence*, but the man obviously had no idea the farce of the military justice system. I am not a lawyer, and I'll never pretend that I know the ins and outs of the legal system, whether civilian or military, but even I could recognize the circus that the Army JAG corps set up for the trials of nine men who were clearly set up to take a fall for one kid who had put an M4 rifle underneath his chin and pulled the trigger without taking into consideration the consquences that would follow for others. Other than the Palace Eight/Nine, Cpt. Allred also took a career hit. So did the first sergeant. And what about the kid's family?

There are really no words to describe the absurdities that were in store for us all over the next six months. It all started when I and twenty other witnesses were picked up from the airport in Fayetteville. A convoy of vans took us all to an old barracks building on the back side of Fort Bragg, and we were all assigned rooms. I was put in a barracks room with a sergeant that had spent less than two months with us at COP Palace but spent a short time as Zisha's team leader. He was a good guy, and I had no issues with him other than the fact that he played Dungeons and Dragons and was a complete nerd.

We weren't left to our own devices. We had escorts, and Charlie Company's first sergeant and Third Platoon's platoon sergeant were with us as well, so it appeared we would be well monitored. A few days into it, the platoon sergeant told me I had a No-contact Order and wasn't allowed to speak to any of the other witnesses.

"Well, that's all fine and good except one thing," I told him.

"What's that?" he asked.

"I'm in a fucking room with another witness," I blurted out. "How the fuck am I supposed to *not* talk to any other witnesses when I'm in a room with another witness. Not to mention I bump into these fucking guys every day."

"Well, there's not much I can do about that," he said.

"I'm calling my fucking lawyer," I said in disgust. "I need a room to myself. This is bullshit!"

"Wait . . . OK," he stammered. "I'll get you a key to a room."

He reached into the consul of his van and pulled out a pile of keys and handed me a key, made me sign for the room, and I was living alone. It was at that moment that I first realized the power contained in the simple phrase *I'm going to call my lawyer*. And don't think for a second I stopped using that phrase to my advantage until I got out of the Army. I was suddenly untouchable, and oddly enough, officers and NCOs alike would cower to the words *I'm going to call my lawyer*. The truth is if I had actually called my lawyer, he would likely have told me to "shut the fuck up and quit bitching" because I had actually never been counseled on a No-contact Order at the time. But I had learned I could typically get my way by using six words: I'm going to call my lawyer. Was I abusing the system? You bet your sweet ass I was, and it was about time I did.

The month of July passed with all the witnesses spending every night drinking heavily, going into town to enjoy the Fayetteville nightlife, and finishing every night with a game of beer pong in the hallway of the barracks. It was complete debauchery. One kid even flew a friend of his in from Chicago who was a tattoo artist, and most of the witnesses, and some of the parents of the witnesses, got tattooed in the barracks while a local prostitute smoked crack in the bathroom. It was out of control while the government was picking up the tab with taxpayer money.

Because of the constant drinking and craziness, I can't say for sure when it was, but Carden showed up at some point and was in the room next to mine. We drank together on a regular basis. Dugas showed up later in the month, and Carden and I went out one night with him and drank a few beers. When we were winding down, I invited Dugas back to the barracks. I thought it would be good for him to see some of the guys from the platoon. Dugas stopped at a beer store and brought a six-pack with him to the barracks. Things were going pretty good, and he was reconnecting with some of the guys. Dugas ran out of beer and started drinking some of my vodka. That's when things took a turn for the worse.

I was lying in bed when I heard banging from the room next to mine where Dugas was staying. I went into the room to find Dugas banging on the window blinds.

"What are you doing?" I calmly asked.

"It's gotta stop!" Dugas yelled at me.

"What are you talking about?" I asked.

"They're out there," he said. "We have to stop it."

He was hitting the blinds on the window, and I was afraid he was going to break them. I pulled him off the blinds.

"Calm down, Dugas," I said and pulled the blinds all the way up. "Is that better?"

I thought I had diverted his attention. He grabbed the cord to the blinds and let them back down and started smashing them until they crashed to the floor. He picked them up and pounded them to pieces. I was stunned, but furthermore, I was financially responsible for the room.

"Do you feel better?" I asked.

He didn't answer and climbed into the bed. I left the debris lying on the floor and went back to my room, climbed into bed, and started to worry more about my friend. Within minutes, I started hearing furniture moving around next door. I got up and found Dugas moving the dresser in front of the door.

"What the fuck are you doing?" I screamed at him. "You need to get to bed. You're fucked up!"

He climbed back into his bed, and I went back into my room. About two minutes later, Dugas was in my room.

"They're coming!" he screamed. "We gotta stop them!"

"Dugas!" I yelled at him. "You need to relax and go to bed. No one is coming. You've had too much to drink. Just go to bed!"

Dugas went into my closet and started pulling all my clothes off their hangers and throwing them onto the floor. He started rolling around on them and curled into a ball, muttering more talk about how "they were coming" before he got quiet again. In my mind, I thought, *Well, at least he's sleeping*. I figured I'd just do laundry the next day.

I was lying in bed and had just fallen asleep when Dugas pounced on top of me and was calling me a motherfucker and throwing punches at me. I pushed him off my bed, and he started lashing at my sheets and ripped all the sheets and blankets off my bed. I jumped out of bed and went next door, grabbed Carden, and begged him for help.

Dugas was out of control, and with Carden's help, we calmed him down and got him to bed. I was completely freaked out and went downstairs and called his wife.

"What the fuck is wrong with your husband?" I asked.

After I told her what happened, she told me not to let him drink hard liquor. All I could think was, *Now you tell me*. She told me to go into my room and hide all my prescription drugs and let her know if anything else got out of hand.

I went back to bed and woke up the next morning for PT. I went into the room Dugas was staying in, and he was gone. I knocked on Carden's door and asked if he was in there. He wasn't. I was starting to panic. I went downstairs and saw a bunch of the guys at the bottom of the stairs.

"Has anyone seen Dugas?" I asked.

"He's asleep in my bed," Hendrick said. "He came into my room last night and asked me to go wake someone up. When I got up, he crawled into my bed and went to sleep."

I'm sure I rolled my eyes, but at least I knew Dugas hadn't been picked up by the MPs, and he was somewhere safe. I ran PT, and when I got back, I found Dugas bouncing from room to room. I asked him what he was doing, but he rambled back something I couldn't understand. I scooped him up and brought him back to my room, where I made him lie down. He slept until late in the afternoon before he went back to his hotel room.

I went to Wal-Mart that day and bought replacement blinds for the ones he'd destroyed, and later that evening, he called me.

"What the fuck happened last night?" he asked.

I recounted his escapades and finished by telling him he was no longer invited to the barracks to drink with us. I was angry with him because of the way he acted. But what I didn't know was how deep his problems had become.

The previous story was just another episode that had occurred while we were staying at Fort Bragg, waiting for the trials to begin, and it really has little impact on this story other than to say that I ignored a serious issue with a close friend. I should have done more, but I passed off the incident as Dugas being drunk and having a simple flashback. His issues were much deeper.

The depravity didn't end with the *Dugas Night of Flashbacks*.

Schwartz's family, Kurt and Laura Schwartz, drove up from Georgia to Fort Bragg for a weekend and rented a cabin at Smith Lake. One night, they invited a bunch of people over to cook out and have a good time. Before the night began, I asked if there was a designated driver. Alley had volunteered to be the designated driver, so I immediately began drinking. Christiansen was one of the guys that invited himself and spent the night drinking off of my bottle of vodka.

I spent most of the night with Schwartz's dad inside the cabin. A couple of us had brought guitars along, and we would get together and play on the front porch of the cabin. It started out as a fun night. Carden was there, and occasionally, he would get next to Christiansen and say, "Before the end of the night, I'm going to punch you." I would laugh because I thought he was kidding. It turns out he wasn't kidding.

Deep into the night, I was sitting on the front porch, playing some songs with Schwartz on the guitar. I heard a ruckus behind me, looked back, and saw Carden punch Christiansen with a crowd of people around the two of them. I jumped up, and when I got there, Christiansen was lying face first on the ground. I grabbed him by the arms and lifted him up. He was crying and had blood pouring out of his nose onto his shirt, and in between sobs, he was trying to say something, but it was unintelligible. I finally got him to stop crying, and we packed some ice around his nose to stop the bleeding.

"We're going back to the barracks," I said and got Alley to ferry us back onto Fort Bragg.

When we got to the barracks, I went to bed. The next morning, I walked downstairs and found Christiansen's room. He was still asleep, and I woke him up. As he sat up I could see his nose was swollen, and he had two black eyes.

"Are you OK?" I asked.

"Yes. I'm fine," he replied, and he slumped back onto his pillow and went back to sleep.

Typically, this sort of brawl ends right there. But the fact that Carden, one of the Palace Eight, was the one who punched Christiansen put the incident into a whole new category. When the platoon sergeant found out about the incident, he passed it along to the prosecuting attorneys for the Zisha trials who kicked it into high gear.

One evening, Schwartz, Alley, Christiansen, and I were loaded into a van and taken to the provost marshal's office. For seven hours, I sat waiting to get interrogated over what had happened at Smith Lake. When the investigator finally pulled me into the room, I was hungry and exhausted.

"Are you CID?" I asked before anything got started.

"No, I'm not," he answered. "I'm a military police investigator."

"Then I'll speak to you," I said.

He began asking me questions about what had happened the evening Carden punched Christiansen. I explained to him that as soon as I found out we had a designated driver, I began drinking, and I had at least three drinks before I even left the barracks.

It didn't matter what he asked me about concerning the incident. I had one answer: I was too drunk to remember anything that happened that night.

The investigator had to have a written statement, so he would write a question on the sworn statement form, slide it across the table to me, and I would write my answer. Of course my answer remained the same, and after the second question came to me, I looked at the investigator.

"You do realize that no matter what you ask me, I was too drunk to remember what happened that night, and that answer is not going to change, right?" I asked him.

"I understand," he responded. "But I have to have this on paper, so just answer the question."

I did, and then the questions started to change. The Q and A looked something like this:

Q: How many drinks did you have that night?
A: I'm not sure. At least thirteen or fourteen throughout the night.
Q: Do you usually drink this much?
A: Are you crazy? If I normally drank this much, I'd probably be dead. So no.

Eventually, the investigator realized he wasn't getting anywhere with me, and they let me go. We got into the van and rode back to the barracks, but the platoon sergeant wouldn't let us out of the van until he saw Carden getting put into another van. I couldn't believe this was happening. There are many times when a brawl in the Army (or between infantrymen) is dismissed as too much testosterone and booze. But in this case, the fact that Carden was already facing charges escalated the entire situation.Carden was being arrested for hitting Christiansen, and he was placed in pretrial confinement.

But there was more to the story. Soon after this incident happened, the barracks got a shakedownThey were looking for Carden's .38 caliber revolver. I tried to tell them he didn't have a revolver. What I didn't tell them was that he did have a .45 caliber weapon in the car he had borrowed from his sister.

Apparently, while Carden was in Alaska, waiting for his court-martial, he had gotten into an incident with a few other soldiers, and somehow he had accidentally shot a hole in the side of the battalion staff duty van with a .38 caliber revolver. I don't know the whole story behind what happened, and I never asked. I felt like the less I knew, the better.

This was just getting better and better, and there was just no end in sight.

TWENTY-THREE

BY THE WAY . . . I TOLD YOU SO!

We few, we happy few, we band of brothers. For he today that
sheds his blood with me, shall be my brother . . .
—William Shakespeare

The following chapter is the culmination of six months' worth of trials and an undetermined amount of American tax dollars. Although I spent nearly the entire next half of the year at Fort Bragg while paying rent on a cabin no one was living in for the most part, I testified at only two of the trials. I wasn't upset about not testifying, but it would have been nice to *not testify* back in Alaska.

Since I didn't attend all the trials, I can only go by what I was told of the outcomes of all but three of the procedures, mine being one of the three I attended. Most of this information came from the Palace Eight, so I believe every word.

United States vs. Holcomb

Holcomb was the first one to go to trial. He was facing at least seventeen years in prison, and it was a media circus.

I sat in the lobby of the Fort Bragg courthouse for a week, reading a book on my Kindle Fire while Holcomb's trial was going on. Since it was the first trail, there was a lot of confusion as to who had to be at the courthouse and when, so everyone that was on a witness list sat at the courthouse, waiting to be called to testify. It was four days into the trial before I was called.

When they called my name, I walked to the witness stand and took the oath. I promised to tell the truth, the whole truth, and nothing but the truth. I was about two questions into my testimony when the prosecuting attorney made an objection, so I stopped answering, thinking that was the right thing to do.

The prosecutor kept talking as the judge was reviewing the legal precedent for his objection. The judge asked the prosecutor to stop talking while he reviewed his documents, but the prosecutor kept trying to plead his case for his objection. I've seen a lot of episodes of *Boston Legal* and other courtroom television series, but I have never seen a judge get shitty with an attorney.

"I told you to be quiet!" the judge screamed at the attorney, and it was loud enough that it freaked me out. Keep in mind my PTSD is triggered by loud noises. I was told later that from that point on I sat on the stand picking my fingers. Holcomb's attorneys asked him if I was retarded. It turned out I wasn't a good witness for either side, and I felt good about that outcome.

When I left the stand, I had no recollection of what was asked of me. I didn't even remember sitting up there past the time the judge yelled at the prosecutor. My only hope was that other attorneys in the pending cases would take this into account when they considered calling me as a witness. I don't know if they did, but I was rarely called again.

I sat in the courtroom at Holcomb's sentencing. He was reduced to E-4, fined about $1,100, and sentenced to thirty days in jail. Considering he was facing seventeen years in prison, this was a slap on the wrist. I sat next to Carden in the courtroom when the sentence was read, and we both laughed.

As far as I was concerned, Holcomb had committed the most terrible of the offenses, and his worst punishment was thirty days in jail. I really thought this was a sign of what was to be the outcome of the rest of the trials, and I wasn't too far off. We all said the attention shown to these trials was blown out of proportion. This was turning into a case of "I told you so."

After Holcomb was sentenced and taken to jail, he gave me the keys to his jeep, and I had transportation for the next thirty days.

United States vs. Offutt

Offutt was the next one to stand trial, and it started to look bad. Offutt cut a deal before his trial, agreeing that he would testify against the other defendants. I wasn't present at his trial or his sentencing, but I can say that Offutt should have had better lawyers. I don't think he even had a court-martial hearing, other than the preliminary actions where he pled guilty.

Offutt was sentenced to six months in prison, a reduction to E-1, and a *Bad Conduct Discharge* from the Army. I never heard from Offutt again, so I can't say why he took this deal, but I do know that he got a raw deal. As far as I knew, the worst Offutt did was put his foot on Zisha's head to let him know his head was too high up to be considered low crawling, and this action was considered assault. Holcomb dragged the kid across the rocks and did thirty days. Offutt did six months. It didn't make sense, but I could remember as far back as when we were at KAF and we were talking to Offutt about his options, we all recommended he try to get better attorneys He trusted the ones he had. He did his time, so there's nothing that can be done at this point, but he deserved better.

United States vs. Dugas

Dugas stood trial next, and I didn't even know his trial was under way when it happened. I really thought I'd be called to testify against him since he and I had consumed alcohol together, and that was one of his charges. Before I knew he was even on trial, I heard that he had been sentenced to three months in prison and a reduction to E-5. He was given ninety days time served for his unlawful pretrial punishment, which included being denied midtour leave and the fact that his weapon was taken from him not long after we arrived at KAF. He did no jail time. The bad part about his conviction was that it opened him up to testify against the remaining defendants.

I felt bad that I wasn't there when Dugas was sentenced, but I didn't even know his trial was under way. After his trial, Dugas was sent back to Alaska to spend time with his wife, but he'd be back, and when he came back, it turned into another circus.

United States vs. Westenrieder

My court-martial was next, but instead of Fort Bragg, my hearing was held at Fort Wainwright in Alaska. On August 18, I got on a plane and flew back to Alaska. I was pretty thankful because the next day was my birthday, and I didn't really feel like spending my birthday flying twenty hours from Fayetteville to Fairbanks.

On August 19 I went to church and spent the day trying not to stress over the next day's event. There's nothing like getting court-martialed the day after your birthday. That evening, I sat on the back deck of my cabin, smoking a cigarette and getting drunk. About one in the morning, I put out the day's last cigarette in a plastic flower pot that was sitting on the bench of the top deck of the cabin, brushed my teeth, and fell into bed.

About 4:00 a.m., I woke up to a loud crash. I don't know if I actually heard the crash or if it was a dream, but in my mind, I thought, *There's a moose outside!* So I got out of bed and went out the back door to the deck to see if I could see the wildlife. I didn't see a moose, but the flower pot that I'd put my cigarette out in was in flames. I freaked out, grabbed a cup of water, and threw it on the smoldering container. It doused the flames, but there were still coals burning. I made several trips inside to refill my cup and eventually was comfortable with the fact that the fire had been put out. Tragedy had been averted. There's no doubt that if I had slept another ten minutes, the log cabin I was living in would have ignited, and I likely would have been burned alive. Apparently, potting soil doesn't make a good ash tray.

After that, I couldn't get back to sleep, so I shaved, showered, and got ready for my trial. I sat at my kitchen table and wrote out a statement for when I had the opportunity to speak on my own behalf. There was nothing more I could do but get to the courthouse on time.

I showed up early and went into the waiting area. I had two character witnesses there to speak on my behalf, and when the time came, the battalion legal specialist called me into the courtroom. There were three people in the courtroom: me, the legal specialist, and the officer presiding over my summary court-martial. He was a major, and I knew he was an infantryman because he wore an Expert Infantryman's Badge (EIB). Oddly enough, I had opted not to wear my CIB in lieu of wearing my EIB. My thinking was that at this point, every infantryman had a CIB, but the EIB was a rare badge. When I saw the major wearing an EIB, I felt a professional bond with him, and it made me feel much more comfortable.

A summary court-martial is a low-key trial roughly the equivalent of a misdemeanor court hearing in the civilian court. Most of the proceedings are scripted. The legal specialist was there to advise the presiding officer on what he could say or not say. It was obvious the officer presiding over my hearing was not a judge but was given the duty of presiding over the court-martial.

The court-martial started, and the officer read what he had to read, and I answered the questions he asked me with the scripted "yes, sir" and "no, sir" answers. There were times when he would say something and then turn to the legal specialist and ask if was allowed to say this or that, and the legal specialist would give him the permission or not.

At the point in the trial where I had an opportunity to call my character witnesses, the officer reviewed some paperwork, asked the legal specialist a question, then turned to me.

"I understand you have some character witnesses, but I'd really like to hear your side of the story," he said.

"Sir, do you want me to tell you what happened?" I asked.

"That's exactly what I want to hear," he replied.

I spent about five minutes recounting the story of the day we were attacked. I told him about running to my CHU and eating my dinner. I explained to him how Dugas was paranoid and came to my CHU in a rage and how I pulled the vodka out and he agreed to drink with me. I admitted to the one drink I'd consumed that night and that Dugas only had two drinks about four hours before the explosion rattled my CHU and sent Dugas into a frenzy. I described the conversation Dugas and I had about throwing a stun grenade over the wall, but since I didn't have one, Dugas told me to throw the frag. And I told him that I was verbally reprimanded immediately afterward by Lieutenant Labowski.

When I was done telling the story, the officer appeared stunned. I thought he was pissed.

"Are you telling me that your throwing of the grenade is this charge of destruction of government property?" he asked.

"Yes, sir," I replied.

"How close was the nearest village to your COP in the direction that you threw that grenade?" he asked.

"Sir, it was at least five hundred meters," I replied. "I've never done the math on that, but I know it was at least half a click."

He rolled his eyes.

"I can't believe they charged you with this," he said.

"Sir, neither can I," I said smiling, knowing that finally someone had made a sensible statement about what had happened.

"Staff Sergeant, I can tell you that this grenade incident will have no bearing on the punishment I decide for you," he said.

"Thank you, sir," I replied.

"But let's talk about this drinking," he continued. "I can't ignore that."

"I understand, sir," I said.

"Here's the way I see it," he explained. "You're a leader of men, and if you break a general order by drinking when you've been ordered not to, how can you tell your soldiers they aren't allowed to drink? If you break the rules, you are setting an example for the soldiers under you, and you're telling them that it's OK for them to break those rules. That's where you made your mistake."

"Yes, sir," I agreed. I knew the drinking was going to bite me in the ass. I had broken an order and took full responsibility for it and I was about to take my punishment.

The officer sat in his chair for a few minutes, and the pause seemed to last forever.

As an NCO at a summary court-martial, I was facing the loss of one rank and the loss of two-thirds of one month's pay. I held my breath.

"I'm ready to rule on this," he said, and I stood at the position of attention. "I'm going to demote you from the rank of E-6 to E-5. I'm not going to take any of your pay from you, but I just can't ignore the fact that you were drinking over there. The grenade incident plays no part in this. You cannot set a bad example for the soldiers who look to you for guidance."

"Yes, sir," was about all I could say. I was disappointed because one of the goals I set for myself when I came back into the Army was to reach the rank of staff sergeant. I had reached my goal, but now it was stripped away. But disappointed or not, I knew the result of all of this could have been much worse, so I was thankful I had gotten my "slap on the wrist."

I was a little bitter because I knew that had Zisha not killed himself, my transgressions never would have come to this. Lieutenant Labowski reprimanded me, and he knew I had enough respect for him to know I wouldn't have continued to drink in Afghanistan, and the grenade incident, as the major had said, was nothing more than a product of being an infantryman. It's like I originally told my lawyer, "It's no big deal."

I went back to the waiting area and told my character witnesses that I wouldn't need them and thanked them for coming. I got in my truck and drove to the clothing sales store, bought some E-5 rank, and in the parking lot of the PX, I stripped myself of staff sergeant rank and replaced it with the rank of sergeant.

The next day, I was back on a plane bound for Fort Bragg.

United States vs. Carden

Carden's case is a little different than the rest because of the Christiansen incident. Originally, Carden had pled to a deal that gave him a summary court-martial and added the provision that he would receive a *General under Honorable Conditions* discharge within ninety days of his sentencing. He was basically facing a demotion of one rank and the loss of two-thirds of a month's pay. It would have worked out fine for him, but when he got tagged with hitting Christiansen, it changed everything.

On August 22, he faced his court-martial for the charges he was facing against the Zisha incident. He was demoted from E-5 to E-4 and fined the two-thirds of a month's pay. But since he went from sergeant to specialist, he was eligible for a stricter punishment for the charges he faced for hitting Christiansen and for shooting a hole in the battalion van.

An NCO is *lucky* when it comes to a court-martial in the sense that anyone with the rank of E-5 or above can only be reduced by one rank in a summary or special court-martial. Now that Carden had lost his NCO status through the deal he made regarding the Zisha trials, he was opened up to much harsher punishment with the court-martial he would receive for hitting Christiansen and shooting the battalion van.

Trust me when I say the irony of all of this was not lost when his second court-martial hit the Army's docket.

The day Carden was sentenced, I sat in the courtroom. The judge seemed to be sympathetic and asked Carden if he realized the consequences he (the judge) could hand down. Carden said he understood and was willing to accept whatever ruling this judge deemed worthy.

We went outside the courtroom during the break to smoke and Carden said he hoped the judge would just kick him out of the Army and that would be the end of it. I could tell he was just tired of being incarcerated and having to deal with all the legal issues that we'd all been put through over the past year. I hated the fact that he would be willing to take any kind of bad conduct discharge, but I understood his frustration.

The judge came back with his sentence, and I was floored. Carden was sentenced to four months in prison and fined $1,001.87 for the damage to the van. He also was demoted to private (E-1) and received a *Bad Conduct Discharge* for striking and pushing another soldier, threatening to harm another soldier, negligently discharging a firearm, and damaging government property, negligently discharging a pistol in a government van, and attempting to impede an investigation.

Carden had already served most of the jail time during his pretrial confinement, but he spent a few more weeks in jail and then was discharged from the Army with a *Bad Conduct Discharge.*

United States vs. Curtis

Curtis was the next to stand trial, but before his court-martial could take place, he struck a deal. I don't know the particulars of the deal, but I sat in the courtroom the day he was sentenced.

As far as I knew, the worst Curtis did was give Zisha a knee to his thigh. When I learned that he'd actually put hands on Zisha, I told him that he deserved anything he had coming to him, and he agreed. Curtis was a good guy. He was a former Marine and demanded respect. I have nothing bad to say about Curtis other than he tended to put his foot in his mouth.

One time at FOB Zangabad, when he learned my first name was Richard and we talked about the nicknames associated with this name, he told me he "preferred Dick." When I said, "Do you ever say something and immediately wish you hadn't said it?" he completely went humble on me.

Another time, at KAF, he said he went to the chow hall to get "black cock" when he really meant to say he went to get the chocolate chip cookies. I don't know how he confused "black cock" with "chocolate chip cookies," but Dugas and Lieutenant Labowski heard it too, so I knew I wasn't hearing things. Curtis tended to say things without thinking.

On the day Curtis was sentenced, I sat in the courtroom as a show of support for my friend. The judge came back with a sentence I thought was fair. Curtis was sentenced to three months in prison after pleading guilty to hazing and maltreatment. He had admittedly assaulted Zisha by kneeing him in the thigh, and as much as I hated to see any of the Palace Eight go to prison, I felt like Curtis's punishment was fair. He was also demoted to E-1 from E-4, and to me that was a more severe punishment than the prison time, but Curtis took the punishment in stride. Since he's been out of prison, I've spent some time with him, and he's none the worse for the time in prison.

United States vs. Hurst

I was called to testify against Hurst, and really, the only negative action I recalled was that I saw Hurst make Zisha do an exercise called Little Man in the Woods, which is basically an exercise where you do jumping jacks from a crouched position. It's not an exercise that is sanctioned by the United States Army, but it wasn't an uncommon form of punishment in the infantry. Basically, I had seen Hurst make Zisha do an unauthorized exercise, but how bad was that?

When I took the stand during Hurst's court-martial, the first thing the prosecution did was mention that I had been demoted one rank, and that I had drank alcohol in Afghanistan. My thoughts while on the stand were, *Did you really just make me look like a loser when you're trying to use me as a witness?*

I was asked some damning questions that I really thought hurt Hurst's case, and when I was dismissed, I walked away from the stand and gave Hurst a look that said I was really sorry if I hurt his case. He just smiled at me, so I don't think I hurt him. Later, his lawyers said my testimony didn't make a difference. My reaction? "Duh!"

Hurst was demoted to specialist, reprimanded, and sentenced to forty-five days of hard labor for negligent dereliction of duty. It was a slap on the wrist, and he would never do the forty-five days of hard labor.

It was another incident where it looked good on paper, but the punishment didn't fit the crime. Hurst was prosecuted because he was Zisha's team leader, but the truth was that he was Zisha's team leader for less than a week when Zisha killed himself. Hurst, like me, was a victim of circumstance.

United States vs. Van Bockel

Before Van Bockel's trial, I submitted a leave form. Van's trial took place just before the Thanksgiving holiday, and my family was planning a family reunion. The lead prosecutor said I was on his list of witnesses but agreed to call me early, so I could take leave. I checked with the legal office, and I was told I wasn't on the defense witness list, so there was no reason I shouldn't have been able to take leave over Thanksgiving.

The prosecution never called me to testify against Van Bockel, so the Sunday before Thanksgiving week, I signed out on leave. When I was in Dallas on Monday, I started getting text messages from people telling me I was being called as a witness. How was I supposed to respond?

"They can call me on the phone," I finally responded. "But I'm in Dallas, Texas. I am not flying back to testify. I was told I could take leave."

So Van Bockel's trial took place while I was drinking vodka and playing guitar with my kids on the back porch of my parent's home. I spent Thanksgiving with my family, and I didn't give Van Bockel's trial a second thought. I know it was stressful for him when the verdict came down, but Van Bockel is a strong guy.

Van Bockel was demoted two ranks to E-4, given a letter of reprimand, and forced to perform sixty days hard labor for his role in the hazing of Pvt. Mikey Zisha but was awarded forty-five days of credit for time served, so he was only sentenced to do fifteen days of hard labor. As with Hurst, he would never do a day of hard labor.

United States vs. Lieutenant Labowski

Lieutenant Labowski was the last one to stand trial. I was at Fort Bragg awaiting his trial. I had testified at his new Article 32 hearing, and I told the truth. I had nothing bad to say about my platoon leader. He followed the rules, and when he saw a discrepancy, he set it straight. Everyone in the platoon had enough respect for Lieutenant Labowski that when he got upset about something, we respected the fact that he was upset, and no one wanted to make it worse.

I don't know the details of what happened with Lieutenant Labowski. He was pretty private about his sentence, but from what I understand, he pled guilty to six counts of Negligent Dereliction of Duty. He received a General Letter of Reprimand and was forced to resign his commission. But these consequences are hearsay, and I respect him enough to know that if he wanted me to tell the outcome of his punishment, he would have told me. I know that I wish him the best, and no matter what the result of his punishment, he will always be the best platoon leader I've ever had.

There are few men in this world that hold more respect from me than Lieutenant Labowski. One is my father. The other is Jake Jegelewicz. Both are war veterans, but Lieutenant Labowski served with me in a time of war. My respect for him is boundless. I love my father and I love Jake, and I hold the utmost respect for these men. I served with Lieutenant Labowski, and he had my ass. The truth is I'd give my life for my father, for Jake, or for Lieutenant Labowski. Truthfully, if you name anyone in this book that I've mentioned, I would give my life for them. Even the ones I've bad-mouthed.

There are some events worth mentioning. Before Curtis or Offutt went to trial, they got into an argument, and Curtis slashed Offutt with a knife. Offutt received about sixty stitches and almost died. The day before Holcomb was released from prison, he tried to hang himself using a towel he tied to the bars of his jail cell. Dugas, on his way back to Fort Bragg, was found in the fetal position in the Atlanta airport and taken to a psychiatric ward in Atlanta, where he spent more than a week. After he was released, he returned to Fort Bragg, and within two weeks, he freaked out again and was admitted to the mental ward at Fort Bragg.

Not long after the last Dugas incident, I was called into the JAG office. The lead attorney sat across the table from me and started to list off problems that had occurred between Curtis and Offutt, the Holcomb suicide attempt, and the issues with Dugas. His follow-up question solidified my contempt for the Army JAG corps.

"What the fuck is wrong with you guys?" he asked me.

I couldn't believe he'd asked me that question. First of all, it was completely disrespectful. The men he was referring to were war heroes. What had he done? My response?

"Sir, are you really going to ask me that question?" I spat back at him with disdain. "You're going to ask me why Curtis knifed Offutt? You're going to ask me why Holcomb tried to kill himself in prison? And you're going to ask me why Dugas freaked out? Let me ask you this. What have you done to help these guys? They've spent the past year dealing with the legal implications of some kid who killed himself, and you're trying to get some kind of conviction out of them. Their legal problems are over, and now they're trying to deal with the PTSD problems that started before this kid killed himself. So let me ask you this: What have you done for them to help them with their mental issues? You haven't done a goddamn thing! So you ask me what the fuck is wrong with us? Sir, what the fuck is wrong with you?"

I got a blank stare, and from that day on, I was nothing but belligerent with the Army JAG corps. I had completely lost respect for military prosecutors. This man had no clue what we went through at COP Palace. He had no idea what we had sacrificed for our country. He claimed he had been an infantry officer, but he was dead to me.

Zisha died at Palace at his own hands. Is that sad? Yes. But my true assessment of what happened in the aftermath of Zisha's death is that nine good soldiers took the fall for someone who had deeper issues than what he had to deal with at COP Palace. Lieutenant Labowski, Dugas, Van Bockel, Hurst, Carden, Curtis, Offutt, and Holcomb were outstanding soldiers. I got wrapped up in the whole mess, and so did Captain Allred and the first sergeant who was in charge at the time, who I haven't even mentioned. Basically, eleven Army careers were ruined because one kid killed himself. That lawyer had the balls to ask me what was wrong with us? What's wrong with eleven men who put their lives on the line for their country? Seriously?

Sir . . . enjoy your freedom, you fucking POG, because people like me earned it for you. That's what's wrong with us. We gave our country our all, only to have people like *you* treat us like criminals.

What's wrong with us?

Sir, *you're* what's wrong with us.

TWENTY-FOUR

THE FINAL CHAPTER

I'm through,
With you.
You're one bridge I'd like to burn,
Bottle up the ashes, Smash the urn.
I'm through with you,
All I wanna be is done!
　　　　　　　　—From "Done" by The Band Perry

After Van Bockel's trial I returned to Fort Bragg from my Thanksgiving trip. While I was in Dallas, I bought a sailboat. Call it a wild hair because I knew nothing about sailing at the time I bought the boat, but I had dreams of living on a boat while I was in Afghanistan. I'd even made up a grand scheme about smuggling Mexicans into America on a sailboat when I got out of the Army. Of course it was a joke but it made everyone think I was crazy, but I really did want to buy a boat, so when I was in Dallas, I found a sailboat slipped on a lake north of Dallas in my price range and bought it.

I had returned to Fort Bragg because Lieutenant Labowski's trial was supposed to be the next court-martial, and there was no doubt I would be on the witness list of the prosecutors or the defense . . . or both. Of all the trials, Lieutenant Labowski's trial was the one I dreaded the most. If there was one person that, in my mind, was completely innocent, it was Lieutenant Labowski.

We moved into a hotel on Fort Bragg in September, and I had a room to myself. The rooms were almost a hundred dollars a day, but the government was paying for it. Well, the American taxpayers were paying for it. It was walking distance to a Class Six (liquor) store, so I had no complaints. While waiting for Lieutenant Labowski's trial to begin, I spent my evenings drinking myself into a coma.

Christmas was coming up, and I was determined to get away from Fort Bragg over the holiday, so I put in for Christmas leave. I was approved to take three weeks, and right before my leave began, the word came down that Lieutenant Labowski had come to an agreement with the government and he wouldn't be standing trial. I couldn't believe it.

The trials were over.

I went to the JAG office and tried to make arrangements to return to Alaska from Dallas, but for some reason, that wasn't going to happen. So I went back to Dallas for Christmas and New Year's, and on January 6, I flew back to Fort Bragg. On January 7, I flew back to Alaska. Call it military intelligence or stupidity, but I thought it would have made much more sense, and it would have been much more cost effective to fly from Dallas to Alaska rather than Fort Bragg to Alaska. At this point, I was done asking questions.

I landed in Fairbanks, and Holcomb picked me up from the airport. He was staying at my cabin along with Van Bockel and Hurst. On the drive from the airport to the cabin, Holcomb told me when we got back he was going to finish packing his stuff and put clean sheets on my bed since he'd been staying in my room.

We got to the cabin, and I started drinking while Holcomb was upstairs, *cleaning* my room. By the time it got dark, which is pretty early in Alaska in January, I didn't know my ass from my elbow. I went upstairs to my room and fell asleep on top of the covers. I woke up the next morning to find Holcomb had moved out. I was a little hurt that he didn't even say goodbye, but as drunk as I was the night before, I figured he may have, and I just didn't remember it.

I went upstairs to clean my room because Holcomb had obviously not done a good job cleaning up after himself. I won't go into too much detail, but letting him stay in my cabin cost more than the money it took to replace the stuff that was lost, ruined, or broken . . . It cost us our friendship.

Luckily, for Holcomb, he had gone to a chapter board while we were still in North Carolina. A *chapter* in the military is another way of saying getting *separated* from the service. In the Army, a soldier that has six or more years of active duty time is entitled to a *chapter board* if the separation is less than honorable. At the board, the soldier can lobby for upgrading the discharge to an Honorable Discharge.

Surprisingly enough, Holcomb received an Honorable Discharge through the board, and when I got back to Alaska, he was basically on his way out the door anyway. Within a few weeks of my return to Alaska, Holcomb was on his way back to his home state of Ohio.

Carden and Offutt had been discharged by virtue of their trial verdicts, so now, including Holcomb, three of the Palace Nine were out of the Army. The next trick was for the remaining six to get an Honorable Discharge. There was no question that we were all getting chaptered because the new chain of command made it clear they wanted us all out the door.

I sealed my deal when the new sergeant major flew to Fort Bragg while I was still there and told me that when I got back to Fort Wainwright, he expected me to go to his office and tell him why I think I *deserve to stay in the Army*, and if I couldn't give him a good enough reason, he would "expedite my chapter paperwork." When he said that, I almost laughed in his face. Why would I want to stay in an Army that had just put me through the wringer?

Time went by, and I ran out of patience; so one evening, I wrote him an e-mail explaining why I no longer wanted to remain in the Army. At the end of the e-mail, I put him on the spot and said, "After considering all these factors, I have to tell you that I can't think of a single reason why I deserve to stay in the United States Army. Respectfully, I am going to hold you to your word and ask that you expedite my separation upon my return to Alaska."

When you put a sergeant major on the spot, they tend to get defensive, and his response to my e-mail came rather quickly. When I read what he wrote back, I knew I wasn't dealing with the brightest NCO in the Army. He wrote, "But under no circumstances have I ever allowed any Soldier to be treated like Private Sitka was treated, or allowed others to be treated in that manner."

First off, he was the one who capitalized *Soldier*. Second, how can you stand up for Zisha when you don't even know his name? And third, this NCO was a product of the Eighty-second Airborne Division. He served in Desert Storm in 1990-91. Are you really going to tell me that this guy never smoked one of his soldiers? Or that he never called another soldier a bad name?

Regardless, the man said he'd expedite my chapter paperwork when I returned to Alaska, so I never bugged him again. I wanted out of the Army so bad I was willing to smoke pot to get out, but if he was going to help and Holcomb had already received an Honorable Discharge, I was more than willing to go through the *process*.

It turns out the process wasn't as easy as you'd think. When I reported in to the company, I was given a checklist of things that I needed to get done to complete my chapter packet. I wasn't interested in wasting time, so I knocked out as much of it as I could get done. Dental held me up, but after a *month*, I had gotten all my dental work done and completed my last Army physical, the Phase 3 physical, before I was finally able to turn my packet in to the company first sergeant.

By this time, Hurst and Van Bockel had already had their chapters read by the first sergeant, which is a formality when a soldier gets separated. Dugas was dragging his feet on his packet, Curtis didn't seem to be in any hurry, and Lieutenant Labowski had been given two weeks to clear and get out of the Army.

Hurst had learned through his lawyer that if he submitted a conditional waiver stating he would decline a chapter board in lieu of an Honorable Discharge, he could get out of the Army much faster. The only catch is that it had to be signed by the battalion commander and the brigade commander. We all had intentions of submitting the waiver, but Van Bockel learned through his attorney that since he was tried under a general court-martial, his waiver would have to be signed by the division commander, and if he rejected it, Van's chapter board could then be settled under a division chapter board. He didn't like his chances with that, so he opted to just go for the brigade chapter proceedings.

Hurst submitted his conditional waiver, and within ten days, it was denied. So much for trying to avoid a separation board.

The whole procedure was mind boggling, and I don't ever remember any chapter proceedings that were as confusing as what we were going through. I've seen people get chaptered out of the Army in less than two weeks, so why were our chapters taking so long? I remembered the words of the sergeant major who had promised to expedite my packet and remembered why I no longer wanted to stay in the Army. If you can't trust a sergeant major to keep his word, who *can* you trust?

During this time, the drinking got a little out of control. Hurst and I were the worst. We were getting drunk almost every night and finding new and stupid things to do. One night, we each ate a raw onion. Hurst threw it up in the sink. Another night, when it was minus thirty-eight degrees outside, Hurst filled a large cup with hot water, and while I was out on the back deck, smoking a cigarette, he came up behind me and threw the water on my back. The hot water crystallized in the arctic air, and by the time it hit my back, it was more like powder. We did it a few more times after that, then we recorded it and put it on YouTube. Another night we autographed each other's arms and drew moustaches on our faces with a Sharpie marker. Those pictures never made it online.

It wasn't all bad. We were working out at a local gym and I was regularly attending church at St. Matthew's Episcopal Church on Sundays where I would sit in the back row and hug the heater pipe at the early service while secretly picking stray hairs off of the pretty blonde woman who sat in front of me.

Finally on March 4, 2013, after having been back in Alaska for almost two months, I was called to the first sergeant's office for my chapter reading. I sat in the office while the first sergeant read the conditions of my chapter.

The chapter called for a General (Under Honorable Conditions) Discharge under *Chapter 14-12c*, which is a separation for "committing a serious offense." In the grand scheme of things, a General Discharge is not bad discharge, but according to my lawyers, family, and everyone else who had two cents to put in, I had an obligation to myself to fight for an Honorable Discharge. So when the first sergeant offered me the opportunity to speak to legal counsel, I took it.

Curtis had his reading right after mine, and I sat next to him during the process. When the first sergeant finished the reading, Curtis declined his right to an attorney.

"Where to do I sign to waive everything?" he asked the first sergeant.

As pages were turned to get to the waiver signature, Curtis turned to me and smiled.

"I just want to get this shit over with, man!" he said, and he signed his chapter packet. When the first sergeant went into the commander's office for signatures, I looked at Curtis in disbelief.

"Curtis, you are entitled to a board," I said. "Holcomb got an Honorable. What makes you think you won't get one?"

"I'm just tired of all of this shit," he said with a resigned look on his face. "This is the fastest way out of here, and I'm taking it. Fuck the board. Fuck the Army. Just get me out of Alaska and on with my life."

I was stunned but jealous at the same time. I wish I had the resolve to just not give a shit and to just take the General Discharge. In my mind, I thought, *What are a few more weeks? I can stick it out, go to a board, and likely get an Honorable. But on the other hand, Curtis is probably going to be out of here in a couple weeks. I'll be here at least six more weeks.*

It was a mental struggle.

The first sergeant came back and told Curtis he'd have final *out date* soon, which would be the day Curtis could sign out of the Army and go home. Then the first sergeant called TDS, and I got an appointment to speak to legal counsel on March 13 . . . more than a week away. I should have taken the long gap as a sign, but I didn't.

In my mind, I figured I would have my TDS, and within a few weeks, I would have my separation board. Typically after that, it would take a couple weeks to clear and get orders to get out, so I was hoping I'd be sitting on my boat around mid-April.

If I back up a little, I have to say that one of the TDS attorneys had already told me that no one at Fort Wainwright could represent me because they were all representing members of the Palace Eight, although she didn't use that language. So on March 13, when I went to the TDS office and watched the separation video, I told them that what I had been told by the other attorney in that office. An NCO escort had followed me to the meeting because apparently, I wasn't allowed to handle the chapter packet on my own. So when the receptionist in the office told me she would contact Fort Richardson to locate an attorney from there, I sent my packet back to the company with my escort and headed toward Fort Wainwright's back gate.

Ten minutes later, I received a phone call from the TDS receptionist. She said I had been cleared to use one of the attorneys at Fort Wainwright, and if I wanted to come back, I would get seen right away.

I turned around and went back to the office. The attorney assigned to my case took me upstairs to her office, and sitting on her desk was the conditional waiver that, if approved, would give me an Honorable Discharge, and I could avoid a separation board. I actually didn't want anything to do with it. Hurst's waiver had been denied, so why would mine be approved?

"I don't think I want to do that," I said to my attorney. "Hurst already had his denied. I don't think mine will get approved. I'd rather just take a board and get out of here faster."

"Your case is different than his," she explained. "You had a summary court-martial, and you have more time in the Army than Hurst. Your waiver has a better chance of being approved."

I thought about it for a moment, and I started to cave. I wanted to believe what my new attorney was telling me.

"Hypothetically, what if it's not approved?" I asked. "How long is this going to set me back?"

"If it's not approved," she responded, "it'll put you back about one week. Two weeks at the most."

How could I argue with that? Signing the waiver would be a small price to pay to walk out of the Army with an Honorable Discharge and avoid the board. Worst case scenario, I'd only be set back two weeks if it was denied.

I signed the paper. Even after I signed it, I felt like I shouldn't have. Before I left the TDS office, my attorney handed me a folder she'd gotten from the receptionist, explaining it was a copy of my chapter packet. I left the office carrying my folder. I sat in my truck and thought about going back into the office and tearing the waiver up and telling her to just schedule my separation board. But I didn't. I trusted my attorney.

A week went by and I didn't hear anything. I called my attorney who told me she hadn't heard anything yet, but she'd "make some calls and let me know" when she heard something. Another week went by, and I still hadn't heard anything. So I called her again.

"I still haven't heard anything," she explained over the phone. "When I hear something, I'll let you know."

"Ma'am, I was talking to Hurst, and he said his waiver only took a little more than a week to come back," I explained.

"I know," she said. "Sometimes these things take a while. I'll call over there, and when I hear something, I'll let you know."

As I was getting off the phone, all I could think was, *A week, two weeks at the most.* I was starting to feel betrayed. I should have known better. In fact, I did know better. I didn't want to sign that waiver, but I'd been led to believe it had a chance to go through. What I should have done was tell her right then on the phone to withdraw that waiver and just schedule a board, but I didn't. I kept playing along.

Another week went by and I was losing patience. I knew a kid that worked in the brigade legal office, so I sent him an e-mail, asking if he knew the disposition of my waiver. His response came back, and I was livid.

"I haven't seen your waiver," he wrote in the e-mail. "In fact, your chapter packet still hasn't made it back here from the company."

It's real anger when you can feel your balls get hot, and my balls were on fire! How could my first sergeant do this to me? The next morning, I went into work and cornered my boss.

"First Sergeant, I talked to legal yesterday, and they said they don't have my packet," I said.

"I know," he said. "It's on my desk. I can't send it back until you've had an appointment with TDS."

"You mean the appointment I had three weeks ago?" I asked.

I got a blank stare for about three seconds.

"I'll get it back to legal today," he said before he turned and walked down the hallway.

I left the company and drove to brigade legal. I went into the office and explained to the guy I knew that the first sergeant would be returning the packet that day, and I asked him again about the waiver.

"I've looked all over the place," he said. "Your waiver isn't here. It's normally in the chapter packet."

"Well, when I signed the waiver, my packet was at the company," I explained. "I'm thinking that attorney should have sent it over here."

"Well, it's not here," he said.

"I'll go to talk to her," I said. "Thanks for your help."

I left the legal office and went to the trial defense office. When I approached the receptionist, I was impressed that she remembered me.

"Did she call you back yesterday?" she asked.

"No!"

"Well, she said that nothing has changed with your status, and she wants you to be patient."

No, she didn't tell me to be patient!

"Are you kidding me? I need to talk to her," I spat at the receptionist.

"She's busy working on cases right now!"

"I don't give a shit," I responded as I was clearly losing my temper. "I need two minutes of her time. I'm not leaving here until I get it!"

And with that, I sat on the couch in the waiting room and waited. A few minutes later, the attorney came downstairs and asked what was wrong.

"Where is that waiver?" I asked.

"I put it in your packet," she responded.

"When did you do that?"

"The day you signed it."

"Well, that would have been hard since my packet was on my first sergeant's desk and has been sitting there for three weeks, waiting for confirmation that I even spoke to a TDS attorney."

"Wait here," she said and went upstairs to her office. When she came back down she said, "I don't even have a copy of that waiver."

What had I gotten myself into this time? Call me insane, but don't lawyers make copies of everything? And I'm pretty sure I had a copy of the waiver in the folder she gave me the day I signed it.

"Ma'am, how can you not have a copy of it?" I asked. "Even *I* have a copy of it."

"Where's your copy?"

"It's at my house!"

"Well, go home and get it," she directed. "Bring it back here, and we'll make sure it gets to legal today."

"Yeah, I don't think so," I said. "I think I'll go home, get that copy, and bring it to legal *myself.*"

"That's fine," she said. She was so nonchalant about the whole thing, and it made me even angrier than I was before.

I left the office and headed home. As soon as I got home, I made a beeline for the folder I had been given three weeks earlier. I opened it up and couldn't believe what I found. Sitting right on top inside the folder was the copy of my signed Conditional Waiver. Right below it was the original. (Let that soak in for a moment!) Having *hot balls* doesn't even begin to explain my anger.

I took the original waiver to the legal office and handed it to the guy I knew and explained what had just happened. He promised he would get it sent up as soon as possible to try to get it approved, especially in light of the delay I had already endured.

Three more weeks went by before the receptionist from TDS called and told me I needed to come in on Friday, April 26, to see my attorney.

"What is this about?" I asked, since it was Wednesday, and I didn't want to wait two days to find out.

"She didn't tell me that," the receptionist answered. "She just told me to call you and set up the appointment."

Forget the fact that I had already been diagnosed with anxiety disorder; it was just rude to set up that appointment with me and give me no information to go on. The best I could do was to assume the waiver had been denied six weeks after I'd signed it. The worst part about all of this is that had I just scheduled the board, I would have gone to the board, cleared, and left the Army in probably five weeks.

On April 26, I went to brigade legal and signed for a board date. The date was set for May 20, which was still three weeks away. I left legal and went to TDS and waited for my appointment with the lawyer. She asked me for a list of character witnesses that I could use for my separation board.

"Is there any way to get this moved up?" I asked her.

"Do you want to waive all of this?" she asked me.

"Are you kidding me? After all this time do you think I'm just going to waive it? I want a fucking honorable discharge! I just want my board to be sooner than three weeks away!"

"That shouldn't be a problem," she said. "When do you want it? Next week?"

"As soon as possible," I said. "I need to get out of here and on with my life."

I left her office, thinking I was wasting my time with her again. She said she'd let me know by the following Monday if she could have it moved up, but I expected to go to the board on May 20.

I had joined a gym in Fairbanks, so I was working out at *Anytime Fitness,* getting crushed by the gym manager's brutal *Ultimate Core* class; and when I was done, I had an e-mail waiting for me on my phone. Much to my surprise, my attorney had not only gotten back to me but had moved my board date to May 7. There was suddenly a light at the end of the long dark tunnel.

In the midst of all this drama, Hurst and Van Bockel both attended their separation boards. Hurst's board took place on March 15, and he received an Honorable Discharge. Van wasn't so lucky. His board took place on April 8, and he walked away with a General (Under Honorable Conditions). Though they had both been through a separation board, they couldn't leave or even start clearing because their final dispositions from their courts-martial had not made it through the clemency portion, and they couldn't be discharged until it had made it through that process and signed off by the commanding general at Fort Bragg. If that sounds confusing, it's because it is, and I don't really know how to explain it. I'm a grunt, remember?

Curtis got a final out date, and on April 15, I took him to the airport so he could fly home to Tennessee. Dugas had a board date for May 6, and he had every intention of asking for retention so he could follow through on a medical separation board. Dugas had his separation board and received a General (Under Honorable Conditions) and wasn't retained as he had hoped, but he still went forward with his medical separation board.

Now I was the final member of the Palace Nine that hadn't been officially chaptered out of the Army, and my board was scheduled for the next day. When I found out Dugas had received a General Discharge, I was a little nervous. We all assumed going to a separation board would mean an Honorable Discharge. After all, Holcomb had admittedly assaulted Zisha by dragging him through rocks, had served a short prison sentence, and still received an Honorable Discharge. After Van Bockel and Dugas both received General Discharges, the board was no longer a given, and now I was nervous.

On May 7, I met my attorney at 8:30 a.m. at her office, and we walked to the courtroom, which was right across the street. It was the same courtroom where I'd received my summary court-martial in August the year before. I had five character witnesses, including Captain Allred, Schwartz, and Dumar. I wanted to call Dugas as a witness to confirm that he had told me to throw the hand grenade, but since the day before he had received a General Discharge, my attorney thought it was best not to call him.

The board convened at 9:00 a.m., and most of the proceedings were scripted. The prosecution didn't call any witnesses, so when it was time to call witnesses, my attorney called the witnesses, and they all gave amazing testimony. When all the witnesses were called, questioned, and cross-examined, it was my opportunity to give unsworn testimony.

When the testimony is unsworn, the prosecution and the board are not allowed an opportunity to ask questions, so it gave me one of the first opportunities I had since the whole affair began to give my side of the story without being cross-examined. I was able to tell what really happened without fear of having to try to explain that which is difficult to communicate to someone who hasn't served in a place like COP Palace.

I don't remember much of what I said when I answered the questions my attorney asked me. I remember my voice quivering because I was nervous. More importantly, I remember standing up for myself for the first time and being able to tell the prosecution they were full of shit.

"Do you regret your actions at COP Palace?" my attorney asked me.

"I regret drinking," I responded as I looked to the three-member board. "I knew it was wrong when I did it. I've never argued that it was right, but I never denied the fact that I drank at COP Palace, and I took responsibility for it from day one. But the grenade incident is something I don't regret."

"You don't regret throwing the fragmentation grenade over the wall at COP Palace?" my attorney asked, seeming a little confused.

"No, ma'am, I don't regret that," I responded. "First of all, we were in a combat outpost in the middle of nowhere, so we often threw grenades over the walls at COP Palace. Do you really think I am the only soldier from Palace to throw a grenade over the wall? Secondly, I was told to throw the grenade by my platoon sergeant. If an infantryman is told by his superior to throw a grenade in a combat zone, do you think he's going to say no? I didn't."

For my final point, I looked directly at the prosecuting attorney. "Finally, I've listened to prosecutors tell me for a year and a half that I was intoxicated when I threw that grenade," I said, glaring at the captain. "I've heard people who were *not* at COP Palace tell me what happened. The truth is I drank one drink about four and a half hours prior to throwing that grenade. I'm not justifying the drinking. That was wrong, but there was absolutely no way I was drunk when I threw that grenade."

After making that statement, I turned to the board members and looked each one of them in the eye. I needed them to see I was sincere.

Following my statement, I was excused from the stand and sat next to my attorney. Both lawyers gave their closing arguments, and the board recessed to make its decision. I was nervous. There was a lot riding on me getting an Honorable Discharge. Additionally, I had a lot of time invested in this board. I could have waived everything like Curtis did, but I didn't. I stuck it out for nearly two extra months to get an Honorable Discharge.

After about fifteen minutes of deliberation, the board returned to the courtroom. The findings were simple: I was separated from the Army for committing a serious offense, and I received an Honorable Discharge.

As the president of the board read the decision to give me an Honorable Discharge, he looked at me. When I heard the words *Honorable Discharge*, I mouthed the words *thank you*, to him, but I'm not sure he saw me.

I was the final chapter in the Palace Nine, and I got the result I had hoped for, but not in the timeframe I had expected, and it wasn't over yet.

EPILOGUE

It finally seemed like it was all over, and in all likelihood, it should have been. After one year and seven months of dealing with the drama, the stress, and the frustration of the whole ordeal, the light at the end of the long dark tunnel was getting brighter.

The powers that be seemed to have a different idea on the timeline. The evening of my separation board, I went to the emergency room with severe stomach pains and was told I was taking too many ibuprofen pills. The next day, the pains were worse, and I was admitted to the hospital with an abscess on my liver due to an E. coli infection. I was transferred to Fairbanks Memorial Hospital later that evening because they had an ICU. Later that day, I was told there weren't facilities to handle the kind of care I needed in Fairbanks, so I was loaded on an air ambulance and taken to Madigan Army Hospital in Seattle. I spent ten days in the hospital before I came back to Fort Wainwright with a drain tube protruding from my chest. Two weeks later, I had to go back to Seattle to get it removed. The whole experience was painful.

I expected to have clearing orders by the time I returned from my first trip to Seattle. After all, it was more than ten days from my separation board.

I had no orders when I got back.

My first sergeant was very helpful. He arranged for me to get battalion clearing papers, so when the post clearing papers came down, I'd be that much ahead of the power curve. The papers looked like a lot of work, and I was still weak from my ailment, so I sat on them for a while.

I made numerous trips to the brigade legal office, and I made even more phone calls than I did visits. I know I was driving the legal specialist insane with my constant badgering, but he took it all in stride. Despite all of his hard work, the paperwork still had not been pushed through even five weeks after the completion of my separation board. Apparently, the separation packet had made its way to the commanding general's desk and was buried, ignored, or just snubbed.

My frustration began to mount again. I still wanted to get out of the Army and get on with my life, but I was on some general's back burner. Everyone kept saying,

"At least you're getting paid." I didn't care about the paycheck. I just wanted to move on and put my Army experience behind me.

I went up my chain of command, spoke to attorneys, and bugged the legal office enough that I'm sure they were sick of hearing my voice and seeing my face. I was a dog backed into a corner, so I had no other option.

I called my congressman.

Apparently, my woes were not important for my congressmen. I tried a senator first, and I'm sure they're pretty busy, so I didn't hear back from him until I had already contacted the member of the US House of Representatives. I didn't want to take up that much of the government's time, so I declined his help. That was a mistake.

The house member I contacted never replied. I gave up hope.

Six weeks after my separation board, I called the legal office again.

"Has my packet been signed?" I asked the legal specialist.

"Let me check," he replied. A few moments later, he came back on the phone. "Nothing yet."

"What is taking so long with this?" I asked with frustration in my voice. "It's been six weeks since my separation board. There's no excuse for this."

"I don't know why," he said. "Usually, these are signed faster. I don't understand it myself."

"Well, I called my congressman a couple weeks ago," I admitted to him. "They never got back to me, so I guess they don't give a shit. I'm not going to call you anymore. I'm just going to sit here on my ass and collect a fucking paycheck. You can call me when it's done."

I hung up the phone and vowed to do as little as I could for the Army. Not that I was doing anything anyway. I had stopped going into the accountability formations a week or two earlier. No one called to ask where I was. No one seemed to miss me.

Hurst and Van Bockel moved out around mid-May into a dry cabin. Everyone anticipated they would be in the Army much longer than me, so they got their own place. They still came by to take showers and do laundry, but it was nice to have some privacy. And to be quite frank, I was tired of them waking me up in the morning when they got ready for work.

My new mantra: "Work is for suckas!" and I continued collecting that government paycheck for doing nothing at all.

I decided to go up and finally clear the battalion, so during the sixth week after my separation board, I went into the company and cleared the arms room, supply, and the other minor items I needed signatures on. When people saw me, I often heard, "You're still here?" I didn't have a good comeback.

When I went into the battalion area to clear, I saw the operations sergeant major. Of course he had to ask too.

"Are you still here?"

"Yes, I am, Sergeant Major."

"What is the holdup?"

"Well, from what I understand, my separation packet is sitting on the general's desk waiting to get signed. Other than that, I have no clue."

He recommended I go play casualty for the medics who were testing for the Expert Field Medic Badge (EFMB). I declined his recommendation.

"Work is for suckas!"

He rolled his eyes and walked away, and I hit all the battalion stops I could make. I was, for all intents and purposes, out of the battalion, but I was still on the roster.

I continued doing nothing more than waking up late in the morning, playing the guitar, and keeping tabs on my fantasy baseball team. In the evenings, I'd mix a glass of vodka with soda and sit on the back deck and swat the wretched Alaska mosquitoes with an electric bug zapper I bought from Wal-Mart with money I was making for not doing anything.

On Wednesday of the third week in June, I got a call from Hurst.

"Guess where I'm going?" he asked.

"You're going to Hell if you don't change your ways!" I answered.

"Well, as true as that may be, I'm on my way to pick up my clearing papers," he said.

This was impossible. He and Van Bockel had been waiting for months for their packets to come back from the commanding general at Fort Bragg, so they could start the hard labor they had been sentenced to perform before they could get out. How was Hurst going to pick up clearing papers? And why wasn't I picking up my papers?

All I could do was roll my eyes.

The next day, Van Bockel found out he was getting his clearing papers on Friday. Anger and frustration can't even describe the emotions I was feeling. On Friday, I made one last attempt to call the brigade legal office. I told the legal specialist I wouldn't call him again, but I couldn't help myself.

"Did my packet get signed yet?" I asked.

"Let me check," he answered, as he did every time. "It's still not back. It was supposed to get signed yesterday, but the general had an appointment. I'll check around and call you if I hear anything."

I got off the phone and considered pouring a glass of vodka at nine o'clock in the morning. Instead, I made a pot of coffee and went out back to kill more mosquitoes. Thirty minutes later, I got a call from the brigade legal office.

"Your discharge was approved," he said to me.

"Already?" I said in my best sarcastic voice. "When will I get my orders?"

"I'll take the packet to transition today or Monday," he said.

"I don't want to sound unappreciative," I said. "But I'd prefer that you take the packet in today, so I can start clearing and get the fuck out of here."

On Friday, June 21, 2013, my separation packet made it to the transition office where separation orders are generated. It only took forty-six days. I considered this a new spin on the old Army adage of "hurry up and wait."

On June 24, I picked up my orders and my clearing papers. My final out date was July 8. Lucky for me it was a post training holiday, so nothing was open for me to clear. I had to laugh at the comedy of the whole thing. I finally got clearing papers and couldn't clear.

The next day, I cleared with Van Bockel. Hurst was done clearing, and his out date was July 3. We made a mad dash of things and finished clearing before the end of the week. I took my paperwork back to the transition office and had my out date amended. On July 3, I signed out of the Army with Hurst and Van Bockel. On July 4, I loaded my car and drove away from Fairbanks, Alaska. Ironically, it was Independence Day. History repeated itself with me yet one more time.

Dugas was the last one left of the Palace Eight/Nine. He was on leave when I signed out, but I had no doubt that he and I would one day cross paths again. He was still waiting on the outcome for his medical board separation, which he told me could take up to 120 days.

"It's an easy paycheck," he said to me before he left on leave.

As I look back on my time in the Army, I wonder if it was all worth it. My three goals included earning my CIB, making staff sergeant, and becoming a jumpmaster. All were achieved, but I stopped wearing my CIB after I got back from Afghanistan because everyone had one. I pinned my EIB back on my uniform before my court-martial. I was demoted from staff sergeant back down to sergeant. I hadn't even done enough jumpmaster duties to earn a star on my jump wings.

I fought the *War on Terror* on two fronts and have nothing but nightmares and anxiety left to show for my deployments. I was ostracized by my last unit, left out to dry, and ultimately ignored. I was involved in a mind-numbing legal ordeal with eight other seasoned soldiers who were treated just as bad and, in most cases, worse.

I've been asked if I would do it all again even if I knew what the outcome would be. My response is a solid "fuck no!" There are things that happened by choice and I own the responsibility and consequence for those. It's the things that happened by sheer chance and circumstance that turned my life . . . and so many others . . . completely upside down. If I could have seen all that coming I never would have done it. It just wasn't worth the sacrifice and cost.

Knowing now what we got into, would you?

CASEY WESTENRIEDER left the United States Army in 2013 after serving as an infantryman during two combat deployments. He has a Bachelor's of Arts in Journalism from Texas Tech University and a Master's Degree in Education from the University of Texas at Arlington. He is now living in North Texas with his Miniature Pinscher, Wrigley, and his Doberman Pinscher, Dugas.